THE OPERA INDUSTRY IN ITALY
FROM CIMAROSA TO VERDI

THE ROLE OF THE IMPRESARIO

JOHN ROSSELLI

Reader in History, University of Sussex

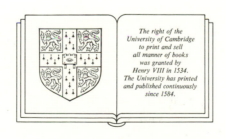

CAMBRIDGE UNIVERSITY PRESS

Cambridge

London   New York   New Rochelle

Melbourne   Sydney

Published by the Press Syndicate of the University of Cambridge
The Pitt Building, Trumpington Street, Cambridge CB2 1RP
32 East 57th Street, New York, NY 10022, USA
296 Beaconsfield Parade, Middle Park, Melbourne 3206, Australia

First published 1984

Printed in Great Britain by
the University Press, Cambridge

Library of Congress catalogue card number: 83–07688

British Library Cataloguing in publication data
Rosselli, John
The opera industry in Italy from Cimarosa to Verdi:
the role of the impresario
1. Opera – Production – Italy – History
I. Title
782.1′07′0945   MT955
ISBN 0 521 25732 8 hard covers
ISBN 0 521 27867 8 paperback

Contents

Illustrations

Acknowledgments

An historian who works on the social and economic history of Italian opera, and who is not a musicologist, needs a lot of help. A fellow historian, Enzo Tagliacozzo, first suggested the impresari as a way into this largely unexplored subject. Generous and helpful advice has since come from a number of musicologists: to name Lorenzo Bianconi, Julian Budden, Jeremy Commons, Pierluigi Petrobelli, Andrew Porter, and Michael Robinson is merely to list the heaviest of my obligations. I have also had valuable advice from the economic historians Aldo De Maddalena and John Myerscough. Whatever in this book remains imperfect is all my own.

I have been helped with local knowledge by Architetto Franco Mancini in Naples, Dr Mario Seghieri in Lucca, and Captain George Glossop in the matter of his kinsman Joseph Glossop. The most persistent of my debts is owed to archivists and librarians, most of them in Italy. There are few collections to which I have not been able to get access; one such, the recently discovered Fondo Lanari – on which Marcello De Angelis has based his study of the impresario of that name, *Le Carte dell'impresario* (Florence, 1982) – is offset by several collections which I have not even tried to get into, because to have done so would have stretched out the period of research beyond all practicable limits: so abundant is the documentation, and yet so little worked.

The Social Science Research Council gave me a grant for research, the British Academy a smaller grant for a preliminary Italian visit, and the University of Sussex a term's leave to write. I am grateful to them, as to all those others without whose help the book could not have been written. To my two sons I offer it as a by-blow of evenings at the opera some of which they enjoyed, some not.

J.R.

Brighton, February 1983

vii

Abbreviations

ASB	Archivio di Stato, Bologna
ASC	Archivio Storico del Comune di Bologna (in ASB)
ASCF	Archivio Storico del Comune di Firenze
ASCM	Archivio Storico Civico, Milan
ASCR	Archivio Storico Capitolino, Rome
ASF	Archivio di Stato, Florence
ASL	Archivio di Stato, Lucca
ASN	Archivio di Stato, Naples
ASR	Archivio di Stato, Rome
ASV	Archivio di Stato, Venice
ATLaF	Archivio del Teatro La Fenice, Venice
ATRP	Archivio del Teatro Regio, Parma
BNF CV	Biblioteca Nazionale, Florence, Carteggi Vari
BTBR	Biblioteca Teatrale del Burcardo, Rome
Dep. Pub. Sp.	Deputazione dei Pubblici Spettacoli
MTS	Museo Teatrale alla Scala, Milan
Piancastelli	Collezione Piancastelli, Biblioteca Comunale, Forlì
Sp. P.	Spettacoli Pubblici

The following abbreviations denote theatre seasons:

C	Carnival
Q	Quaresima (Lent)
P	Primavera (Spring)
E	Estate (Summer)
A	Autunno (Autumn)
F	Fiera (annual fair)

(C season usually started on 26 or 27 December of the previous year; C1837 started on 26 December 1836)

References to certain theatre histories that are arranged chronologically year by year do not give page numbers if the year referred to is obvious.

TO
MARK AND DAVID

Giuditta Pasta as Medea in Mayr's *Medea in Corinto*.

1 · *A season in the life of an impresario*

An Italian town even today is a place of stone, a meeting-ground for citizens who live and work tightly stacked, unlike an English or American town many of whose inhabitants surround themselves each with his own grassy homestead. In 1783, or for that matter in 1823, a town of north or central Italy – say Parma or Padua or Florence or Lucca, capital of a small state or a region – cut itself out still more sharply against the countryside. It was walled, or at least gated; at the gates strangers must explain their business and produce papers; carts must be searched, merchandise perhaps unpacked, for each town levied a tax on goods coming in. Within the town grass grew, but scarcely on lawns: rather from the many cracks in buildings and streets, for these, among the oldest towns in Europe, had had centuries in which to decay. Some had slid down gradually from a point of prosperity reached perhaps around the year 1300. Others had kept going in some branch of manufacture or trade, but their looms or hammers had then most of them fallen silent, the goods they once made priced out of nearly all markets by the late seventeenth or early eighteenth century; by that time a good third of the population of these towns were literally in rags, set down in official registers as *miserabili*, destitute.

By 1783 such a town might well have found a little more to do; it might have tidied itself up over the past half-century and put up some new public buildings; but it also very likely held more people than in 1683. Fewer perhaps were ragged or idle, but for many of those in work what they could buy with their pay had decreased. Even then, as in India or Africa today, almost everyone living in a town was better off in some years than a great many people living in the countryside. In a town such as we have looked at, with a princely court or at any rate a governor, with an archbishop, with convents and military barracks, with a school or two, perhaps a university, with inns and shops and law courts, there was nearly

1

Giuditta Pasta, this time in a comic opera, Gnecco's *La Prova d'un'opera seria*. In spite of his surname Luigi Lablache was a Neapolitan equally famous in bass parts both serious and comic. He created the parts of Giorgio in *I Puritani* and Don Pasquale, and, with Giulia Grisi, Mario, and Antonio Tamburini, made up what was perhaps the most celebrated quartet of Italian singers of the nineteenth century.

always some kind of living to be picked up, even though some people kept alive by begging and many others existed on starch, a few vegetables and cheap wine, and spent the winter in unheated rooms. But in the countryside, where the vast majority of Italians lived, the growing number of landless labourers could, in some years – 1764, 1800–1, 1816–17 – die of typhus and dysentery following malnutrition; in the worst famine years peasants were found dead by the roadside with, in their mouths, the grass they had tried to eat.[1]

In town one of the high spots of the year was the carnival season: coming near the end of a cold, though short, winter it licensed, for a week or two, freedoms which the Church, despotic governments, and strict codes of propriety at other times repressed. Women as well as men could go about masked (though masquerades were more tightly regulated in 1823, when governments had always in mind the perils of revolution, than in 1783). In 1817 King Ferdinand's younger son drove along the packed main street of Naples on a float in the shape of a warship whose cannon fired sugared almonds into the crowd.[2] All who could ate, drank, and danced in expectation of the rigours of Lent.

For the nobility whose palaces lined the fashionable streets, for the officers of the military garrison, the civil servants, the better-off doctors and lawyers, and the students of the university, the heart of the carnival season was the opera house. An Italian town would have several theatres, some built wholly of wood, others (perhaps after a wooden structure had burnt down or fallen down) of neo-classical stone and plaster. All of them embodied the plan worked out in Venice for public indoor theatres when opera had first become popular in the 1630s: several tiers of boxes arranged in horseshoe or oblong shape and enclosing the stalls area, in many theatres only part-filled with seats (mostly benches). These theatres were all likely to be busy at carnival time, with plays, or comic operas, or acrobats, or demonstrations of animal magnetism (mesmerism). Some theatres might put on opera of every kind in the other main seasons of the year, spring and autumn, but up to the 1820s, during carnival time, only one theatre as a rule presented the entertainment acknowledged as the right one for the upper classes: *opera seria* (mythological or historical opera), the intervals between its acts being filled with *ballo grande* (spectacular ballet, also on mythological or historical subjects). In some cities such as

3

Bologna where a different season was the fashionable one, one of the theatres enjoyed the same monopoly during that time.

The carnival season was supposed to begin on St Stephen's night, 26 December, and lasted until Shrove Tuesday. From about seven o'clock till midnight on all but one or two evenings in the week, the upper classes of the town were to be found in the opera house. There they met, talked, ate, drank, gambled, and were entertained. Not only was the theatre the centre of social life; before the 1848 revolutions it was 'the one field open to the manifestations of public life', a substitute for a parliament or a free press.[3]

One of the paradoxes of Italy before unification was that although fragmented into nine or ten small states whose populations spoke dialects none too easy for their neighbours to grasp, it did have – like the ancient Hellenic world – a certain cultural unity. In the towns at least, enough people understood the dialects of 'foreign' cities to make the *commedia dell'arte* – the improvised theatre based on comic figures attached to particular towns and speaking their dialects – widely popular. *Opera seria*, unlike *opera buffa*, was far too high-minded a genre to deal in anything less than literary Italian at its most formally poetic. But it too was an all-Italian form; those who carried it on, singers, composers, librettists, impresari, travelled an Italian circuit – which in practice took in, at the turn of the eighteenth century, the whole of north and central Italy, Naples, the three chief towns of Sicily, and, as outposts, those non-Italian courts and capitals where Italian opera had become the fashionable entertainment, ranging from London and Cadiz to Haydn's Ester-háza. There was, in Italy (unlike Germany), no stable company of singers apart from minor itinerant troupes performing comic opera, no theatre director or *Intendant* in a fixed official post. Nearly everyone was on the move.

So if we visualise the key figure in putting on the carnival or any other opera season, the impresario, we need to see him too on his travels. Whether in 1783 or 1823 the date was within a day or two of 1 December. The impresario had probably just finished running an autumn season in another town, ending on 29 or 30 November, and now he was approaching Parma or Padua or Florence or Lucca, either toiling over the Apennines in a hired carriage or crossing the river Po by ferry. With him he had perhaps one or two of the leading singers or dancers who happened to be travelling the same way; but others would be coming from other directions in other carriages. He probably also had with him a son or nephew or other young man with better handwriting and spelling than he to act as secretary, a couple more hangers-on, and at least one trunkful of papers: contracts, accounts, correspondence, for an impresario lived by the written word, at least until he reached the *piazza*, as people called the town where the season was to be given.

The earliest papers in the trunk were letters exchanged with the mayor of the town, or the governor, or the reigning duke's superintendent of theatres, or the nobleman representing a committee of boxholder–proprietors, or possibly the nobleman who owned a theatre outright: their purpose was to agree terms on which the impresario would have the concession (*appalto*) of the theatre, whether for the one carnival season or for a number of seasons. The impresario was essentially an intermediary, a fixer: unlike the *capocomico* or head of a permanent troupe giving a large number of plays (and sometimes of small-scale comic operas), he had no ready-made company, no repertoire to deliver. Hence the negotiations by letter between the impresario and the authority that controlled the theatre – undertaken possibly a whole year or nine months earlier – had been elaborate: nearly everything had to be gone into in detail: operas, ballets, soloists, scenery and costumes, to say nothing of financial terms. Even while he negotiated with the authority the impresario had been engaged in a parallel correspondence with singers, dancers, composers, and agents to see who was available and on what conditions. His correspondents meanwhile were dealing by post with yet other impresari and agents, not just for the carnival season that was now about to begin but for intervening seasons as well; and so was the impresario himself. The whole of operatic Italy was criss-crossed by this continual postal traffic, helped by a service that was, by late twentieth-century standards, extraordinarily regular: in the 1820s, a letter from Naples to Milan would have taken eight days, but at least one was not left wondering whether it was going to take three or thirteen. Two decades later, during the 1848 revolutions, Verdi was to be shocked when the post failed to get through.[4]

Part of the impresario's correspondence would have been with private individuals in the town who could help him to arrange his season. He would have to have a local man of substance as his guarantor: most impresari were, to quote an official description of one of them, 'speculators with little capital and no real estate';[5] and governments, by the late eighteenth century, had come to insist on their providing more caution money than before. Then the impresario needed someone, probably a local lawyer, to help the correspondence along by talking to the authorities direct, and perhaps to engage instrumentalists and chorus singers and hire lodgings; in the eighteenth century, and often even up to the 1820s, it was part of the impresario's contract with his leading soloists that he should put them up, sometimes in his own house – a sign, this, of the family character of the business, and a ready cause of friction. Now and then the impresario might also find it politic to take on a local man as his partner in running the season: 'bell-tower patriotism' (*campanilismo*) ran strong in Italian towns and an outsider in charge of the leading theatre might be resented. Whether there had been correspondence with a local scene designer and with the head of a costume workshop depended on how much was to be done on the spot. Some impresari ran their own costume workshop, for their own use and for hire; if our man was one of these he dictated, at some point on the journey across the Apennines, a note bidding his underlings at home remember that the costumes (due to follow a little later by cart) must be the right ones, clean and in good order, and must leave in good time to avoid getting held up by customs.

We think of Italian operas – those few that survive in the repertoire out of the thousands composed – as the work of Cimarosa, Rossini, Bellini, or Donizetti. That was not necessarily how contemporaries looked at them. They did not ignore the individuality of the composer, but at least until the early nineteenth century the composer mattered less than the singers: this was demonstrated by his being paid a fraction of a star singer's fee. The impresario might accordingly sign up a composer when he already had the singers under contract; all composers up to Verdi wrote their operas for particular singers, to suit their vocal resources.

Eighteenth- and early nineteenth-century composition – certainly in Italy – was a kind of musical journalism, done to order, for a specific occasion and in a hurry. The prima donna who in 1807 wanted a clause in her contract entitling her to approve the libretto four months before the start of the season was being optimistic;[6]

it took Bellini's genius – recognised almost at once as something special – to impose on the opera world his need for time, which meant that he had to have seven weeks or so to write an opera from scratch and disliked writing more than one a year.[7] If our impresario was at work in 1823 he could have commissioned an opera from the young Donizetti or from Giovanni Pacini, both of them prolific and fast workers. Pacini, who carried the journalistic habits of his youth into another age, was to be still capable in 1852 of not knowing on 4 December what libretto he would set for the coming carnival season, and yet having the first two acts ready within three weeks.[8] In the early years of the century, when instrumental and choral writing was simpler, not only Rossini and Donizetti and Pacini but the academic veteran Zingarelli would normally compose an opera in anything from two to four weeks.[9] If, for the carnival season we have in mind, the libretto – of the first act at least – had reached the composer sometime in late September or early October, the impresario could rest content; libretto writers too were journalists, and the best of them, Felice Romani, had to an exasperating degree the journalist's combination of dilatoriness and bursts of quick work. If things went wrong the composer might still be waiting in mid or late November for even the first part of the libretto with which he was to open the season on 26 December.[10]

Suppose our impresario knew on 1 December that the libretto was safely written and had got past the censorship that operated in all Italian states; he would still expect the composer to be writing the second or third act in the course of rehearsals and perhaps almost up to the first performance. If he himself arrived at the *piazza* on 2 December he would look for the rest of the company to turn up by the 4th or 6th: that was the date specified in their contracts, unless these read 'early December', which by one of the unwritten customs of the Italian theatre meant 'up to 10 December'.[11] The composer, if he had sent the music of the first act ahead of him, might not turn up until the middle of the month. If on the other hand a singer was still missing by the contractual deadline the impresario hastened to register a legal *protesta* – a statement disclaiming responsibility on grounds of breach of contract.

For the next three weeks everyone was hard at work rehearsing and preparing the new opera. Early vocal rehearsals were by custom held at the prima donna's lodgings, where a keyboard instrument had been installed. The kind of early or mid eighteenth-century opera that had several star soloists, a stately plot, and no chorus was easy enough to stage with the principals brought together only for the last few days.[12] By 1783 things had begun to change; by 1823 operas by and large had more concerted pieces, more scenes with chorus and extras, sometimes more historically conscious sets requiring more elaborate movement; orchestration too, though conservative Italian audiences disapproved, was growing more complex. Theatres which had made it a point of honour to put on two new operas each carnival season, like La Fenice in Venice, were beginning to find such a programme unmanageable.[13] They had to fall back on presenting one opera new to their own town but not expressly composed for it; sometimes, if the first opera of the season was a flop, the impresario might be called upon to rush onto the stage a fall-back work (*opera di ripiego*) while the second main opera contracted for (*opera d'obbligo*) was still being rehearsed, and perhaps written. The notion of repertory opera, with singers coming along to appear at the drop of a hat in a work everyone more or less knew, was not to develop fully until the 1840s; but already in the 1820s a famous tenor like Giovanni David could turn up to rehearse one of 'his' parts with five days to go to the opening – three or four more than many of his late nineteenth-century successors would be asked for.[14]

Meanwhile our impresario, unless he was contracted to one of the biggest and best-funded theatres, had only a single roster of soloists, possibly not even one understudy: if a singer failed to turn up, if he or she fell ill, disaster threatened. An opera might have to be given incomplete – in extreme circumstances, with an apologetic notice put up to warn the audience that the tenor hero's part would simply be left out.[15] To be left on 20 December still without a prima donna or a comic bass, one impresario lamented, was enough 'to make a poor wretch like me spit blood': he then got his singers, but in order to open – late – on 13 January he had to 'put a knife to everyone's throat', and even then he feared the singers would reach the first night unready and sung out. That was the comic opera season (carnival 1816) when Rossini, shivering with the singers in the freezing cold of January nights, rehearsed his early *L'Italiana in Algeri* and went on to dash off *Il Barbiere di Siviglia*.[16]

For this kind of reason the chances were high that the impresario's forces would reach the first performance exhausted. Dress rehearsals sometimes ended at three o'clock in the morning on the day of the performance; singers learnt their parts as these were being written, rehearsed them, and sang performances of the season's first opera, all at once, within a few days of the opening; in a minor theatre they might on occasion virtually learn the work that very day. The result was unpredictable: the company might, like track runners on the last lap, snatch a success through one more burst of nervous energy,[17] or they might sound as tired as they felt and the first night might be a near-failure: this happened with *Norma* and *Il Barbiere*. The cause was not – or not only – a national habit of improvisation: compared with those of the London musical stage, Italian methods of rehearsal could, in the early nineteenth century, seem 'careful and gradual'.[18] The trouble was the relentless rhythm of the seasons and the need to be forever producing new work with, often, barely adequate resources.

In these conditions each first night was a gamble. The new work or the new singer might rouse '*entusiasmo, furore, fanatismo!*' as impresari liked to put it. Even the impresario himself might be carried away: 'he throws his hat into the air', it was reported of one of them, 'tears off his toupee, and shouts like a man possessed'.[19] On the other hand the first night might be the worst kind of *fiasco*. This meant, as a rule, not just a scatter of applause or a cold silence. It meant shouts, insults and whistling (the Italian form of hissing), with some members of the audience blowing through house keys or whelk shells to make even more noise. It might mean, at the extreme, a riot outside the impresario's lodgings.[20] The despotic governments of the Italian states all forbade demonstrations of this kind, but their minute regulations could seldom hold out against an audience determined to hiss, even when police picked out the ringleaders and marched them off to jail. Opera stood at the heart of town life: disorder must be stemmed. So the authorities and the theatre owners served the impresario with written notice that he must within days put on another work, hire another singer, at the cost of yet more frantic correspondence and rehearsal.

Suppose, though, that the impresario's first offering was a success or at any rate was deemed acceptable. The audience on succeeding nights would still not fill the theatre – only something quite unusual could do that – but it would be adequate. This meant that the leading families of the town were coming pretty regularly night after night and occupying their boxes.

They did not come alone. Such families moved about with a retinue of servants. In 1783 these servants milled about the passages and stairs in the intervals of preparing food, drink, and ices for their masters (each box had a dressing-room across the passage where this could be done) or of carrying messages. They also relieved themselves on the spot instead of using the perhaps inadequate buckets provided – into which they sometimes threw rubbish from the dressing-rooms. Matters were not much better on the stage side of the footlights. A late eighteenth-century theatre, even the grandest, stank with the result.[21] Yet other liveried servants might have a space set aside for them in the gallery; at La Scala the *cappe nere* or black cloaks – the noble family's secretary, accountant, major-domo, and other more exalted servants – had cheap entry to the stalls area, so that their masters need lack for nothing they could command at home. By 1823 this overpowering servant presence had abated somewhat: revolution and short-lived democracy had intervened, and the more ostentatious forms of display were gone; lavatories too had been improved. It marked a shift of social tone when La Fenice, rebuilt in 1837 after a fire, no longer had grilles at the back of the boxes for servants to peer through.[22]

It sometimes appears that this audience did little besides talk, eat, drink, gamble, and visit each other. At La Scala up to the 1820s one could draw the curtains of the box and make it into a closed-off drawing-room; at the Teatro Regio, Turin, in the eighteenth century, the royal box had mirrors that allowed gamblers to turn their backs on the stage without losing sight of it.[23] Even in an age when few audiences anywhere preserved a religious silence, foreign visitors were startled by the noise during the performance: Italians might be relatively quiet when the ballet came on, the German composer Nicolai reported, but 'during the opera they all chatter like canary birds that cry all the more sharply the louder the music is played'.[24]

Yet the same Nicolai noted the hair-trigger sensibility of an Italian audience: they might be in tears at a pathetic scene (it was not unknown for someone in a box to cry out during a stage murder 'but he's really killing her!');[25] let the singer utter a false note, though, let a dog bark, and the whole audience would burst out laughing.[26] All this had its positive side. The audience did listen to their favourite passages – which they might be hearing for the twentieth time that season; and they listened as audiences in India today listen to a sitar recital, as active participants, phrase by phrase. 'Without interrupting the performance', the eminent English baritone Charles Santley recalled of his own early days in Lombardy, 'they express their approbation with a murmur of satisfaction, or short sharp "*bravo!*," very encouraging to the performer.' To shy beginners they showed some mercy ('*coraggio!*'); pretty women they greeted with cries of '*bella!*' and a shower of kisses in the air. If they were quick to hiss, that – Santley pointed out with the complacency of an artist too good to have suffered himself – was understandable: it was the only way they could avoid enduring the same bad performance twenty nights in a row.[27]

If no one fell ill or sang out of tune, if both the operas contracted for were reasonably successful, if no epidemic threatened and no princely death intervened to close the theatres, the impresario could count himself fortunate. The routine of the season was then more paperwork: inventories of scenery and properties he had taken over from the owners, returns of ticket sales, returns of boxholders' payments (often in arrears), correspondence with the theatre owners and the government superintendent's office (*Deputazione degli Spettacoli*) over matters of day-to-day running. If two ballet dancers quarrelled and came to blows in the wings, if a singer refused to appear out of caprice rather than genuine indisposition, that, under the old Italian governments, was a matter for officialdom, quite possibly to be dealt with by summary arrest and a short spell in prison. On the morning of every performance a poster announcing it would have to be printed and, with police approval, put up outside the theatre; cast changes of any importance had to be cleared with the *Deputazione* and the theatre owners. But the biggest paper explosion was caused by what the impresario hoped might be a high spot in the box-office returns – a leading singer's benefit night.

Unlike benefits in London this was not a great money-maker: there was in Italian towns little enough money for any purpose. Still, it made a difference – not only to the singer but to the impresario if, as was common, they had agreed to go halves, or if, as was less common, the benefit was a sham and they had agreed on the impresario's pocketing the lot. A benefit night in 1823 and probably a good deal earlier showed just how closely the opera season locked into the social life of the upper classes. The first step was a printed slip which the singer had had distributed to the houses of all opera subscribers and other leading citizens. The famous contralto Rosmunda Pisaroni – so runs an example – was to sing between the acts on her benefit night a scena and rondo by Rossini:

Not this slight addition, but that vivifying genius that animates every individual on this illustrious soil, leads her to flatter herself that the night in question will bring her honour; and that will be the highest prize for one who never did nor will neglect any pains whereby she may make herself worthy of your benevolence and sympathy.[28]

After such an exordium it was only fitting that the lady should be found standing in the foyer as the audience arrived, wearing full costume and with a bowl by her side into which well-wishers deposited offerings in cash; more personal presents – flowers, lace, jewels, perhaps cash as well – went straight to the beneficiary's lodgings. At one time around 1800 the singer whose night it was took to going round the boxes with her collecting bowl, but this seems to have been thought too pressing a call: back went bowl and singer to the foyer, until in the 1830s the practice began gradually to die out.[29] With it died the old Italian custom of throwing into the auditorium sonnets (perhaps printed on silk) in the singer's honour: at Urbino in carnival 1816 a dove bearing a sonnet tied to each foot had flown to the prima donna on stage with a purse containing ten silver coins in its beak.[30]

The other high spot of the carnival season was the series of masked balls and banquets that ended it. These were held in the theatre, often after the performance; they might well bring in more money on any one night than the opera and ballet ever had. By then the impresario was probably glad of this extra income. His first task (after that of propitiating the local authorites) had all along been to see his company paid: night by night for most of the stage staff and sometimes the orchestra and chorus, in four instalments (*quartali*) for the soloists.

This meant that the impresario needed cash in hand, right at the start of rehearsals when the first *quartale* was due. The impresario, that man of – as a rule – little capital and no real estate, was accordingly an anxious figure, his correspondence thick with yet more letters about credit notes due, delayed, discounted, repudiated.

Those who had contracted with him for the season had at the back of their minds the worry that he might not pay: theatrical gossip was full of impresari who had left their company in the lurch, the *quartale* unpaid, after fleeing the town in the middle of the night. Most impresari in most seasons did not fail or run away, though many went through anxious moments; enough did fail to keep suspicion alive.

What if the season did go badly and the impresario failed? The chances were that something had gone wrong from the start – through bad luck, the impresario would maintain, though others put it down to his incompetence. Take Augusto Pecori, an impresario who ran a carnival season a quarter-century later than the period we have been dealing with, but in conditions little changed. The place was Siena, as a rule a sleepy, decaying city, but now – in the time of revolution, 1848–9 – suddenly called upon to house the Grand Duke of Tuscany and his court. In spite of this apparent boon Pecori's season got off on the wrong foot: there was bad feeling in the town, some of his singers were ill, the prima donna was 'so hoarse that she sounds like a rook croaking'. Orchestral parts turned out to be missing from the hired score, the stage staff were 'a chain gang', yet another singer fell ill: in four performances he had taken altogether about 92 francs; 'nothing goes right'. Pecori then got in a new prima donna who took the stage with three days' rehearsal. But by 17 January he was falling behind with some of his payments. He tried to get an advance from the court or from the academy – really an aristocratic club – that owned the theatre, but in vain. Then the Grand Duke, frightened at the latest revolutionary turn of Tuscan politics, fled the state. That finished Pecori: the theatre was virtually empty; he could not meet the third *quartale*. The academy agreed to pay it and end his contract; it handed over the remaining performances to the artists, who banded together to share out what little there was to be earned. Pecori undertook to pay off his other creditors in instalments.[31]

He had got off more lightly than another, more experienced impresario who failed at Parma in carnival 1819. Osea Francia was usually known as *il signor Osea*: he was a Jew and surnames for Jews were still a novelty. Thirty years earlier he had helped to launch a new opera house at Faenza; as the impresario there for the first ten years he was supposed to have put Faenza on the operatic map.[32]

13

He was well known at Parma, for he had put on repeated opera seasons at the Teatro Ducale, certainly since 1811 and possibly as far back as 1801. He had worked at Bologna, Reggio Emilia, and Florence, and at the important summer fair at Senigallia on the Adriatic coast. He was thus an impresario of much experience in a wide area of central Italy.

On 26 December 1818, however, the first night of his Parma season was a disastrous flop. The audience took a violent dislike to the singers; it was so incensed that the Duchess of Parma's government did what the old despotic governments sometimes did: it arrested Osea on the spot and put him in the town fortress. He was let out four days later, but his papers were seized; by 19 January the Duchess (none other than Marie-Louise, Napoleon's separated wife, who had been allotted Parma in the peace settlement) cancelled Osea's contract with his agreement and put in his stead a government commission. She was furious both with him and with his local guarantor. The Ducale was her court theatre (performances did not begin until she turned up or gave leave); what she saw as the two men's 'negligence' seemed to her a personal affront. She therefore directed that the cost of hiring new singers – those who had caused the trouble had been sent packing for fear of worse riot – should fall on Osea; the commission must entertain no claims other than those strictly necessary to keep the season going.

The odd situation therefore arose in which Osea was legally responsible for paying some of the artists, but the commission was collecting the theatre takings. It could not go on: even the governments of Restoration Italy could be brought to a sense of legality and fitness in commercial matters. After receiving a number of anguished petitions from all concerned, the Parma government gave Osea enough money from the subsidy it laid out on the carnival season to enable him to pay his debts and leave on 15 March, as he put it, without dishonour. Part of the trouble all along had probably been that the subsidy allotted to the impresario was too small to meet the demands of the Parma audience; at any rate the Duchess raised it by a quarter within three months.[33]

Not that these failures marked the end of Osea Francia or Augusto Pecori as impresari. Osea went on to run seasons at Modena in 1823 and 1824 and was planning a particularly lavish one when he died in March 1824, leaving debts. He had failed at least twice before the

Parma business, at Florence and again at Senigallia during the economically troubled years that preceded and followed Napoleon's downfall, but had managed to keep going none the less. As for Pecori, a smaller operator, we find him running seasons at Cremona and in a Parma bereft of its former status as late as the 1870s.[34]

The impresario of our model season might not have proved so resilient. It was not unknown for an impresario of long experience to kill himself – as did the first one to run seasons at the new Teatro La Fenice in Venice: in 1794, overwhelmed by losses, he took poison.[35] But such drastic endings were few. It was more common for a bad season to end messily in a series of contractual disputes and lawsuits. The impresario then entrusted the legal business to his lawyer on the spot and himself went off the moment the season ended.

All through it, in spite of excitements and crises, he had been firing off letters to get the coming spring season under way in another town, to plan the autumn season in a third, to negotiate a fresh contract for next year's carnival, to sandwich in a 'sacred drama' (in effect an opera on a biblical subject) during Lent, to set up twenty performances at one of the summer trade fairs.

In one or other of these seasons the impresario would preside over the creation of Bellini's *Norma*, or Donizetti's *Lucia di Lammermoor*, or Verdi's *Nabucco*, or – if he was the kind of impresario who ventured beyond the Alps – Mozart's *Don Giovanni* or Weber's *Euryanthe*. But these works, our main reason for taking an interest today in the economic and social workings of the opera business in the late eighteenth and early nineteenth century, loomed no larger in the impresario's mind than any other production of his – unless he could hire them out after their first season and make a fresh profit. In a business much closer to Hollywood of the 1930s or to television of the 1980s than to the museum opera we are familiar with, the opera that counted was this season's and, after that, next season's: the one that, with any luck, would rouse '*entusiasmo, furore, fanatismo*' and cause a run on the box-office. For the impresario the show must, in the most literal sense, go on.

Stage design by Paolo Landriani for Rossini's opera seria, *Aureliano in Palmira*, Milan, La Scala. 1813.

2 · *A profession of sorts*

Almost anyone could become an opera impresario. But those who did were most of them already involved with opera or ballet; they were also likely to come of musical or theatrical families.

Italy was a conservative country where birth and family did most to determine people's future. Guilds lasted well into the eighteenth century and, in some cities, into the nineteenth; but even after guilds were suppressed most urban crafts and trades went on being run through family organisation and apprenticeships. The lyric theatre was no different. The horn player's son became a horn player; if the town had a permanent orchestra the father would strive to bring in his son as second horn and then leave him the post of first horn when he retired. Nearly everyone who had a fixed post in a theatre, whether as prompter or as ticket collector, tried to do the same; the King of Naples decreed in 1816 that jobs in the royal theatres should not be passed on by inheritance, but several years later an usher still expected to be able to pass his job on to a relative.[1]

So too there were dynasties of ballet dancers, like the Taglioni, and briefer dynasties of singers; there were so many Bassi singers and musicians that one of them, a famous baritone of the mid nineteenth century, marked himself off by taking the name De Bassini. Much of this can be found in the theatrical life of other countries. But family organisation in the Italian theatre seems to have been particularly strong. People who made a success took along with them fathers, brothers, nephews, some to do jobs of work and others as hangers-on; there was a cant term for these – *procoli* – and they were supposed to be particularly demanding. It comes as no surprise that a good many impresari were the sons of impresari or of other theatre people.

Perhaps a majority of professional impresari were former singers, dancers, and choreographers. The ex-singers had mostly failed or had had undistinguished careers: if they had been successful and had managed their earnings sensibly they would not have needed to be impresari. Almost the only clear exceptions – the well-known tenors G. B. Verger and Berardo Calveri Winter, impresari in the 1840s and 50s, the one at Barcelona and Palermo, the other at Naples – had finished their singing careers; both came to grief financially, and they may have had money troubles earlier as well.[2] The comic bass Carlo Cambiaggio, who acted as his own impresario in the 1830s and 40s while still singing in good second-rank theatres, was a distinguished example of a type common in the eighteenth and early nineteenth centuries, the singing leader of a comic opera troupe. He ended as an agent.[3] Other impresari occasionally sang when someone was ill, but only then.

The choreographers turned impresari were more inclined than the ex-singers to go on with their old line of work. The organising skills needed to devise the ballets of the time with their elaborate plots and scene changes and their crowds of extras were after all akin to those of management in general. Dance is an evanescent medium: the names of the leading choreographers who became important impresari – Onorato Viganò, Lorenzo Panzieri, Livio Morosini, Domenico Ronzani – now mean nothing to anyone except a few specialists. Viganò helped to launch the career of his still more famous son Salvatore, author of *The Creatures of Prometheus* and other grandiose ballets. Ronzani, 'the last of the great Italian choreographers of the nineteenth century', had a mixed career as an impresario in the 1850s; after a series of financial disasters he fled to the United States, where he ran a touring ballet company while the wife he had left behind became Cavour's last mistress.[4]

For similar reasons scene designers and especially the owners of costume workshops found it easy to become impresari. In the seventeenth century a noted impresario in Venice and Munich, Francesco Santurini, had been in the first place a designer of scenic vistas. By the late eighteenth century costume design and manufacture seems to have become a readier path to taking on the organisation of an opera season. Both scenery and costumes were given high importance. The impresario's contract generally stressed the need for 'splendour'; in leading theatres everything had if possible to be new; leading singers' costumes must be made entirely of silk and velvet. The head of a costume workshop was often described as a '*capitalista di vestiario*': it was not unknown for him to offer to take on a season as a means of getting a return on his stock,[5] and then press for a particular opera to be done because it would suit what he had available.[6]

Plenty of musicians took on the running of a season, but usually as a last resort when a professional impresario had failed part way through or when none would come forward: it was a way of keeping the orchestra employed. Otherwise few musicians became impresari. Rossini and then Donizetti were successively involved with the *impresa* (management) of the Naples royal theatres, but as musical directors and shareholders rather than as heads of the enterprise. Near the start of the nineteenth century a composer then of some note, Gaetano Andreozzi, had taken over the Naples *impresa*, briefly and disastrously. Haydn's cellist from Esterháza, Valentino Bertoja, did little better in Venice about the same time. Of the better-known nineteenth-century composers the only one to have dabbled in opera management – in partnership with others – was Pacini. In the difficult last years of his long career, around 1860, he started a theatrical agency; whether this was the cause of his financial troubles or an attempt to remedy them is not known.[7] With exceptions like these, impresari by and large were not musicians; most of them had little or nothing to say about the musical (as against the commercial) merits of particular scores.

But although the lyric stage was deeply traditional and run on family lines the profession remained open to anyone with cash, dedication, or effrontery. Like other branches of the theatre it was free because not wholly respectable: opera provided, for instance, one of the very few ways for women to make a career and run their lives as they chose.

In Italy, as in other parts of Europe, the early nineteenth century saw an attempt to make the theatre world more proper. Singers and dancers, a well-informed writer asserted in 1823, were now often 'persons of the best birth and breeding and of unexceptionable conduct'; at about the same time the Naples government was busying itself with making sure that men's and women's dressing rooms were kept separate and backstage visitors banned, and was being assured by the impresario (with some exaggeration) that 'the theatre has become a chapel'.[8]

True enough, the upheaval of the revolutionary and Napoleonic years had impoverished some landed families and driven their children to seek a living on the operatic stage. One such, whose singing career petered out, became an impresario and agent. He complained in after years that with his noble birth and natural 'unbounded sensibility' he had to live 'buffeted by the moral deficiencies of many creatures compounded of bad faith with whom I unfortunately must be in frequent contact'.[9] This need not be taken too seriously. He was writing to an official: people in the opera world used one language to the great and another – racy, slangy, often bawdy – among themselves. Even people like Donizetti and Verdi who girded at the corruption of the theatre noticeably failed, when they had made a lot of money, to leave its freemasonry behind.

A member of the upper classes who had held on to his land and fortune could choose to turn impresario. In the middle decades of the eighteenth century, sometimes until its close, it had been normal practice in some leading theatres – those of Turin, Milan, and Bologna in particular – for an association of nobles to act as impresari and elect a directorate to run the opera season. At La Pergola in Florence up to the 1750s the *impresa* was often in the hands of one or more nobles. In Venice and some other northern cities like Modena, individual noble families owned theatres and played an active part in running seasons.[10] By the 1820s the association of noble impresari was generally recognised as extravagant and expensive; an attempt to revive it in the Turin royal theatres between 1824 and 1833 only confirmed this.[11] On the same grounds, associations of boxholder–proprietors like those of La Fenice, Venice, did their best to attract professional impresari. In Venice and other cities – with Rome a notable exception – family owners had mostly given way to boxholders' associations or to professionals in controlling and running seasons.

Where members of the upper classes controlled theatres there was a standing temptation for them to take part in the running of the season even if a professional impresario held the contract. The directors of La Fenice were – one leading professional impresario complained – fussy to the point of 'prolixity';[12] among them Giuseppe Berti, a landowner, and Carlo Marzari, probably a lawyer, had an important share in putting on new works by Donizetti and Verdi.

Some members of the upper classes who took an active interest in opera *impresa* had singers or ballerinas as their mistresses or wives; it is not generally clear which came first, the interest or the liaison. The Marchese Cavalli, who gave Rossini his first chance at a minor Venice theatre, had first come across him when, as a thirteen-year-old accompanist, Rossini had laughed at an unfortunate cadenza uttered by Cavalli's mistress, a mediocre though beautiful singer.[13] It was characteristic that Cavalli was prepared to put vocal qualities ahead of sexual claims. There is little evidence that noble 'protection' helped incompetent singers to make a career they would otherwise have missed: the public was too exacting. Matters may well have been different in ballet, where technical demands were less than they became later in the century. But even here we do not find in the nineteenth century the flamboyance of the mid eighteenth, when one noble theatre owner's mistress, a prima ballerina, went about with him dressed as a man in clothes identical to his, and another noble impresario had a male dancer, presumably a rival in love, beaten up by thugs when the man was naked drying himself after the performance.[14] Discretion had come in.

Cavalli, who ran several seasons in the Napoleonic period, seems to have been more of a genuine impresario than the odd noble who put on a season to show off a particular singer. Among these last were two expatriate members of the English gentry, Joseph Glossop and Rowland Standish. Standish was content to run a few minor seasons for his soprano.[15] Glossop went further. He was married – legally or not – to two leading singers in turn. A fit of dangerous optimism led him to take on in 1824–5 both of the biggest *imprese* in Italy, those of the Milan and Naples royal theatres. The venture lasted only a few months; Glossop was bailed out by his family in England (whose purse had already been taxed by his share in financing the London theatre that became the Old Vic) and his passion for opera was fulfilled only by his grandson Augustus Glossop-Harris, who as Sir Augustus Harris was to run famous Drury Lane and Covent Garden seasons in the late Victorian period.[16]

In contrast, Duke Carlo Visconti di Modrone, whose tenure of La Scala in 1833–6 was cut short by death, seems to have begun as a speculator; at first he put in a deputy, but when things went wrong he took over and seems then to have behaved much like a professional impresario, conducting correspondence, interviewing singers, and taking rehearsals himself.[17]

Though there were these noble amateurs, or amateurs turned professional, what we hardly find in Italy is the kind of bourgeois impresario who flourished in Paris in the middle decades of the nineteenth century, with some education, a professional or journalistic background, and an aptitude for speculative ventures of different kinds. A solitary exception is Angelo Petracchi, impresario of La Scala from 1816 to 1820. Under the brief republican régime this former lawyer had been a member of the legislature, then a diplomat; he became private secretary to the redoubtable Finance Minister, Prina, in Napoleon's Kingdom of Italy. He was also a poet, had been a rival in love of the great poet Foscolo, and in later life promoted insurance against hailstorms. At La Scala he enjoyed the backing of a trio of Milanese bankers; he seems to have carried on his seasons decently but at a loss. He then wrote a book – rather abstract in its argument though well documented – urging that opera houses should be run by the state through a permanent administration. By a permanent administration he may well have meant one run by himself. Soon afterwards he went to London as director, in effect stage manager, of the King's Theatre in the Haymarket, which at that time housed the Italian opera, but he seems to have made little mark.[18]

Petracchi is significant in showing what impresari were not. They did not write books (though a few wrote libretti), practise law (for purposes other than bringing suits over theatre contracts), or move in the same circles as Foscolo. Indeed it is doubtful whether many of them had heard of Foscolo: literature seems to have interested them exclusively as a quarry for opera and ballet plots, and after reading thousands of their letters it comes as a considerable surprise to find one – G. B. Lasina, an amiable man who played rather a subordinate part at La Fenice in the first productions of *Rigoletto* and *La Traviata* – quoting Dante.

'Clerk, printer, tradesman, busybody, and now impresario as well': this description of the Naples impresario Vincenzio Flauto gives some notion of the social groups impresari came from when they were neither members of theatrical or musical families nor upper-class amateurs. Flauto, it is true, once told the ailing Verdi that he had been a doctor, but that was probably a joke in bad taste. His firm had for generations done the San Carlo's printing and, like some other theatrical printers, he had drifted into opera management.[19]

Those impresari who were not ex-singers or choreographers or members of the upper classes fall into three main groups; they include some of the men who made a deep mark on nineteenth-century Italian opera. The three groups are: tradesmen; agents and journalists; and gambling promoters.

If we say that tradesmen who became impresari were shopkeepers, mainly dealing in food and in luxury articles, that alone does not get us far. In a country with few manufactures and many poor those were in any case the trades most likely to be carried on. But why did the successful jeweller Andrea Campigli, with a shop on the Ponte Vecchio, choose to become a powerful theatrical agent and manage the leading Florence opera house, La Pergola, for fourteen years in the 1770s and 80s?[20] We do not know. A much later Florentine businessman, the eccentric Girolamo Pagliano – inventor of a successful herbal elixir – built his own huge opera house and ran it some of the time as impresario; but he was a failed singer with a passion for music.[21]

Where we can observe a group of tradesman impresari at work, in nineteenth-century Rome, the key to their theatrical activity is their relationship with the nobles who owned the main theatres. Rome, until unification a near-stagnant city compared with the more advanced Milan and Turin, kept up several practices that had grown obsolete in opera seasons elsewhere: it may therefore point to similar conditions in other cities at earlier, less well-documented periods.

From the early years of the nineteenth century to 1880, Rome opera seasons were run at nearly all times by a handful of impresari who were all tradesmen and who in their theatrical undertakings seldom ventured outside the city and its region.* Giovanni Paterni (1779–1837) was a distiller–shopkeeper and owner of house property; he seems to have dabbled in other lines of trade, for in 1828 he got a licence to import from Naples a kind of paint or dyestuff (*imbratta*); for some years he held a government concession as inspector of weights and measures (*dogana dei pesi e misure*), with the right to pocket fines.[22] Pietro Cartoni (1776–1848) was a grocer

---

* The other big city where a few locally rooted impresari dominated the theatre was Genoa.

(*droghiere*) who traded, among other things, in chocolate; his four brothers joined him in some of his ventures and one of them, Felice, was a manufacturer of high-quality masks.[23] Aniceto Pistoni (died 1828) was a café keeper.[24] Vincenzo Jacovacci (1811–80), a famously mean man with a squeaky voice who dominated Rome opera seasons for forty years, was a fishmonger; he seems to have inherited the fish business and had it run by his brother while he attended to his theatres.[25]

What these men had in common was their dependence on the papal government and on two or three noble families who owned theatres: the Sforza Cesarini, who had built the Argentina in 1731 as a speculation; the Capranica, owners of the palaces that housed the Capranica and Valle theatres; and the Torlonia, rich bankers and landowners who bought the leading Rome theratre, the Apollo, in 1820 and went on to buy up most of the others in the 1840s and 50s. Cartoni (who put on the first performance of Rossini's *La Cenerentola*) had his flat and shop in the Marchese Capranica's palace and supplied Capranica's household with chocolate and candles besides running some of his theatre seasons; Pistoni seems to have regarded himself as a kind of steward to Capranica for theatrical purposes; Paterni was Capranica's creditor as well as his impresario. Though we lack documentation of Jacovacci's ties with the Torlonia they were certainly close.

One archaic Rome practice was that the papal government still sometimes gave one man a monopoly of theatrical production; even when there was no legal monopoly the tendency remained for one man to try to corner the *impresa* of all the main theatres. Hence a prolonged war of petitions and lawsuits between Paterni and the Cartoni family from 1820 until Paterni's death in 1837. It started when Paterni outbid Cartoni for the monopoly by offering the papal government a mixed lot of antiques, including 200 Etruscan vases for the Vatican Museum. Cartoni claimed (unsuccessfully) the right of first refusal and offered to match the antiques within ten months.[26] The limits to what these men might trade in were clearly flexible. From 1840 there was a briefer but sharp struggle between Cartoni and the rising Jacovacci. Even when Jacovacci was securely established one of his subordinates wrote that he was

as jealous of his theatre as a Turk is of his favourite, and he would do anything to prevent other theatres from playing while his is open. I need not tell you how much he dislikes other impresari. He would like to see them all ruined and indeed none of them so far has succeeded [in Rome].[27]

There were economic reasons, to be discussed in a later chapter, for the restrictive outlook of these Rome impresari. But by the time Verdi dealt with him over the first performance of *Un Ballo in maschera* (1859) Jacovacci's penny-pinching had come to seem absurdly out of date. When Verdi complained that the women singers were all poor Jacovacci replied that the house was full anyhow: 'Next year I'll get hold of some good women singers, so the opera will still be new for the audience. This year half – later the other half.' There were other episodes when Jacovacci tried to bargain over the hire of Verdi scores; Verdi at one point invited him ironically, if he could not afford proper fees, to help himself to the old operas of Paisiello, Gluck, and Lully, hallowed and costing nothing.[28]

These shopkeeping impresari with their dependence on noble patrons and their traffic in vases and chocolate seem to have survived from a world before the French Revolution. The figure who represents the agent or journalist type of impresario at its most successful, Bartolomeo Merelli (1794–1879), was unmistakably of the nineteenth century. He lived by the word rather than by scales and ledgers; he came from the region that was most advanced economically, Lombardy; he depended on noble patrons only in the general sense that all impresari did, and indeed he nursed for some years a passionate desire to prove his own noble origins.

Merelli's father was steward to a noble family of Bergamo; the young Bartolomeo was destined for the law, but soon got into the way of writing verse for the still younger Donizetti to set as prentice exercises; he also claimed to have helped Donizetti to a touch of literary education.[29] What happened next has been disputed but can now be plainly established. Merelli, aged about eighteen, was arrested in 1812 and charged with attempted theft from the house of a noblewoman (probably a relative of his father's employer). Nearly six months later a court decided that there was insufficient evidence, but none the less ordered that he should be detained for three more months while inquiries went on; after that it ordered his release, but on bail and under police surveillance.[30] This seems to have been a traumatic event. Merelli made his way to Milan; there he got into the world of theatrical agents and was quickly able to set up on his own. At the same time he went on writing libretti for Donizetti and others.

Merelli's long career is ill-documented; much of his vast correspondence seems to be lost. What is clear is that throughout it he was first of all an agent, a man concerned with placing artists at maximum profit. He was one of the few agents to develop a system of giving artists long-term contracts and then trying to make a profit by selling their services; when he became an impresario – at La Scala and La Fenice in partnership with the two older impresari Crivelli and Lanari in 1828 – at least one of his partners thought he was too preoccupied with his other commitments as agent to put his best efforts into the business.[31] It was none the less Merelli who took over when Crivelli died in 1831 ten days before the first night of *Norma*, and who saw the work through to its uncertain start.[32] From then until the 1848 revolution he was actively concerned with La Scala and its sister theatre, the Cannobiana, at first on behalf of others and then, from 1836, as impresario himself. At the same time he took on the Kärntnertortheater, the Vienna opera house, which he ran – as he did some seasons in the north Italian provinces – through a partner, with himself always the master agent.

Merelli became a rich man. He kept English horses. In his villa outside Milan he accumulated a collection of old masters. He relished the title flatterers gave him of 'the Napoleon of impresari'. In the 1840s he spent years (and, according to his own account, nearly 300,000 francs) trying to prove his aristocratic origins so that he could send his sons to a college for the sons of noblemen.[33] This seems to have been his life's passion. But the Austrian Emperor would not consent; there is a hint that the old theft charge stood in the way.

Meanwhile Merelli seems to have deliberately behaved like a gentleman and to have been treated like one. His surviving letters avoid all bad language – unusual enough in the theatre of the time; more unusually still, his sometime partner Lanari, a tough old professional, avoided bad language in writing to him. That he was now and then described as a swine or scoundrel was only common form in the hard-pressed world of opera, where the same person would denounce you one year and call you friend the next. But Merelli, without – to our knowledge – having done anything plainly scandalous, attracted more than his share of distrust and dislike; he seems also to have been a good hater.[34] His real failing, probably, was glibness: he remained the agent who assumes that all is well when the right 'package' has been put together, and does not follow through. Verdi, who owed Merelli a great deal – it was Merelli who launched him, and who got him out of his depression after the deaths of his wife and children and into the composition of *Nabucco* – nevertheless refused to let La Scala put on any more of his works after experiencing Merelli's shabby productions. Donizetti, who may also have owed Merelli something, complained of careless staging and cavalier treatment of his music.[35]

Merelli came to grief in the 1848–9 revolutions and wars, which damaged him financially as they did other impresari. He was, besides, suspected of being an Austrian spy, though no evidence was produced; he was certainly pro-Austrian[36] – not in itself unusual up to 1848, particularly in the opera world, which tended to be apolitical or pro-government. He withdrew to his Vienna *impresa*, kept it until 1859, but then lost it. After a last fling in 1861–3 as impresario in Milan and Turin his financial troubles caught up with him; he lost most of his fortune and retired to the hills near Bergamo. When over eighty he published an anonymous booklet, ostensibly his recollections of Donizetti's youth but in part a puff for his own 'gigantic theatrical operations, bound up with so many events important and glorious for Italian Musical Art'.[37]

No other agent attained Merelli's eminence as impresario. Three agents who branched out with some success as impresari were Pietro Camuri and Antonio and Alessandro Magotti, father and son.

Camuri was a Modenese agent who often acted as impresario in his native city as well as in Bologna and other northern towns; for several years in the 1830s he ran the leading Rome opera season. In contrast with Merelli he was described by an authoritative source – the great dialect poet Belli, who knew a lot about the inner workings of the Rome theatre – as an honest man. His surviving correspondence is plain and businesslike and there is no reason to doubt this judgment. In the midst of the 1848 revolution, when he was ill and in deep financial trouble, he was able to appeal successfully to his fellow Modenese to support him by attending a benefit night.[38]

The Magotti between them carried on an important Bologna agency from the 1820s to the end of the century. Antonio Magotti was an ex-singer whose operatic career seems not to have got off the ground. Besides doing every kind of agency work he and his son specialised in furnishing entire companies for minor opera houses, first in their own region and in central Italy from the 1840s, then in southern Italy and Greece as those regions were opened up. They seem to have taken shares in *imprese* and represented outside impresari in Bologna rather than become ostensible impresari themselves, though Alessandro would go down to a place like Bari in the 1870s to take one of his companies through the last few days' rehearsals. Rather than creative men they seem to have been steady and expert packagers.[39]

In the last quarter of the nineteenth century Carlo D'Ormeville (1840–1924) had a busy career as agent, poet, librettist, and journalist, besides acting now and then as impresario, but by that time the impresario's role was devalued.

Gambling promotion was an entry to the running of opera seasons for the simple reason that as the centre of social life the opera house was usually the place where the upper classes gambled: that was the purpose of the spacious foyers in eighteenth-century Italian opera houses. The old Italian governments sometimes permitted games of chance, sometimes not; but even when faro and roulette were forbidden operagoers were allowed to bet small sums on milder games like backgammon. In the eighteenth century the normal practice was to forbid games of chance everywhere else but to grant a monopoly concession to the impresario of the opera house. This monopoly was abolished at various dates between 1753 and 1788 as 'enlightened' principles spread through the Italian states; but from 1802 the new states of Napoleonic Italy revived it as a means of raising badly needed revenue.

Large garrisons, free-spending governments, and wartime upheaval between them made Milan, Naples, and the spa of Bagni di Lucca centres of gambling on an unexampled scale; between 1802 and 1810 those impresari who had the gambling concession enjoyed a bonanza. But the Restoration governments once again suppressed the monopoly, in north and central Italy from 1814 and in Naples and Sicily from 1820. Only the tiny Duchy of Lucca went on upholding the monopoly – and financing opera seasons at Lucca of unusual quality for so small a place – until its own disappearance in 1847.[40]

Eighteenth-century impresari as a matter of course organised gambling, provided cards and dice, and collected profits of which part had to be paid over to the state or to a charity. That did not make the impresari crooks, though it must have coloured the atmosphere they worked in. One who was a crook, a Neapolitan called Giuseppe Affligio, began as a cardsharp around army camps and managed to become a colonel, a rich man, and impresario of the Vienna court theatres from 1767 to 1779. In the latter year he was arrested for forgery and sentenced to the galleys.[41]

The impresari who came up with the Napoleonic gambling monopoly were not like that. They were a close-knit group, or more likely they became one after having started out as rivals. They were to dominate opera in Milan for a quarter-century, in Naples and Vienna for longer still.

Of these men two were already professional impresari: Francesco Benedetto Ricci, who ran La Scala throughout the Napoleonic years – one of its most splendid periods, at least in ballet and scene design – and Giuseppe Crivelli (died 1831), who had started in Turin but moved on to Milan and Venice. Little is known about them. Ricci made a great deal of money out of the Milan gambling; with it he bought land. Crivelli was said to have once employed three thugs to beat up a nobleman who had forced him to pay a debt.[42]

The Villa brothers were rooted in Milan; they appear to have been men of means – financiers and perhaps building contractors – independently of their opera and gambling concerns, which they carried on as local partners of one of the big impresari. The head of the family, G. B. Villa (died 1848) seems to have been the type of the shrewd, laconic Milanese businessman: favourite phrases were 'I'm laughing it off' and 'if this doesn't suit you do whatever you like'.[43]

The two leading impresari in this group started out as gambling promoters. Carlo Balochino (?1770–1850) was the son of a Piedmontese pharmacist and seems himself to have been the typical dour, close-fisted Piedmontese of legend. In later life he described his father as an attorney. He also told people that he himself had started as a *tailleur*, which they took in its normal sense of 'tailor'; he had in fact been a croupier or card-cutter (likewise *tailleur*). When the gambling monopoly started up in Milan in 1802 Balochino was turned away from the La Scala card-tables; he then contracted to run the gambling in a house patronised by General Joachim Murat, Napoleon's brother-in-law, who for a few months tried to set up a gambling network in northern Italy in opposition to the official monopoly.[44]

Not long afterwards there arrived together in the foyer of La Scala two new portents: a former café waiter and billiard player called Domenico Barbaja (1778–1841), and the roulette wheel. It was Barbaja who introduced roulette, a recent French invention; he subcontracted from the impresario, F. B. Ricci, who did not realise at first the potential of this new form of gambling – 'democratic' in that it allowed far more people to take part at any one time than did older games. That was in the carnival of 1805. Within a year Barbaja not only was rich, with houses and land to his name; he and Balochino had joined forces. As the French armies took over other parts of Italy after Napoleon's victory at Austerlitz, Balochino opened up the gambling monopoly in Venice while Barbaja similarly conquered Naples. Within two months (April–May 1806) the Barbaja gambling syndicate came to control not only these cities and Milan but twenty other towns in northern Italy; to these were added, in 1809, Lucca and, after further Napoleonic conquests, various former papal and Austrian cities.

Meanwhile, in tune with the Italian habit of attaching any gambling monopoly to the theatre, Balochino had become in 1807 impresario of La Fenice. Barbaja achieved in the same year a share-out of the La Scala management with Ricci, Crivelli, and the Villa brothers. In Naples, where Barbaja settled, he himself in 1809 took over the San Carlo and other royal theatres, though Ricci in the following year paid him back in his own coin: by judicious counter-bidding he forced Barbaja to grant him a share in the Naples management.

Barbaja and Balochino were oddly contrasted: Balochino stubborn but controlled, writing educated Italian in correspondence that was at times querulous but gave little away; Barbaja exuberant, scarcely literate, such letters as he wrote in his own hand spelt phonetically in Milanese Italian and bespattered with vigorous multiple dashes and underlinings as well as with swear-words. There was no doubt of who was boss. Balochino spent most of his Italian career working as Barbaja's subordinate in Venice and Naples or else in partnership with other members of the syndicate in Milan and, again, Venice;

later, from 1835 to 1848, he was Merelli's partner and man on the spot in Vienna. Balochino was always cautious; in his last Vienna years he seems to have lost touch, to the extent of refusing one of the best German operas of the period, *The Merry Wives of Windsor* by his own musical director Nicolai.[45]

Barbaja on the other hand became a millionaire and lived like one. His millions came not just from the gambling monopoly but from army contracts in the Napoleonic period, and then from large-scale building contracts employing thousands of men: in Naples the neo-classical church of San Francesco di Paola, new government offices, the new Teatro San Carlo (rebuilt after a fire) were all his firm's work.[46] Barbaja quickly developed the tastes of a millionaire: diamonds, racehorses, a picture collection that would have been remarkable even if only half the attributions were correct,[47] a villa on the coast built to his own 'eccentric' design as well as a house on the main street of Naples.[48] The great soprano Isabella Colbran was his mistress until she left him for Rossini (with the three of them remaining friends).

Amid all this Barbaja ran the Naples royal theatres with only brief interruptions over thirty-one years; he also took on La Scala and the Vienna opera for a few years in the 1820s, setting up a kind of opera shuttle service as he had once run a many-centred gambling syndicate. He was thus responsible for putting on some of Rossini's most ambitious *opere serie* as well as Weber's *Euryanthe* and others by Donizetti, Pacini, and Mercadante.

'Murderer', 'thief', 'crook', were some of the insults Barbaja let fly with ease, for he was irritable and vain and had a strong streak of self-pity:

for 15 years for my sins I've been doing *this infamous job as impresario* – and I've been an honest man – and when I give my word I keep it – I know all the crooked ways of these *theatrical scoundrels* and my worst enemies are those who drink my blood – there isn't much left – and one of my *chief enemies is that fool my son* but one day he will be sorry indeed to have acted like this but poor fool it'll be too late.[49]

His vanity went to the length of asserting, improbably, that he might have displaced Rothschild in making a loan to the Kingdom of the Two Sicilies.[50] Yet Barbaja also had a strong streak of generosity and even of naïvety. He liked to describe himself in the third person as 'that animal Barbaja', 'that ass [*coglione*, literally "testicle"] Barbaja'. If you stood up to his bluster he relented: '"All right, you old crook" – and he ordered a plate of spaghetti and we made peace.'[51]

His contemporaries praised him for the magnificence and good taste of his productions: there was no expense spared.[52] Yet he could bargain as shrewdly as anyone, whether with the government or with fellow impresari. The truth was rather that Barbaja had considerable organising genius. Nothing short of that could have run a gambling syndicate across large parts of Italy, regularly collecting money from subcontractors in each city and – what the governments that licensed him appreciated above all – paying on the nail himself. That may suggest something like an urban mafia chief of later times. There is no doubt that Barbaja did his best to achieve the legal right to collect a rake-off on all private gambling, achieved it briefly in Naples, and, according to his enemies, had all along been collecting it unofficially. But the mafia too has its efficient and inefficient operators.

Part of that efficiency was to make himself indispensable. Like Jacovacci in Rome, he detested any possible rivals for the Naples opera *impresa* and did his best to thwart them; he made short work of Glossop, that hopeful black sheep of an English gentry family.[53] Unlike Jacovacci, he aimed at grandeur and put on, with ups and downs, some of the finest seasons in the history of the Naples lyric stage. Towards the end of his career he too ran into financial trouble, tried to sell off some of his pictures, and left a fortune much diminished. He died of apoplexy when lending a hand to some workmen on an extension to his villa. The theatre audience that night filed out in silence at the news, and his funeral was attended by artists some of them so old that they had to be supported. At his memorial service the work sung was Mozart's *Requiem* – not what might have been expected if the ceremony had marked the passing of a vulgarian.[54]

Barbaja had gone from running a concession only indirectly connected with the lyric stage to producing opera and ballet on a grand scale. An impresario who did things the other way round was Andrea Bandini. From 1819 on he was active in Parma, Bologna, and other northern cities as well as, for a few troubled years in the 1830s, in his native Florence. There seems to have been little remarkable about his work and he himself was repeatedly called arrogant and difficult; we have an account of him coming down from a carnival banquet, full of food and drink, and blackguarding the theatre ushers as dishonest.[55]

Just when he was in apparently severe financial difficulties in Florence in 1838 Bandini took on, with a banker as his partner, the concession of salt and tobacco taxes for the neighbouring Duchy of Lucca: the partners were to pay the Lucca government just over 500,000 francs a year. In 1843 they also made the duchy a loan of another half-million or so, and two years later Bandini offered (unsuccessfully) to take on the running of a new land survey. He claimed to have been 'experienced in the direction of enterprises (*imprese*) of every kind, [and] favoured by many royal governments with the task of carrying out important and delicate speculations'.[56] Even if the claim had some substance it is surprising that Bandini should have been able to branch out as a moneylender and tax farmer on this scale. Lucca still allowed a gambling monopoly (farmed out, at least nominally, to two Frenchmen) and the roulette tables at Bagni di Lucca drew adventurers from all over Europe: one might suspect that Bandini's suddenly enlarged means were in some way connected with that. At all events his career shows how long the relationship lasted between opera management and the running of government concessions characteristic of the *ancien régime*.

Precisely because the impresario was a go-between, a fixer, opera *impresa* was seldom a distinct profession. A man who could fix an opera season could fix a lot of other things. Yet an ideal of the professional impresario did exist. So far as it was embodied in any one man that man was Alessandro Lanari (1787–1852).

There is some temptation to believe this simply because we know more about Lanari than about any other impresario: the 15,000 or so items of his surviving correspondence (only a fraction of his total archive) fill in detail on a scale unmatched elsewhere. But we need not rely on our own conclusions. Those virtues of Lanari's that struck contemporaries were his knowledge and competence in all branches of his business, and his care for what are now called production values, especially the finish and historical authenticity of sets and costumes. They are well attested. Donizetti, without any obvious axe to grind, wrote that there was 'no impresario more alert than he or more dedicated to serving the public well'.[57] Verdi trusted him with *Macbeth*, well aware that it needed careful production, and was – unusually – willing to prepare a revival of it with Lanari once again the impresario.[58] Fairly early in Lanari's career, which ran from at least as early as 1819 until his death, an observer stressed his talent as a producer: 'costumes, scenery, even part of the ballet are directed by him, and he is expert in all of them. I see him on stage in the evening doing what few people could manage, always coolly and without getting upset.'[59]

Although – or rather because – he was the most peripatetic of impresari, Lanari insisted on getting a detailed account of all the scenery and costumes needed well before the libretto was finished, let alone the score: 'you know I like to do things properly', he told Donizetti in August 1836 when he wanted to start preparing a new opera for the ensuing carnival.[60] Yet he was not concerned only with the look of the stage. To the well-known scene designer Pietro Venier he wrote that the tribunal scene in *Beatrice di Tenda* must indeed have a 'very majestic and rich throne', but that a deep set (such as Venier clearly wished to build) would not do. It would be effective in itself, but 'since both the choristers and Ronconi have to sing from where they are placed...the effect of the music would be lost'[61] – a piece of advice worth recalling today.

Lanari came from Jesi, a small town in the Marches of eastern Italy. A brother of his stayed on and seems to have had a part in running the theatre there. Alessandro is first heard of as impresario in 1819 in Lucca, by which time he was married to a successful singer, Clementina Domeniconi, a member of a well-known theatrical tribe; soon afterwards, however, they appear to have separated and from then on Lanari lived with a minor singer, Carlotta Corazza. In 1823 he took over, from an impresario who had just died, both a costume workshop in Florence and the task of running the main theatre there, La Pergola. The workshop became one of the two main influences that shaped Lanari's career; the other was the practice he developed during the 1820s of giving promising singers long-term contracts and then trying to place them at a profit.

Workshop and agency both led him to form circuits where his costumes and his singers could be exploited with the fewest possible gaps. One circuit took in Florence, Lucca, and the secondary towns of Tuscany and Umbria, particularly Pisa, Leghorn, Siena, Perugia, and Foligno. In the minor towns Lanari either put subordinates in charge of the theatre or had a regular understanding with the local impresario. In Florence he did not, like Barbaja or Jacovacci, wish to run everything himself, but he was determined to hang on to La Pergola, if not as impresario then at least as costume supplier; on two occasions when he failed in this he conducted a 'war' on La Pergola by running a season in a rival theatre.

The larger circuit on which Lanari operated took in almost the whole of operatic Italy except for Turin, Genoa, and Trieste. He had long runs of seasons at La Fenice, Venice, and at the Senigallia fair; he also worked at various times in Bologna, Parma, Verona, and Ancona, in some smaller towns of northern Italy, twice in Rome, once in Milan, and once in Naples when Barbaja was out of things. Because he often worked in partnership with others his role has not always been clear, but he was responsible for launching two of Bellini's operas, two of Verdi's, and five of Donizetti's, including *Lucia di Lammermoor*. He also helped to launch some of the finest singers of the day, in particular the French tenor Duprez, whose discovery under Lanari's guidance in Italy of the 'chest high C' changed the development of the tenor voice.[62]

All this was done with the impresario constantly on the move, firing off letters to partners and subordinates elsewhere while he rehearsed new works for the season he had chosen to run himself. While Lanari was away his widowed sister, a semi-literate woman, ran the costume workshop; a nephew accompanied him as secretary; other relatives and retainers, among them a couple of broken-down ex-impresari, did various jobs at his Florence headquarters.

He was running what was for Italy a fairly large and complex business. His understanding of his craft was wide. Yet he remained a harsh, narrow, driving man. The only expression of unaffected warm feeling that has come down to us dates from his youth; it was addressed to Rosa Morandi, a famous contralto, and her husband, slightly older people who both came from his native Marches and who had befriended him. He was genuinely moved at Rosa's early death.[63] For the rest, to paraphrase Coolidge, the business of Alessandro Lanari was business.

He drove a hard bargain. When his common-law wife Carlotta exclaimed on first hearing Duprez's voice at rehearsal Lanari slapped her – by praising it she might drive up the young tenor's price.[64] Nothing was too small for him to scrutinise. When away from Florence he insisted on trying to control the number of sequins bought for the workshop and the price paid for cloth. If the price seemed too high he complained that he was being 'assassinated'. Because he was suspicious he did not delegate authority clearly: the people he left in charge then quarrelled among themselves. He snapped at his subordinates when they failed to consult him ('I ought to be everywhere'); he snapped at them when they pestered him with detail ('I don't know how you expect me to deal with such matters from here').[65] An incompetent retainer, rather like an old dog, who was supposed to help in running the costume workshop once asked exceptionally for a fifth-tier box at La Pergola; Lanari let him have it but added 'I am sure your going to the theatre won't lead you to neglect the workshop.'[66]

A story of Duprez's rings true even though it had probably improved with time. When he saw Lanari about signing a long-term contract – he was then twenty-four – Lanari was in his bath, to which he was often confined by severe piles. Duprez tried to push up the price. '"Alas! You want to make me die, I can see! A poor impresario who is in such pain! To torment him like that! Look!..." and, willy-nilly, I saw!' Hardly knowing whether to laugh or commiserate, Duprez signed.[67]

Yet Lanari had every reason to drive and be driven. His finances were precarious. He depended on a complex traffic in credit notes that might or might not keep him solvent; at several points in his career he was in serious difficulties. Probably it was his tireless attention to the price of sequins, as well as to the detail of costumes and scenery, that kept him going. In the end the 1848 revolutions were disastrous for him as for others. He announced in 1849 that he would no longer act as impresario, though he was keeping on his agency and his costume workshop. But already in the following year he was coming back and running seasons in Bologna, though not under his own name. Before he could recover fully he died in 1852. His son, trained as a lawyer, took over but went bankrupt ten years later. Scores, scenery, the stock from the costume workshop – everything went.[68]

Alessandro Lanari had shown that a hard-working impresario could make, though with difficulty and at the cost of unremitting work, a career on a national scale – indeed international, for Lanari's agency had a branch in Paris and at various times he supplied singers for European cities and for the fast developing

American market, especially Havana and New York.[69] In the next generation the brothers Luciano and Ercole Marzi managed to run still more seasons at any one time than Lanari had. But they alienated Verdi by what he saw as their carelessness and ineptitude, they were financially unreliable, and they failed several times over in this city and that. Lanari had been haunted by the fear of 'sfigurare', 'cutting a bad figure'; in his circle bankruptcy had been equated with 'civil death'.[70] The change probably had to do with more than personal quirks. By 1875 an agent could recommend a candidate to run an opera season as 'a distinguished person, not a common impresario [*un impresario volgare*]'.[71] To be an opera impresario was becoming less a profession than a disease.

The interior of the Teatro La Fenice, Venice, before the fire that destroyed it in 1836. Note the large amount of standing room in the stalls area. Such seating as there is in the stalls is on benches.

The interior of the Teatro La Fenice, Venice, shortly after rebuilding in 1837. There is now rather more seating in the stalls – still on benches.

3 · An industry in a hierarchical society

Opera was an industry. Yet it was also a means of displaying the hierarchical structure of Italian society and the ascendancy within it of the upper classes.

'A great industry', Cavour was to say, 'with ramifications all over the world'. At least as early as 1780, and from time to time throughout the nineteenth century, the argument was put forward that opera stimulated trade, tourism, and the circulation of money; it gave employment not only to theatre people (said to number some 3,000 in Milan alone by 1889) but to ancillary trades; it provided invisible exports reckoned in the 1880s at over 5 million francs a year.[1] The impresari who carried on this great industry went some way to bear out the description by referring to themselves as tradesmen (*commercianti*, *negozianti*); only in the more advanced economic environment of France did Berlioz call their fellows *industriels*.[2]

Yet, as we have seen, most impresari led insecure lives; it was common to regard them as both poor devils threatened with bankruptcy and unscrupulous rogues – and there was enough truth in both views to keep them current. How could a great industry be run by people who – as legend had it and as actually happened from time to time – might flee the town where the opera season was being given, leaving artists and staff unpaid?

The answer lay in the relation between the impresari and their social superiors. That relation was ambiguous. Impresari were not necessarily dependent on any individual member of the nobility, and the very touch of roguery that marked some of them conferred a kind of freedom. Yet they were deeply dependent on the upper classes as a whole, first for their concessions and then – crucially – for the means of making up an almost certain loss.

The Italian opera house of the nineteenth century has commonly been spoken of as a meeting-place of all classes.[3] The Austrian

39

government of Lombardy–Venetia went so far as to call La Scala the only such meeting-place.[4] What this conventional view ignored was the acute sense of hierarchy that ran through the Italian theatre. There was no single meeting-place and no single mixture of classes. On the contrary, there was a well-understood hierarchy of theatres, of areas within the theatre, of audiences, of seasons, of genres; on every count, *opera seria* – the old eighteenth-century heroic opera on mythological or historical subjects, gradually evolving into the mid nineteenth-century historical or domestic tragedy of Verdi – stood at the top.

The superior status of *opera seria* was demonstrated in the most practical way: it cost more. It cost more to put on than the sentimental *opera semiseria* (an invention of the late eighteenth century), which in turn cost more than the straightforwardly comic *opera buffa*; this was because *opera seria* was understood to demand lavish and historically accurate sets and costumes, the most expensive singers, a larger chorus, and more extras.[5] It also cost more to get into: only in 1838 did La Scala, as a rule the pioneer in making changes of this kind, start charging the same price of admission for serious and for comic opera.[6] Finally, if the impresario got a subsidy it was higher for serious opera.

The theory of the matter – it was set down, as often happens, just when the old hierarchical arrangement was breaking up – was that *opera seria* was better suited to the well off, whereas the less well off preferred *opera buffa*.[7] This might have been true enough in 1750, when *opera buffa* was still fairly new. In 1850, when the statement was made, it was at best doubtful; its real point was to maintain old distinctions.

According to these distinctions, not only did the three kinds of opera form a hierarchy; they all (unless the comic opera was of a low form often called *farsa*) stood a little higher than spoken plays, which in turn stood higher than equestrian spectacle, acrobats, demonstrations of animal magnetism, and so on down to performing monkeys.

The most aristocratic audience was to be found at the *opera seria* in the leading theatre of the town during the carnival or other fashionable season; audiences then became progressively less aristocratic and more plebeian as one went down the scale of seasons, theatres, and genres. Members of the upper classes did go to second-

or third-rank theatres where they could find such early nineteenth-century entertainments as a mixed evening of plays, circus, and *balletto pantomimico*, but they probably went once, for amusement; to the opera they went night after night in the same way that their English male contemporaries went to their club.[8]

The sense of hierarchy in the theatre depended only in part on who owned the building. Some Italian theatres belonged to monarchs, some to municipalities, some to individuals – in the eighteenth century these were generally noble – some to associations of boxholders.

Often there was mixed ownership: the building might belong to the government or to a noble family while most of the boxes were the property of boxholders who, in many theatres, could sell, mortgage, or let them – within limits which the period of revolutionary and Napoleonic rule tended to break down. The boxholders of the Reggio Emilia municipal theatre had originally been forbidden to sell out to non-citizens of the town, to 'mechanics', or to Jews, but in 1814 Jews were allowed to buy boxes in the third tier.[9] The reason for mixed ownership was either that the sale of boxes had originally helped to finance the building of the theatre or that an existing owner had resorted to it to raise capital. By the late eighteenth century individual property in boxes was common and boxholders (often represented by an elected committee) had a good deal of say in the running of the theatre even where they were not full owners.

There were exceptions. Some theatres remained under direct government control, particularly in those monarchies that had never known the ascendancy of the medieval and Renaissance city state: Piedmont, Naples, and (in the hereditary lands of Austria) Trieste. At the Regio, Turin, and the San Carlo, Naples, both of them attached to the royal palace, the question of which families should be allowed to rent a box (or for that matter to give it up) was an affair of state. In Turin the king saw to it himself each year; at the Restoration he insisted on allocating the first three tiers to the aristocracy, thereby angering the Turin bourgeoisie, which through nearly twenty years of French rule had grown used to living on an equal footing with nobles.[10] In both Turin and Naples the king could reallocate boxes if tenants fell into arrears (a common problem, worse than ever in times of economic slump), or if they sublet, or even, in Turin, if they failed to turn up often enough. In practice, noble boxholders were treated gingerly: after repeated pleas from the impresario Domenico Barbaja the Naples government agreed to take away defaulters' boxes, but it did so slowly and reluctantly.[11]

In Trieste, a virtual creation of the Austrian monarchy and a city of newly rich merchants from many countries, the opera house in the late eighteenth century was municipally owned, but the music-loving governor and chief of police between them controlled it at least as tightly as the kings of Piedmont and Naples did theirs. One boxholder had his box taken away for having sold it without authority to an unsuitable person – the young son of an apothecary – and for anyhow being himself too poor. Not until 1847 was control effectively transferred to the municipal council and the boxholders.[12]

In Rome, where ownership of theatres by individual noble families prevailed well into the nineteenth century, the Teatro Valle in the 1820s appears to have had no boxholder-proprietors: the theatre owner could assign all the boxes to the impresario for letting, merely keeping one back for himself. But because ambassadors to the Holy See had a history of quarrels over precedence in the opera house almost as long as that of opera itself, the papal government controlled the seasonal letting of boxes in the 'noble' tiers even of second-rank theatres like the Valle and even as late as 1846: the declared aim was a proper hierarchical arrangement.[13]

There was no doubt in any leading theatre, whatever its structure of ownership, which were the 'noble' areas. The seating arrangements were hierarchical in the most visible way. The second tier of boxes (out of four, five, or six) was always the most aristocratic: except in commercial ports like Trieste and Leghorn it was largely or wholly occupied by nobles, at least in the fashionable season. The first or the third tier in some theatres enjoyed equal standing with the second. More often both were a little lower in esteem and price; in leading or second-rank theatres boxholders' lists show a mixture of nobles and professional men – lawyers, doctors, civil servants, not to mention the Reggio Emilia Jews, some of whom were bankers. The status of the tier or tiers above the third was lower still but varied with the theatre. It was not unknown to find the odd (presumably impoverished) noble in a top-tier box. Taking out the partitions in this top tier to make a gallery was a signal that the lower classes – however defined – were being let in. Two leading theatres most heavily dominated by aristocratic boxholders were late in making this change: the Carolino, Palermo, did it about 1830, La Fenice, Venice, not till 1878.[14]

So conscious were boxholders of belonging to a particular tier that, in the statutes proposed for a boxholders' association that owned one of the Lucca theatres, the executive body was to be made up of eight men, two of them elected by each of the four tiers; for meetings to be valid, at least one from each tier must be present. A refinement in the small town of Recanati gave boxholders in the top tier only half a vote.[15]

Nor did the dominance of the nobility end in the boxes or in the passages and dressing-rooms behind them. Part of the stalls area at La Scala – we have seen – was filled by the upper servants of the nobility, who were admitted at a special price. There and in many other theatres liveried servants accompanying their masters had free entry. In some theatres they had free or specially cheap entry to the gallery; at Padua the Teatro Nuovo had its top tier wholly reserved for them until 1786.

Where French rule from 1796 to 1814 brought about substantial social change, as in Milan with its emerging middle class, these practices came to an end and did not return. At the other extreme, the Carolino, Palermo, had the servants of the nobility filling the back of the stalls area well into the nineteenth century. Other places fell somewhere in between. At the Piacenza municipal theatre servants' virtually free entry to the gallery was dropped sometime after 1812; by 1850 their masters had to pay for them to get into the building, though at a special low rate. But at Bologna two years later servants still had free entry to the building, and their masters needed reminding that they had to pay full price to get into the gallery.[16] From about 1800 the arrangements that gave noble households visible privileges all over the theatre were in silent retreat, but it was a piecemeal retreat and in some places it dragged on all the way to unification.

This was true of other forms of hierarchical pricing. It had been common in the late eighteenth century to charge men more than women, nobles and 'foreigners' (from outside the state or the city) more than citizens. These distinctions had vanished, again piecemeal, from leading theatres by the early 1830s, though as late as 1839 a minor Florence theatre – owned by an academy of no doubt conservative-minded nobles – still maintained a full set of price differentials; it even had a special price for bankers, who were deemed to stand halfway between nobles and citizens.[17]

Even when these particular differentials were done away with there remained in many theatres the distinction between the military and civilians. This too was in part a price differential: by government decree, military officers (and, in Lombardy–Venetia, civil servants) enjoyed a discount. But the most visible distinction, found in Naples and Bologna as well as in Milan and in other garrison towns, was the reservation for military officers of the first row or rows of stalls. This did not just show up the white tunics of Austrian officers in the tense years after the 1848 revolutions. Italian officers – of the papal army – could choose to stand instead of sitting, and so prevent the rest of the audience from seeing the stage: this happened at the leading Bologna theatre in the fashionable season, and all the impresario could do was to appeal to the military command by way of the government supervisory body.[18] After 1859–60 the new Italian state kept on the discount for military men and civil servants but dropped the reservation of the front rows.

Who else was in the stalls, or in the next-to-last tier of boxes in those theatres provided with a gallery? The answer varied from time to time and from theatre to theatre. It is hazardous to speak of a bourgeois audience everywhere. True, at La Scala by 1821 habitual attenders at the back of the stalls and in the (presumably upper) boxes were described as 'well-bred men and women' ('*galantuomini e donne di garbo*') who did not dress elegantly, had no carriage, and might arrive dusty or muddy from the Milan streets.[19] These well-bred people were probably lawyers and doctors of the less fashionable kind, civil servants, engineers, pharmacists, the better-off tradesmen and shopkeepers. In university towns like Padua and Bologna the stalls audience included many students; in tourist towns like Venice, Florence, Rome, and Naples, many non-Italians; almost anywhere, a number of out-of-town Italians passing through. On a night of pouring rain in Florence 'foreigners' were almost the only people to turn up.[20]

When, in Rome, two theatres gave opera on the same night the people who went to the second-best theatre were mainly shopkeepers, many of them grocers or otherwise engaged in food trades.[21] In the provincial town of Cremona the stallholders were so little 'well-bred' that by treading with muddy boots all over the seats of the new theatre (to get from row to row in a hurry) they made it necessary to re-upholster the benches within two years of its opening in 1809.[22] As one went down the hierarchy of theatres, seasons, genres, and seating areas, the audience in a pre-industrial country tended to consist more and more of shopkeepers and artisans. That was what a visitor observed at a decidedly minor Naples theatre that never put on anything 'higher' than comic opera: many boxes were occupied by families 'of the lower cittadini [citizen] class, even to the livery-boy and the baby'.[23]

Still further down the hierarchy, the audience in the gallery at La Scala in the same year (1820) was defined by a civil servant as the '*minuto popolo*' or '*menu peuple*'.[24] This too meant artisans, though not of a kind likely to keep livery-boys, and other providers of petty services. A celebrated dialect poem about misadventures and near-riot in the La Scala gallery in 1813 involved a fireman, a lamplighter, several soldiers, and a tailor employed as assistant to an old clothes dealer.[25] What the La Scala gallery did not contain was a representation of the lower classes as a whole – of labourers, let alone peasants: not when admission cost about as much as a builder's labourer could earn in a day.[26] Contemporary statements that 'the people' or 'the lowest class' were to be found in the gallery suggest, more than anything else, the restrictive definition of 'the people' common in the early nineteenth century. Labourers, peasants, beggars were not 'the people'.

Where some of the humblest members of society did appear was not inside the theatre at all. While the king or duke or governor or at least the representative of the official supervisory body sat in his box, not in the attitude of a guest but in that of a master (old King Charles Felix of Sardinia was so much at home in his Turin royal theatre that he would sit there during the performance munching breadsticks);[27] while the nobility chatted and visited one another in other boxes; while the officers in the front row ogled the ballerinas' legs; while the military guard, perhaps as many as thirty or fifty strong, kept watch over the theatre, with sentries posted at the outer and inner doors, at the box-office, one man by the government box, two in the gallery, two at the stage door, and members of the ruler's civil police, too, on hand in the foyers and the orchestra,[28] a member of the audience who slipped out early might have seen standing outside the stage door a knot of people without the price even of a gallery ticket: they were listening to what they could catch of the sounds wafting from the stage and the orchestra pit, and some were singing the tunes.[29]

The opera house was one of the last Italian institutions to surrender to the liberal–individualist tenet that men should have equal access to the good things of life on payment of an undifferentiated cash sum (sometimes put as 'all men have an equal right to dine at the Ritz'). In the first two-thirds of the nineteenth century the theatre was still backing away, at different speeds in different parts of the peninsula, from the older view of society as organically divided into estates. According to that view, the upper ranks of society were at once responsible and privileged. In most Italian towns that meant the nobility, flanked in varying proportion by rich merchants, bankers, and successful members of the professions. Nowhere was this better shown than in the opera house, physically by the hierarchical disposition of audience and attendants, financially by the way seasons were paid for.

A theatre, one might think, is a piece of capital equipment; its owners can do no better than to run it themselves at maximum profit, without letting in middlemen. Yet that is not how any Italian theatre was run or thought of; it is not even how many theatres are run today.

For the owners to run the opera season themselves was not unknown. But this '*amministrazione economica*' (from the old sense of 'economy' as 'household management') was generally acknowledged to be the reverse of economical. Governments or boxholder–proprietors might have to resort to it in difficult times when no impresario would contract for the season: this happened at La Scala in 1815–16 and again in 1821–4, at La Fenice in 1823. On these occasions there was plenty of 'splendour'; La Fenice put on a lavish Rossini season that included the first performance of *Semiramide*. But the losses were alarming. Nor did they improve when a professional impresario was put in charge, not this time at his own risk but answerable to a committee of the owners. The upper classes were expected to be lavish. The point was made by a leading agent to a bass who wanted an impresario to pay him a fee as high as another bass had been paid by the board of directors (*Presidenza*) of La Fenice in a season under direct management: 'the case is very different when an artist is engaged by a Presidenza rather than by an impresario'; he must now be content with less.[30]

This kind of reasoning had led some eighteenth-century governments to farm out tax collection – as the nineteenth-century governments of Rome and Lucca still farmed out weights and measures to Paterni and salt and tobacco revenue to Bandini. Such governments lacked the necessary administrative apparatus to do the job themselves without running into wasteful loss. In the opera house too the impresario's first task was to stand between the ruling groups and the extravagance expected of them. At the same time he was supposed to be accessible and answerable to his superiors.

The same habits of mind that farmed out tax revenues occasionally granted an impresario a so-called monopoly of theatres, that is, of theatrical management in a particular city. As with other monopolies this could amount in practice to a mere power of licensing competitors and getting a rake-off. In this form the impresari of La Scala enjoyed it between 1790 and 1814, together with a guarantee that no new theatres would be permitted to open, but the guarantee was breached in 1814 and the system appears not to have gone on.[31] A more literal monopoly of theatre management survived in backward Rome down to the early 1830s.

Opera management, then, was a concession, potentially a monopoly: even if the impresario did not himself enjoy an official monopoly the owners who granted him the concession often had the sole right to put on a particular type of opera in a particular season. But what was temporarily handed over to the impresario was not the opera house as a whole. It was not thought of as a single economic entity which he could exploit to greatest advantage. Just as the boxes were physically and socially distinct from the rest, so they – or some of them – might not figure in the theatre takings at all.

Italian opera-house takings were made up as follows. Anyone entering the theatre – except, sometimes, those who owned or rented boxes – paid admission to enter the building (*ingresso*); you could buy a season's subscription for this purpose. Since the opera house was the centre of social life you might pay *ingresso* merely to visit friends or gamble. In some eighteenth-century theatres, and occasionally in those of the nineteenth century, one therefore paid separately to enter the orchestra or stalls area, and again separately for one of a small number of fixed seats which an attendant unlocked.

In other theatres – at La Scala the arrangement dated from the return of the French in 1800[32] – the *ingresso* let you into the stalls as well. There you found in most theatres a good deal of standing room at the back as well as unnumbered bench seats, though you could still pay separately for a locked seat; or you might pay extra for any kind of seat, in which case the number of benches provided varied with the impresario's judgment of what the traffic would bear.[33] The general movement during the nineteenth century was towards filling the stalls with fixed and numbered seats.

The gallery, if there was one, had a separate entrance. It was often sublet for a fixed sum. The Milanese dialect poem already mentioned describes the two subcontractor–impresari of the La Scala gallery making their way through the waiting crowd with a lantern and a key to let loose a free-for-all scramble up the stairs.

What happened about the boxes varied according to the ownership pattern and the management contract. Boxholder–proprietors were not ordinary customers. In many theatres they could sublet their boxes at a profit, thus in effect competing with the impresario for custom; this was something that impresari at La Scala tried in vain to stop.[34] On the other hand they could contribute a levy (*canone* or *tratta*) either by voting one as a corporate body, or else by agreeing individually to use their boxes on payment of the levy set by the impresario; a boxholder who disliked the terms could give up his box for the season.[35] The levy might be in lieu of a seasonal subscription or might supplement it; there were intermediate arrangements under which the levy was fixed for a term of years as the normal subscription. In theatres where there was no property in boxes, those renting them merely paid a subscription. In all theatres any boxes not subscribed for could be turned over to the impresario to be let nightly.

Before Italian unification, finally, all prices were controlled both by the theatre owners and by the government superintending body, which had to agree to changes.

When boxholders paid a levy this was usually shown in the accounts not as part of the takings but as part of the endowment (*dote*). Where this happened the boxholders were by implication acting not as undifferentiated consumers but as a privileged group who – perhaps with government help – provided a service, with the impresario as their intermediary. They appeared partly as consumers since they got the benefit of the opera season in return for their money – but also as producer–patrons; their contribution to the endowment can be thought of as a management charge.

As the matter was understood in Italy at the turn of the eighteenth and nineteenth centuries, all theatre seasons run by impresari had an endowment. This could consist of a cash sum, of privileges (generally that of running some form of gambling or lottery), or of rights in boxes. The cash sum could consist of the boxholders' levy, or of a subsidy allowed by the government or the municipality, or both together, the whole supplemented by the rent of the refreshment rooms and other ancillary services of the theatre. The gambling privilege could be, as we have seen, highly profitable in Napoleonic times when it meant the monopoly of games of chance; after 1814 (in Naples after 1820) it meant at best a few tombola evenings or a tame lottery with prizes in kind.[36] Endowment in boxes for nightly letting remained common, but where we can follow over several decades the relations between owners and impresari we notice a change, with some backslidings, from endowment chiefly in boxes in the later eighteenth century to endowment chiefly in cash in the nineteenth.[37]

Regular government or municipal subsidy in cash seems, in eighteenth-century Italy, to have been uncommon away from the Turin and Naples royal theatres. Elsewhere a municipality like that of Senigallia on the east coast would contribute a small sum to encourage an *opera seria* season during the important summer trade fair; or a duke of Modena would give a 'present' to make up part of the loss on an opera season in a privately owned theatre.[38]

The official gambling monopoly, until its temporary suppression in the later eighteenth century, probably yielded at most times and in most places a good deal less than it would when revived in the hectic wartime conditions of Napoleonic Italy: a British visitor of the 1780s thought more money was lost and won at one club in St James's in a week than at La Scala during the whole carnival season.[39]

None of these endowments, subsidies, or privileges could guarantee an impresario against loss. We might expect that, with only marginal help from the government, impresari in most seasons would balance the costs of production against the theatre takings and the endowment from the boxholders, and perhaps manage a small profit besides. If we find impresari going bankrupt in the early nineteenth century – like Osea Francia, whom we saw being arrested on the first night of the Parma carnival season at the end of 1818 – we might be led to think that some change must have intervened to upset the old balance.

That is exactly what some nineteenth-century impresari did assert, and with them some of the officials concerned with the theatre. A full list of their complaints was drawn up in 1823: singers were demanding ever more money; good ones were becoming scarce; the public wanted ever more complex productions, with more singers and dancers, more extras, more musicians, more lavish sets and costumes. On the other hand resources were finite or shrinking; men with capital were not coming forward and management was falling into unsuitable hands.[40] In twentieth-century language, this meant that production costs were outstripping consumers' purchasing power and the industrial product, opera, was pricing itself out of the market.

The trouble with this diagnosis is that most elements in it can be found asserted at intervals all the way from the 1680s to the 1880s.[41] Just one new element entered the catalogue in the early post-Napoleonic period: impresari started blaming the increased fees demanded by singers on offers from abroad higher than Italian theatres could safely meet.[42] We shall need to look at this new element on its merits. But just as farmers' complaints about the harvest need to be checked, so a diagnosis of imbalance in the economics of opera made at intervals over two centuries cannot be taken at face value.

Nor can it readily be accounted for by the 'income gap' to which the modern economists Baumol and Bowen have pointed.[43] From their study of the performing arts in nineteenth-and twentieth-century America they conclude, briefly, that the gap between the cost of performances and box-office takings has steadily tended to widen. The reason is that the performing arts by their very nature can raise productivity only a little, whereas productivity in the economy at large has risen markedly, and with it real wages and other production costs. But in the Italian economy of the eighteenth and nineteenth centuries it is not clear that productivity rose in anything like the same way.

We can none the less try to get hold of series of actual costs, takings, and endowments over the period and see what trends emerge. (For a discussion of the evidence and of the problems it sets, see Appendix.)

Table 1 embodies an attempt at working out such a series. It expresses items that went to make up costs of performance in any one season as percentages of total cost; it also expresses the season's takings in the same way.

We know that absolute costs went up throughout the period from the early eighteenth century to the 1860s. What the table suggests strongly is that the relative cost of some of the main items did not change much; some imaginary but well-informed model accounts published in 1879 still break down in much the same way.[44]

Let us look at some of these costs. Production (scenery, costumes, lighting, and the cost of stage staff) is unfortunately the most elusive. This is because of changes in accounting practice that make it impossible now to tell how much was spent on each component; the percentages given offer no more than an indication, and some of them certainly express incomplete figures.

What we can say (even though the figures are too scattered to appear in Table 1) is that the relative cost of lighting seems to have gone down. In the 1701, 1749, 1819, and 1819–20 seasons it accounted for 7, 11, 7, and 9% of total costs; in the 1825, 1827, and 1834–5 seasons for no more than 4, 4, and 2%. This probably reflects technological change. Eighteenth-century contracts called for the stage and especially the auditorium to be lit by pure wax candles; in the first half of the nineteenth century all parts of the theatre (dressing-rooms, stage, auditorium, foyers, the lot) had to be lit, until gas came in, by now unimaginable quantities of pure olive oil. The change may have meant a saving in itself, and in the second quarter of the nineteenth century the price of oil was depressed.

Orchestral costs also present problems. In a number of towns the opera orchestra was the royal, ducal, or municipal orchestra, some of whose members received until 1859–60 an annual salary out of public funds; when they played in the theatre the impresario was

Table 1. Cost components and takings as percentage of total costs, 1701–1865

(All figures are percentages of total expenditure on a single opera season)

Theatre	Fontanelli, Modena	Marsigli, Bologna	Malvezzi, Bologna	Malvezzi, Bologna	Malvezzi, Bologna	Regio-Ducale, Milan	Nuovo (later Comunale), Bologna
Date & type of season	1701, pastoral	1711, seria	1733, seria + ballet	1739, seria + ballet	1742, seria + ballet	1749, seria	1763, seria + ballet
Soloists	56	46	49	45	41	51	34
Music (composer's & allied fees)	3	5	4	4	2	6	3
Orchestra	13	?	8	8	?	13	7
Production	22	12	16	24	30	30	32
Rent	0	?	2	3	2	0	2
Other	6	37	21	16	25	0	22
Takings as percentage of costs	75	75	84	67	63	?	73

Theatre	Nuovo (later Comunale), Bologna	Argentina, Rome	Ducale, Parma	La Scala, Milan	Grande (later Comunale), Trieste	Pantera, Lucca	Comunale, Bologna
Date & type of season	1778, seria + ballet	1804, seria + ballet	1819, seria + ballet	1819–20, all types + ballet[a]	1822, seria	1825, seria	1827, seria
Soloists	32	47	59	40	37	49	49
Music (composer's & allied fees)	0	?	1	3	?	0	1
Orchestra	6	10	?	11	16	17	13
Production	32	?	28	31	33	20	24
Rent	1	?	0	0	0	0	0
Other	29	43	12	15	14	14	13
Takings as percentage of costs	60	84	40	62	53	38	62

Theatre	Valle, Rome	Ducale, Parma	Valle, Rome	Valle, Rome	Valle, Rome	Valle, Rome	Valle, Rome
Date & type of season	P1828, opera[b] + plays	1829, seria + ballet	P1830, opera + plays	A1830, opera + plays	A1831, opera + plays	C1832, opera + plays	P1832, opera
Soloists	59	56	50	53	51	51	34[c]
Music (composer's & allied fees)	?	?	?	1	1	2	1
Orchestra	7	2	7	}31	29	24	41
Production	?	26	11		8	20	14
Rent	6	0	8	7	11	3	10
Other	28	16	24	8			
Takings as percentage of costs	86	46	73	66	90	100	84

Theatre	Valle, Rome	Valle, Rome	Valle, Rome	Valle, Rome	Valle, Rome	Valle, Rome	Valle, Rome
Date & type of season	A1832, opera + plays	C1833, opera + plays	P1833, opera + plays + acrobats	A1833, opera + plays	C1834, opera + plays	P1834, opera + ballet[d]	A1834, opera + plays
Soloists	50	36	61	45	42	43	55
Music (composer's & allied fees)	2	8	1	8	1	3	1
Orchestra	}33	25	22	29	26	26	31
Production		25	12	9	23	11	7
Rent	9	6	3	9	8	17	6
Other	6						
Takings as percentage of costs	91	95	63	111	95	44	88

Table 1. (*cont.*)

Theatre	Valle, Rome	San Carlo and Fondo, Naples	Comunale Nuovo, Modena	La Pergola, Florence	Comunale, Trieste	Comunale Nuovo, Modena
Date & type of season	C1835, opera + plays	1834–5, all types + ballet[e]	1841, opera + ballet	1845, opera + ballet[f]	1859, opera	1865, opera + ballet
Soloists	48	54	48	64	44	47
Music (composer's & allied fees)	6	3	0	4	3	3
Orchestra	}21	7	4	?	19	14
Production		19	36	23	22	14
Rent	18	0	0	0	0	0
Other	7	17	12	9	12	22
Takings as percentage of costs	82	53	42	91	57	?

[a] Three seasons (Autumn, Carnival–Lent, Spring)

[b] Opera at the Valle was generally *buffa* or *semiseria*, but *opera seria* was occasionally given. Ballet, when given, was *mezzo-carattere* (less formal than *ballo grande*)

[c] Malibran sang two performances in this otherwise cheap season. Percentage is based on the assumption (documented by A. Cametti, *La Musica teatrale a Roma 100 anni fa*) that her actual fee was half that stated in the accounts

[d] Interrupted season: theatre closed after disturbances

[e] Long season at the two Naples royal theatres (129 performances at San Carlo, 118 at Fondo), run by joint-stock company. Percentages arrived at by eliminating from the published accounts figures relating to stock operations; results remain doubtful

[f] Figures from incomplete accounts covering first 23 performances of carnival season

C = Carnival   P = Primavera   A = Autunno

All percentages have been rounded up or down to the nearest unit. The word 'opera' is used in describing later seasons because from about the 1840s the old categories became blurred and theatres started mixing them in any one season. Up to that period the seasons covered are each the main or most fashionable season in the theatre in question with the following exceptions: (i) Teatro Comunale, Bologna, 1827; this was a spring season of *opera seria* with star singers, but without the ballet that accompanied it in the fashionable (autumn) season; (ii) Teatro Valle, Rome, 1828–35: this was a 'minor' theatre which up to 1830 had the monopoly of opera (always *buffa* or *semiseria*) in the autumn and spring seasons; in that year the monopoly was successfully challenged but the theatre went on for some years with a policy of putting on mixed bills of opera and plays in most seasons. It often engaged leading singers but had not the means – and legally was not allowed – to compete with the 'major' theatre that put on *opera seria* and *ballo grande* in the carnival season.

Sources: A. Gandini, *Cronistoria de Teatri di Modena,* Modena, 1873; G. Cosentino, *Il Teatro Marsigli-Rossi,* Bologna, 1900; C. Ricci, *I Teatri di Bologna,* Bologna, 1888; A. Paglicci-Brozzi, *Il Regio-Ducale Teatro di Milano nel secolo XVIII,* Milan, 1894; ATRP, carteggi 1819 (accounts of Commissione Amministrativa), 1829 (impresario's accounts); A. Petracchi, *Sul reggimento de' pubblici teatri,* Milan, 1821, p. 217; BNF CV 393/117 (accounts of Lucca season), 348/144 (accounts of La Pergola, Florence, season); Archiginnasio, Raccolta Malvezzi, cart. 147 n. 1 (u) (accounts of Bologna 1827 season); C. Bottura, *Storia del Teatro Comunale di Trieste,* Trieste, 1885; *Almanacco de' Reali Teatri San Carlo e Fondo dell'annata teatrale 1834.* Naples, 1835, in the Biblioteca Lucchesi-Palli, Naples; M. Rinaldi, *Due secoli di musica al Teatro Argentina,* Florence, 1978; BTBR Fondo Capranica, Teatro Valle, bilancio dell'impresa, autunno 1828, and cart. 6–10, borderò, bilanci.

usually called upon to take over payment of their salaries or to pay them a supplementary fee, but an element of disguised government subsidy probably accounts for some of the low percentages recorded. In Rome, where there were no stable orchestras in the first half of the nineteenth century, their relative cost appears to have been lower than elsewhere; at the Teatro Valle some of the instrumentalists who took part in the first performances of *La Cenerentola* and of Donizetti's *Il Furioso* were barbers, goldsmiths, or upholsterers who played in their spare time. This may explain the low esteem in which Rome orchestras were held by Berlioz and Verdi.[45]

Even if, as seems possible, the relative cost of the orchestra changed little between the early eighteenth century and the 1870s, its size was going up steadily at least from the 1770s; the chorus (non-existent in the old *opera seria* of the early eighteenth century) grew alongside the orchestra. This is shown clearly in Table 2. The reasons were the growing complexity of scores from the later decades of the eighteenth century, and the fashion that started about the same time for bringing the chorus back into *opera seria*. It was the influence of Paris – of the spectacular grand opera typified by the work of Meyerbeer – that hit Italy from the 1850s and raised numbers to unprecedented levels.

If orchestral numbers were rising but their relative cost was not, some players' real wages must have been falling. There is in fact scattered evidence that in some orchestras the rise in numbers was coped with by squeezing the differential between the wages of the best-paid players and those of the worst paid: at Turin, where the eighteenth-century royal orchestra had included some celebrated players, leading instrumentalists by the 1820s were relatively and even absolutely worse paid than some of their predecessors.[46] Again, this may help to explain the strictures on nineteenth-century Italian orchestras by visiting composers like Spohr, Berlioz, and Nicolai.

The relative cost of the most basic component of opera – the music – seems to have changed little. Up to the 1840s the composer was paid a fee for writing a new opera, supervising rehearsals, and accompanying the first three performances at the keyboard. If the opera was not new, he or, in the nineteenth century, his publisher had to fend off pirated scores that could be had cheap. Composers' fees went up, in absolute and probably in relative terms, from 1815, through the renewed enthusiasm for opera stirred by Rossini. By the

Table 2. Orchestra and chorus – numbers

Venue	Section	Year	Number
San Carlo, Naples	Orchestra	1737	45
San Carlo, Naples	Orchestra	18th c.	50/60
San Carlo, Naples	Orchestra	c. 1810	70
San Carlo, Naples	Orchestra	1837–48	80
San Carlo, Naples	Orchestra	1848–50	93
San Carlo, Naples	Orchestra	1850–61	96/97
San Carlo, Naples	Orchestra	1861–80s	100
San Carlo, Naples	Chorus		[a]
San Carlo, Naples	Chorus	1837–44	36
San Carlo, Naples	Chorus	1844–	40
San Carlo, Naples	Chorus	1850–61	58/60
San Carlo, Naples	Chorus	1861–62	100
San Carlo, Naples	Chorus	1864–	80
San Carlo, Naples	Chorus	1869–72	90
San Carlo, Naples	Chorus	1872–3	94
San Carlo, Naples	Chorus	1876–80s	80
La Scala, Milan	Orchestra	1860s	82/86
La Scala, Milan	Orchestra	1880	100
La Scala, Milan	Chorus	1811	36
La Scala, Milan	Chorus	1855	100[b]
La Scala, Milan	Chorus	1859	80
La Scala, Milan	Chorus	1873	100
Comunale, Modena	Orchestra	1850	48
Comunale, Modena	Orchestra	1866	62
Comunale, Modena	Orchestra	1873	50
Comunale, Modena	Chorus	1850	30
Comunale, Modena	Chorus	1855	60
Comunale, Modena	Chorus	1873	30
Comunale, Bologna	Chorus	1850	27
Comunale, Bologna	Chorus	1855	30
Comunale, Bologna	Chorus	1871	60
Comunale, Bologna	Chorus	1914	100
Regio, Turin	Orchestra	pre-1770	36
Regio, Turin	Orchestra	1800	60/70
Sociale, Voghera	Orchestra	1820	9
Sociale, Voghera	Orchestra	1828	23
Sociale, Voghera	Orchestra	1845	32
Sociale, Voghera	Orchestra	1889	46[c]

[a] Chorus supplied by boys from the conservatories; [b] Special effort; season included Le Prophète; [c] Toscanini conducted.

Sources: M. F. Robinson, Naples and Neapolitan Opera, Oxford, 1972: Prospetti di appalto per lo R. Teatro di S. Carlo, 1837–99, in the Biblioteca Lucchesi-Palli, Naples; ASM Sp. P. parte moderna 20 (contract for concession of Imperial Royal Theatres, 1811); B. Jouvin, Hérold, Paris, 1868, p. 93; A. Basso ed., Storia del Teatro Regio di Torino, Turin, 1976; P. Cambiasi, La Scala, 1889 edn.: A. Gandini, Cronistoria dei teatri di Modena, Modena, 1873; A. Maragliano, I teatri di Voghera, Casteggio, 1901, pp. 24–5, 30, 67; H. Sachs, Toscanini, London, 1978, p. 32; ASB, Archivio Storico Comunale, Deputazione Spettacoli Titolo I rub. I, 1850, 1855; L. Trezzini, ed.: Due secoli di vita musicale: Storia del Teatro Comunale di Bologna, Bologna, 1966.

1830s Bellini could command a fee of 16,000 francs for a new opera in Italy; in the following decade Verdi received 20,000 francs.[47]

After the Austro-Sardinian copyright treaty of 1840 publishers were able gradually to suppress piracy. The result was to make the fee payable to the composer by any one impresario lower than it had been at the peak, since the composer was no longer dependent on the first production for almost all of his income. But even at the peak Bellini's or Verdi's fee had sometimes been less than that paid to one star singer.[48]

Rent is the item in Table 1 that looks at first sight most puzzling. Charging the impresario rent for the use of the theatre was, by the turn of the eighteenth century, an obsolete practice; like other obsolete practices it went on in Rome a good deal longer than anywhere else. Although the percentage of costs accounted for by rent at the Teatro Valle is, in some years, startling, the relation between the Marchese Bartolomeo Capranica, owner of the Valle, and the impresario Paterni was far from a simple one of lessor and lessee.* It all seems to amount to an old-fashioned mix of personal dependence and commercial ties, and obscures the true cost of rent. Still, the rent – which had been raised in 1822 to help to pay for the rebuilding of the theatre – was probably too high for the Valle's capacity; the same was probably true of Capranica's policy of putting on opera with leading singers. Capranica complained at intervals that Paterni had lost money and lowered the prestige of the theatre, but this may have been an excuse for the failure of his own ambitious policy at a time of rising costs.[49]

The most striking item in Table 1 is the cost of soloists. This term includes dancers (and, at the Valle, actors) as well as singers, but in most mixed seasons singers accounted for the greater part of the cost. The table is fragmentary; there are gaps in it, as well as extremes that may or may not be significant. But in most seasons the cost of soloists falls somewhere between 45% and 55%. It seems clear, first, that soloists made up at all times by far the greatest single cost of an opera season in a leading theatre, and secondly, that in spite of complaints renewed over two centuries their fees rose in the

---

* The 1829 contract that set the rent also allowed Paterni a salary, established a complex profit-sharing arrangement, and gave either man a cut if the other should get the monopoly of Rome theatre management; outside the contract, Paterni was also Capranica's creditor.

long term no faster than other costs, though there may have been short periods when they fell behind or raced ahead.

A cost of this magnitude needs to be looked into in detail. Tables 3 and 4 give series of fees paid in leading theatres in four Italian cities over a century and a half. These are, again, fragmentary but reasonably reliable. The theatres can be compared in that they all stood at the forefront of opera production (true, the Regio, Turin, never fully recovered in the nineteenth century the standing it had had in the eighteenth, while the San Carlo, Naples, was in decline from the 1860s, and La Fenice in 1806–7 had been in difficulties).

The fees listed in the tables represent the working of a market. 'The price' – as Alessandro Lanari wrote – 'must be a thermometer [of quality].' Singers were frankly and almost uniformly concerned with earning all they could: 'the first who offers me more – that one I shall accept', the prima donna Marianna Barbieri Nini wrote to an agent.[50]

Many singers came from modest families; a singing career was one of the few ways of making a fortune, but it was often short. In the nineteenth century the fee paid by one impresario to another to secure a singer's release was – like a transfer fee in football today – directly proportionate to the singer's recent performance.[51] Singers (like dancers and composers) travelled readily, often to a tight schedule, so as to get in the maximum number of seasons.

If we ignore fluctuations in the general price level and look at fees in simple money terms, Tables 3 and 4 suggest no marked increase in the eighteenth century. Turin fees were enormous – the highest were about equal to the annual salary of the Piedmontese Prime Minister[52] – but if anything they may have decreased slightly, since early eighteenth-century singers received much payment in diamonds and gold snuffboxes, to say nothing of chocolate. There are signs of a temporary rise to meet the Napoleonic inflation – hinted at in Elisabetta Gafforini's 1811 fee at Naples. But for evidence of a marked general rise in leading singers' fees we have to wait till the 1830s; it had probably begun in the late 1820s.

The rise in the 1830s is unmistakable in all four cities, and the evidence does not depend on the extraordinary fees paid to the two singers reckoned each to be unique, Giuditta Pasta and Maria Malibran: other front-rank singers like Amalia Schütz, Carolina

Table 3. *Fees paid to leading singers in carnival seasons (in francs)*

Regio, Turin	La Fenice, Venice	La Scala, Milan
1730 Faustina (pd) 11,280		
Senesino (pu) 11,280		
1737 Senesino (pu) 11,500		
1739 Cuzzoni (pd) 9,400		
Gizziello (pu) 8,400		
1741 Carestini (pu) 10,400		
Visconti (pd) 8,000		
1744 Turcotti (pd) 6,000		
Caffarelli (pu) 9,400		
1762 Gabrielli (pd) 11,120		
1773 Agujari (pd) 13,348		
1778 Pacchierotti (pu) 10,567		
1785 Marchesi (pu) 12,235		
1788 Marchesi (pu) 15,573		
	1806 Pinotti (pd) 5,750	
	1807 Balsamini (pd) 9,360	
1822 Pasta (pd) 11,000	1822 Velluti (pu) 16,000	
Ferron (pd) 9,000		
Tacchinardi (t) 11,275		
1823 Tacchinardi (t) 13,000		
1829 Bonfigli (t) 8,000		
Genero (t) 3,500		
1833 Verger (t) 15,000	1833 Pasta (pd) 35,000	1833 Lalande (pd) 32,000
		Poggi (t) 19,500
		Deméric (mus) 10,250
		Pedrazzi (t) 20,000
	1834 Donzelli (t) 35,000	

Year	Singer	Fee	Year	Singer	Fee	Year	Singer	Fee
1837	Schutz (pd)	28,000	1837	Taccinardi Persiani (pd)	32,000	1854	Novello (pd)	20,000
			1847	Tadolini (pd)[a]	26,100			
			1848	De la Grange (pd)	20,880			
				Varesi (bar)	16,530			
			1851	Mirate (t)	17,400			
				Varesi (bar)	12,180	1859	Marchisio sisters (pd)	8,700
1858	Mattioli (bar)	8,404		T. Brambilla (pd)	8,700	1860	Lafon (pd)	30,000
			1853	Varesi (bar)	13,920		Corsi	13,920
1872	Prudenza (t)	4,000						

pd = prima donna; pu = primo uomo (castrato); t = tenor; mus = musico (mezzo–soprano or contralto singing breeches part); bar = baritone; [a] = fee offered but refused.

The carnival season generally began on 26 or 27 December of the previous year and ran until Shrove Tuesday. It was extended by about a month to take in most of Lent, at Turin from 1848, at La Fenice from 1830, at La Scala from 1783: fees for seasons at or after those dates cover, in general, a period about a quarter longer.

Fees paid in the early eighteenth century, and occasionally later, exclude some payment in kind; fees paid at later periods exclude, as a rule, a benefit performance (or a half-share in one) and often the provision of lodgings. But in Italy – unlike Britain or the United States – the low level of theatre takings meant that a benefit seldom brought in more than 1,000-odd francs or, in the best-paying theatres, 3,000-odd francs.

Sources: Basso ed., *Teatro Regio*: La Scala contracts, 1859–60, ASCM Sp. P. b. 112/1; ATLaF, Consuntivi, atti anteriori al 1818 (accounts for 1806), Processi verbali convocazioni, b. 3, 5. Autografi diversi s. v. De la Grange, Tadolini, Varesi; S. Dalla Libera, 'L'Archivio del Teatro La Fenice', *Ateneo Veneto*, n. s. 6, vol. 6, no. 1, 1968; BNF CV 343/10, 344/132, 395/129, 131, 175; Piancastelli Autografi s. v. Verger; A. Mackenzie-Grieve, *Clara Novello*, London, 1955, p. 233; B. Jouvin, *Hérold*, Paris, 1868, p. 101; E. Rosmini, *La Legislazione e la giurisprudenza dei teatri*, Milan, 1872, I, p. 394; E. Verzino, *Le Opere di Gaetano Donizetti*, Bergamo, 1897, p. 149 n.

Table 4. *Fees paid to singers at royal theatres, Naples (San Carlo and Fondo)*

		monthly (ducats)	monthly (francs)	annual (ducats)	annual (francs)	per perform-ance (francs)
1785	Roncaglia (pu)			2,886	12,265	
	Morichelli (pd)			2,340	9,945	
	Mombelli (t)			1,638	6,962	
1811	Gafforini (pd)	1,083	4,766			
1819	Morandi (pd)ᵃ	300	1,320			
	Colbran (pd)	909	3,958			
1820	Galli (b)	600	2,550			
1823	Lablache (b)	300	1,290			
1825	Lablache (b)	500	2,175			
	Nozzari (t)	600	2,592			
	Fodor (pd)				70,000	
1826	Pasta (pd)		7,200			
1830	Boccabadati (pd)	650	2,775			
	Tosi (pd)				36,000	
1834	Malibran (pd)	4,755	20,730			
	Ungher (pd)	2,775	12,100			
	Tacchinardi Persiani (pd)	863	3,763			
	Duprez (t)	690	3,008			
	Ronzi (pd)	1,813	7,905			
1838	Ronzi (pd)					424
	Toldi (pd)	450	1,908			
	Barroilhet (bar)	500	2,120			
	Nourrit (t)	600	2,544			
1871	Aldighieri (bar)ᵃ		3,700			
1872	Monti (b)		1,000			
1874	Polonini (bar)		1,000			
1883	Singer (pd)		8,000ᵇ			
1892	De Marchi (t)ᵃ		6,000			

pd = prima donna; pu = primo uomo (castrato); t = tenor; b = bass; bar = baritone; [a] fee offered but refused; [b] approximate; contract was for 25,000 francs for carnival-Lent season.

In the early nineteenth century the Naples season ran almost the year round, starting sometime in the spring (30 May eventually became the traditional opening date) and going on, with breaks for religious festivals, until just before Easter. In other periods the season was shorter and usually ran from November till spring. The usual practice was to engage leading singers for a few months at a time. A singer engaged at an annual salary did not necessarily sing in Naples throughout the year: she or he might be hired out elsewhere for part of the year. Besides fees, a singer might be allowed a benefit or a half-share in one. About 1820 there were other fringe benefits – singing in the Chapel Royal and at private concerts – which according to Rossini were lucrative.

Sources: ASN Casa Reale Antica f. 970, contracts and receipts; Min. Interno II inv. f. 706, Stato dell'importo delle compagnie di canto e ballo; ibid. f. 4356, Glossop petition, Lablache contract; Teatri b. 98, Barbaja to Lonchamp, 11 April 1811; G. Radiciotti, *Lettere inedite di celebri musicisti*, Milan, 1891, p. 44; Rossini to P. Cazzioletto, 1820, Piancastelli 406.32; Quicherat, *Nourrit*, III, pp. 192, 247; M. Ferranti, *Giuditta Pasta e i suoi tempi*, Milan, 1935, pp. 89–90; G. Badolisani, *Per la signora D. Luigia Boccabadati...*, Naples, 1832, p. 21; Zavadini, *Donizetti*, pp. 464–5; *Almanacco de' Reali Teatri...1834*, Naples, 1835; MTS CA, Canedi contracts, Coll. Casati 835; Archiginnasio Coll. Autografi XLI/11.107.

Ungher, Giuseppina Ronzi, Domenico Donzelli, and Henriette Méric-Lalande earned twice or three times as much as anyone ever got in the eighteenth century. There is also corroborating evidence from elsewhere.[53]

This standard of payment (to judge from scattered evidence in other theatres) seems to have been kept up into the 1840s. But revolutions and wars in 1848–9, following on the scarcity and depression of 1847, brought down fees all round; in some, perhaps most, theatres they did not recover fully until the mid 1850s. This is clearly illustrated in Table 3 by the fees paid to the baritone Felice Varesi at La Fenice in 1848, 1851, and 1853; in the latter two seasons he created the roles of Rigoletto and Germont. Near the start of the slump a leading agent was getting plaintive letters from singers who declared themselves 'astounded' and 'mortified' at the 'shameful' level of fees offered, but who none the less ended by taking them.[54]

Evidence from the late 1850s and 1860s is thin, but when two front-rank tenors demanded 30,000 and 38,000 francs to sing at La Scala in carnival 1869[55] – possibly expecting to get a little less – it does not look as though there had been much advance on the level of the 1830s.

As early as 1819, we have seen, an impresario blamed the 'excessive' rise in singers' fees on competition from abroad. The Rome impresario Jacovacci was to point to that as the reason for his bankruptcy in 1848.[56] How true was it that international demand was exerting an upward pull on the Italian market?

Table 5 presents evidence – again fragmentary but reasonably reliable – of fees paid in three capitals between the 1740s and the 1850s.

The Vienna figures are close to what singers of this eminence were being paid in Italy in the same period: they suggest that, at least in the 1830s and 40s, Vienna and leading Italian cities were on a single opera circuit; indeed the Vienna concession was then held by Merelli and Balochino in common with La Scala.

The Madrid and London figures tell a different story. To judge the Madrid figures we have to realise that fees paid in Italy for the carnival season (or other fashionable season) were higher than those paid in the other two main seasons, possibly by as much as 50% to 100%.[57] If we take the carnival fees paid in Turin in the

Table 5. *Italian singers' fees in Madrid, London, and Vienna (in francs)*

1. Madrid		yearly	monthly	per performance
1740s–50s	Mingotti (pd)	28,500		
	Mingotti (pd)	32,300[a]		
	Peruzzi (pd)	25,650		
	Elisi (pu)	31,350		
	Manzuoli (pu)	26,600		
1794	Todi (pd)	30,000		
1835	Manzocchi (pd)	58,960		
1850	Alboni (mus)		21,333	2,666
	Frezzolini (pd)		13,333	
	Barroilhet (bar)		6,666	
1852	Novello (pd)		6,000	

2. London		April–July season
1807	Catalani (pd)	c.125,000 (incl. benefits)
1809	Balsamini (pd)[b]	25,000 (+ benefit)
1817	Pasta (pd)	10,000
1821 to 1827	Camporesi (pd)	41,250/38,750/48,000
1821 to 1827	Curioni (t)	15,000 to 36,250
1821 to 1825	Ronzi (pd & b)[c]	30,000 to 55,000
1824–5	Garcia (t)	25,000/31,250
1827	Pasta (pd)	57,500 (+ benefit)
	Velluti (pu)	57,500

3. Vienna		Spring season	
1840	Ronconi (bar)	10,000	
	Moriani (t)	26,100	10,440
1843	Tacchinardi		
	Persiani (pd)	30,000 (+ benefit)	10,000
	Ronconi (bar & pd)[c]	20,000	
1852	Baucardé (t)	13,920	

pd = prima donna; pu = primo uomo (castrato); t = tenor; mus = mezzo-soprano or contralto singing breeches part (musico); bar = baritone; b = bass; [a] not clear from the sources whether the two figures for Mingotti refer to different seasons or whether one of them is wrong; [b] fee offered [c] fee covers an expensive singer and her/his spouse with much smaller earning power.

Madrid fees of the mid eighteenth century exclude fairly lavish payment in kind, and travelling expenses. In London, benefits (of which there were probably more than are shown) and other fringe earnings could be highly lucrative.

Sources: P. Metastasio, *Tutte le opere*, Milan, 1954, IV, p. 6; Mary N. Hamilton, *Music in Eighteenth-Century Spain*, Urbana, Ill., 1937, pp. 125–7, 140; J. Ebers, *Seven Years of the King's Theatre*, London, 1828, pp. 12–13, 387 *et seq.*; MTS CA 6921–8; BNF CV 343/12, 346/155, 396/14; Mackenzie-Grieve, *Clara Novello*, p. 229; Rosmini, *Legislazione*, I, p. 499; Balochino papers, Wiener Stadtbibliothek (Tacchinardi Persiani contract, Lanari, Ronconi correspondence).

eighteenth century (Table 3) and compare them with the annual fees paid in Madrid to singers of the same eminence, we must conclude that Madrid paid roughly half as much again as a singer might have earned in a year in Italy. In 1850 Marietta Alboni's fee of 2,666 francs per performance was, again, well ahead of Italian standards. Pasta, Ronzi, and Malibran – prima donnas with at least Alboni's drawing power – had set in the 1830s an Italian record of 1,000 francs a performance or just over. This standard represented a goal: rather than take less, Ronzi threw in two extra performances for nothing. There is no sign of its being exceeded before the 1870s.[58] It seems that the Madrid opera – drawing on the resources of a poor but centralised country – consistently outbid Italy.

As for London, in the early nineteenth century it was notoriously the milch cow of Italian musicians, composers as well as singers. The figures show how the fees paid in the 1820s were double or treble anything available in Italy.

For most of the eighteenth century, Italian singers going to foreign cities other than London were attached to a court, often with a title and for a year or more at a time. Such courts were few. By the end of Napoleonic wars commercialisation had set in, with more and more theatres in places like Manchester, Constantinople, Odessa, and Amsterdam offering Italian opera, and with singers now paid by the season and in cash. It was probably this development that accounted for the steep rise in Italian fees in the 1830s.

As late as 1828, putting the young Giulia Grisi under long-term contract seemed to an experienced man like Merelli to be financially risky unless her earning power could be exploited outside Italy.[59] She presently settled the matter by breaking her contract and running off to Paris and fame on her own; but her former employer, Alessandro Lanari, was able in the 1830s to place the most expensive artists such as Carolina Ungher within Italy and at enhanced rates. Italian costs had risen to meet the competition – at least in some cities.

Again, after its slump of 1848–53, the Italian opera industry was able to restore the 1830s level of fees, though perhaps under increasing strain: this was the time when it started feeling the need greatly to expand orchestra and chorus, and to take on the spectacular panoply of Parisian grand opera.

How was the rise in fees paid for? Not, for the most part, by raising

Table 6. *Average takings in Italian opera seasons*

(Takings per performance, in francs, exclusive of subsidy)

Theatre	Season	Type of opera	Average	Remarks
Regio, Turin	C1764–74	seria	1,930	
	CQ1877	opera	2,452	
	CQ1878	opera	2,183	1877–81 minimum: 414
	CQ1880	opera	2,022	1877–81 maximum: 5,041
	CQ1881	opera	2,216	
La Scala, Milan	A1778	seria	1,389	opening season
	C1872	opera	8,250	*Aida* first production (20 performances); excludes subscriptions and gallery
Pantera, Lucca	C1825	seria	161	
Comunale, Bologna	P1827	seria	821	
San Carlo, Naples	1834–5	seria	3,245	excludes carnival balls
	1834–5	carnival balls	2,497	
Fondo, Naples	1834–5	buffa/semiseria	862	
Valle, Rome	C1832–5	buffa/semiseria	1,420	
	P1830, 1832–4	buffa/semiseria	585	
	A1830–4	buffa/semiseria	892	
Senigallia	F1816–29	all types	500 to 700	very rough averages
	F1830–44	all types	1,000	very rough averages
	F1835	all types	714	poor season
	F1846, 1850–4	opera	750 to 900	very rough averages
	F1856–8	opera	900	very rough averages
	F1862–8	opera	500 to 900	irregular seasons
	F1877–90	opera	under 500	save in exceptional season; very irregular
Alfieri, Florence	C1839	seria	405	
Ducale, Parma	C1829	seria	613	opening season
	CQ1837	seria	1,108	
	P1870	opera	over 1,000	excluding *ingresso* subscription; special season (*Les Huguenots*)
Argentina, Rome	P1840	buffa	700	first 10 performances
			410	14th to 21st performances
			under 300	last 10 performances (forecast)
La Fenice, Venice	CQ1851	opera	1,713	includes *Rigoletto* first production; capacity of house 2,473 francs

Takings of carnival seasons down to the 1860s include a (diminishing) number of carnival balls and banquets. In spite of the San Carlo figures for 1834–35, these often brought in more money than did opera performances.

Sources: Basso ed., *Teatro Regio*, I, pp.148–9; Depanis, *Concerti popolari*, I, pp. 125–6, 153–4, 193, II, pp. 95, 132; Verdi, *Copialettere*, pp. 275–6; Dalla Libera, 'L'Archivio del Teatro La Fenice', p. 139; C. Vianello, 'Il "Bordereau" degli introiti della prima stagione della Scala', *Archivio Storico Lombardo*, ser. 8 vol. 2, 1950, pp. 303–7; ATRP carteggi 1829 (Bilancio dell'amministrazione... carnevale 1828–9), 1870 (accounts); Gazzuoli to Lanari, 1837, 1839, BNF CV 364/102–18, 365/51 *et seq.*; Cartoni to Lanari, 1840, *ibid.* 353/94–102; Lucca accounts, *ibid.* 393/117; Senigallia accounts, 1835, *ibid.* 346/41; Radiciotti, *Sinigaglia*, pp. 204–5; BTBR Fondo Capranica, Teatro Valle, cart. 6–10, borderò, bilanci; Archiginnasio, Raccolta Malvezzi, cart. 147 no. 1 (u); *Almanacco de' Reali Teatri San Carlo e Fondo dell'annata teatrale 1834*.

prices of admission. All the evidence points either to formidable resistance to price increases or to government reluctance to authorise them, or both.

Table 6 gives a series of average nightly takings in a number of theatres, all of them leading or second-rank opera houses (but for the Alfieri, Florence, and that was giving a season of unusual quality). The only word for the nineteenth-century average takings, until we reach *Aida* at La Scala in 1872 – a special occasion, in any case – is pitiful.

This is evident if we compare the Italian figures with takings in Paris at the Théâtre-Italien – the Italian opera house – and the (French-language) Opéra. In Italy in the first half of the century even leading theatres – other than La Scala, the San Carlo, and La Fenice – could not manage much more than an average of 1,000 francs a night, and often fell below that. In Paris the Théâtre-Italien at various times in 1820–1 was taking about 2,500 to 3,000 francs.[60] The much larger Opéra was taking, during what look like two routine months of 1818, averages of 4,599 francs and 3,156 francs exclusive of subscriptions; in 1826–8 it is said to have been taking an average 2,000 to 3,000 francs, rising to about 4,000 francs in 1829–30. Prices rose after 1830 and with them takings.[61] These are workaday figures: at high points in the 1830s and 40s we find averages of 9,700 francs, about 12,000 francs, and 6,842 francs a night.[62] There is no sign that any Italian opera house could come anywhere near this, even on special occasions, before the late 1860s.

Not surprisingly, the basic price of admission to the Paris Opéra after 1830 – 4 francs for a stalls seat bought on the night – was over one-third higher than the then highest Italian equivalent, at La Scala and the San Carlo. The two most striking things about Italian theatre prices in the nineteenth century are, first, the rigidity of the nightly *ingresso* price, and secondly the relative ease with which subscription prices rose once governments allowed them some free play.

The nightly *ingresso* price remained unchanged at La Scala from 1823 to 1859 (with a brief downward movement in 1825, fully retrieved by 1831), at the San Carlo from 1823 to 1860, at the Regio, Turin, from 1821 to 1845, at the Senigallia Fair season from 1816 until about 1860. In the miniature capitals Parma and

Modena the price, to the despair of impresari, remained at one franc for *opera seria*, until 1857 in Parma and, in Modena (where it had occasionally fallen lower still), until 1860. When, following unification, the Modena price was raised to 1·20 francs there was hissing in the theatre. At the Valle, Rome, the first increase (from about 1·08 francs to 1·60 francs) 'raised a shout throughout the town' in 1814; the increase was made to stick for a few scattered seasons during the theatre's best period in the 1830s, but was later given up altogether as owners and impresari backed away from opera.[63]

Yet the Valle had been able to raise the subscription price of its boxes by more than half in 1805–7 (when the *ingresso* remained unchanged) and, after an 18% fall in 1810–11, to a level, by 1822 and subsequent years, nearly double that of 1805.[64] This looks like a flexible response, in a theatre with a single noble owner and no boxholders' committee, to the Napoleonic inflation, to the bad years 1810–11, and to the post-war craze for Rossinian opera. At La Scala the subscription price for *ingresso* and a seat in the orchestra for the carnival-Lent season went up by half between 1823 and 1834; by 1847 the 1823 price had doubled; it fell again after the 1848 revolution but returned in 1854–9 to the 1847 level. Here we seem to see the Austrian authorities, with their relative flexibility in economic matters, allowing an increase which the Neapolitan government would not tolerate: after an experiment with price freedom in the early 1820s, subscription prices as well as nightly *ingresso* to the royal theatres remained unchanged from 1823 to 1862.[65]

Even when government price control was removed after unification, nightly admission prices rose much more slowly than did subscription prices. This is shown clearly in Tables 7 and 8.

What is the explanation? In Venice, those who bought tickets on the night were authoritatively said to be either outsiders (*forestieri*) or people who went very few times during the season.[66] Prices can hardly have been kept down to attract non-Italian tourists: as things were, they marvelled at how little it cost to get in.[67] The policy seems to have favoured people, especially young men, with little money but with professional aspirations – students, military officers, minor civil servants, struggling doctors, lawyers, and pharmacists, the stuff of political agitation in the Risorgimento period and also of theatrical

Table 7. *Index of admission and subscription prices, Teatro alla Scala, Milan, 1780–1885)*

(*Carnival–Lent seasons*)

		1823 = 100	
	Nightly admission (ingresso)	Subscription (admission including ordinary stalls seat)	Subscription (admission not including ordinary stalls seat)
1780–96	122	80	
1823	100	100	
1824	100	115	
1825	84	120	
1827	92	120	
1831	100	120	
1834	100	150	
1835–9	100	160	
1843	100	200	
1849	100	170[a]	
1850	100	138[a]	
1851	100	115	
1854–9	100	200	
1860	100	193	
1861	115[b]	207	
1862		414	230
1865		402	207
1866		483	276
1868		529	299
1869	134		276
1872		552	299
1874		621	322
1875		598	299
1878		667	322
1879–84		598	299
1885		644	322

After 1869, the price of nightly admission fluctuated from performance to performance, and it gave less and less right to a seat; by 1886 it gave one a right to standing room only.

From 1862, a new, separate subscription was introduced giving a right to an ordinary stalls seat (*sedia comune*), which had previously been included in the subscription price for admission; by 1880–3 only five, then four rows of seating were available without this, and by 1886 none was available.

[a] Adjusted to allow for shorter season (carnival only).

[b] Autumn season.

Source: P. Cambiasi, *La Scala*, Milan, 1889 edn.

Table 8. *Indexed prices of boxes at Teatro San Carlo, Naples, before and after Italian unification*

1823–62 = 100

	Subscription 1st tier	Subscription 2nd tier	Subscription 3rd tier	Nightly letting 3rd tier	Subscription 6th tier
1785–6	141	141	136	83	50
1823–62	100	100	100	100	100
1864–5	129	165	116	102	97
1865–6	159	206	131	125	97
1869–70	186	241	153	137	112
1872–3	233	291	201	137	117
1876–7	235	294	203	149	117
1891–2	235	294	203	157	117

The index of subscription prices is adjusted to allow for variations in number of performances from one season to another. Prices indexed are for the best boxes in each tier.

Sources: ASN Casa Reale Antica f. 970 bis; *Prospetti d'appalto per lo R. Teatro di S. Carlo.*

faction fights and disturbances. Such was the fear of offending this section of the public that, when Pasta was engaged for the 1833 carnival season at La Fenice for an unprecedented fee of 1,000 francs a performance, a proposal to raise the *ingresso* price barely got through the association of boxholder–proprietors; Pasta herself then took fright and insisted that there must be no increase lest she should be blamed. The impresario, who was bound by contract to supply her services, was locked in.[68] The relatively slow rise in the nightly *ingresso* price after unification suggests that the stalls audience were still seen as allowing little flexibility, whether from poverty or from their potential for making trouble.

At the same time the old governments had tried – rather more half-heartedly, except in Naples – to keep subscription prices from rising too fast (Table 8 shows this). Once the lid was taken off after 1862, subscription prices for the second tier of boxes at the San Carlo – the most fashionable tier, occupied almost exclusively by the nobility – trebled within ten years. The removal of the old governments brought out how far they had gone to subsidise the upper classes in their favourite social resort.[69]

Opera had probably been subsidised at most times since its birth in the early seventeenth century, though in ways not always obvious. One arrangement, in force at Trieste and Turin, was for other theatres to pay 10% or 20% of their takings to the leading opera house. This was highly unpopular and was abolished in those cities in 1841 and 1852.[70]

The main form of subsidy, in force through much of the eighteenth century and again during the Napoleonic years, was the gambling monopoly. When this was abolished at La Scala in 1788 the only way that the authorities could persuade an impresario to risk involving himself in opera management was to allow him to economise: new operas need no longer have been expressly composed for Milan, in short carnival seasons only one new opera need be put on instead of two, artists need not be *di cartello* (with a record of success in leading theatres), costumes need not be quite new. All these changes seriously detracted in contemporary eyes from the 'splendour' of La Scala seasons.[71]

When the gambling monopoly was again abolished in 1814 all over northern Italy (and in 1820 in Naples) matters were no longer so simple. Audiences had had a decade and a half to get used to the unexampled 'splendour' typified in Milan by the grandiose mythological ballets of Salvatore Viganò, in Naples by such *opere serie* of Rossini as *La Donna del lago* and *Mosè in Egitto*. The authorities in Milan deemed it unthinkable to cut down on standards that dressed all the chorus and extras playing medieval Scots in Mayr's *Ginevra di Scozia* (La Scala, carnival 1816) in satin. A few years later the official committee that was trying (in vain) to attract impresari to La Scala gave its opinion that 'in a city where there are many other theatres, and which is used to continual new and grand productions, to cut down even though minimally on their splendour would be the same as to destroy them and to drive away the public'.[72]

That meant official subsidy in cash. Detailed study of the affairs of La Scala, the San Carlo, and La Fenice shows in 1815–26 a recurrent struggle between impresari and theatre controllers over the terms of proposed contracts. At La Scala and La Fenice the upshot was, in several of those years, expensive direct management; or else impresari once again agreed to take on a season or seasons with no more precise obligation than that their productions would

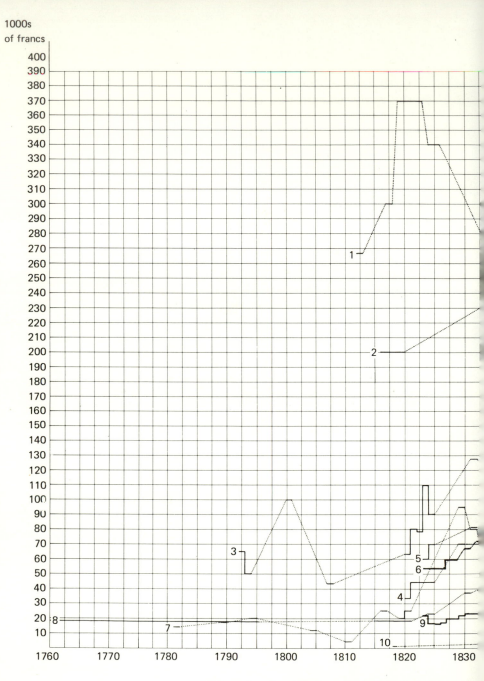

KEY: 1: Royal Theatres, Naples (San Carlo & Fondo)
2: La Scala and Cannobiana, Milan
3: La Fenice, Venice (total endowment)
4: La Fenice, Venice (municipal subsidy)
5: Teatro Grande (later Comunale), Trieste

Fig. 1 Levels of endowment of opera seasons, 1760–1910

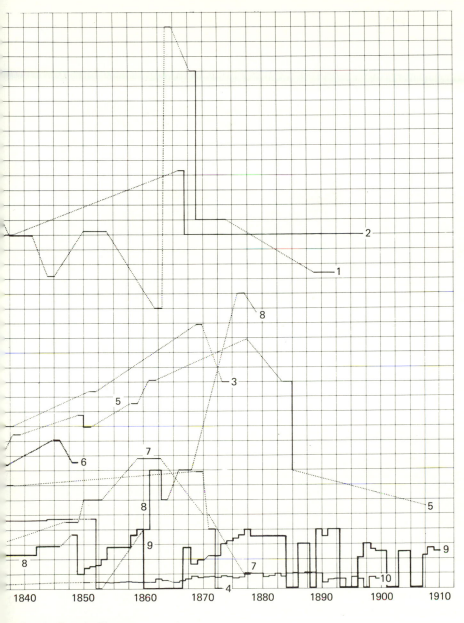

1840	1850	1860	1870	1880	1890	1900	1910	

6: La Pergola, Florence
7: Teatro Ducale, Parma
8: Teatro Regio, Turin
9: Teatro Sociale, Mantua
10: Teatro Sociale, Voghera

'suit the decorum of a leading theatre'. Eventually governments brought themselves (or compelled municipalities) to pay subsidies at a rate that would attract impresari.

The result may be seen in Figure 1: a general rise in subsidies in the 1820s, sustained in some theatres up to 1848; then, after the 1848–53 slump, a standstill or a further rise until unification. The two major exceptions are Naples, where the financial outlay of the Rossini period could not be kept up, and Turin, where an early result of the granting of a parliamentary constitution in 1848 was the cutting off of the subsidy.

The relation between subsidy and costs is not a simple one. If we look, in Table 1, at the percentage of costs covered by takings – and by implication at the 'income gap' to be covered by endowment or subsidy if the impresario was not to make a loss – we notice two extremes. On the one hand, all but one of the completed seasons whose takings covered more than four-fifths of their costs took place in Rome theatres – the Argentina and Valle. On the other hand all but one of the completed seasons whose takings failed to meet even half their costs took place in the leading theatres of Parma, Modena, and Lucca.

This can hardly be accidental. The two Rome theatres were owned by nobles. The papal government kept up an aloof and restrictive stance. It would grant no subsidy at all before 1829; even then it gave one only to maintain a carnival *opera seria* season in one theatre (not shown in our table). The Argentina and Valle seasons enjoyed neither boxholders' levy nor government subsidy; their seasons had to be run on a tight budget, if possible at a profit or at least close to breaking even.[73] Parma and Modena were the states that most noticeably stood out against raising the *ingresso* price even while they demanded a high standard of opera performances as a matter of policy. The figures suggest a deliberate decision to allow substantial losses and cover them through subsidy (though still not enough to save Osea Francia at Parma in 1819).

The remaining figures form no particular pattern. But the eighteenth-century seasons – none of which seems to have attracted an official subsidy, apart from a small ducal 'present' at Modena in 1701 – were all run by associations of noble impresari: we can take it that they were prepared to stand the loss. In the nineteenth century matters were rather different. Professional impresari (who ran all the seasons shown other than those at Trieste) might take a loss now and again, but they could not be expected to take continual losses. Endowments and subsidies were granted to make possible a quality of product which the government and the upper classes wished to see, and which they could not or would not secure by adequate price increases.

Did subsidies rise enough between the 1820s and the 1860s to match the international rise in costs? We lack the kind of series of costs, takings, and subsidies that would yield a clear answer. Impresari and theatre controllers themselves seem often to have been unsure of what the relation between the likely takings and the endowment (usually incorporating a subsidy) ought to be if it was to cover the 'income gap'.

Where an impresario received a subsidy equal to about twice the takings he was able to mount a successful season and make a small profit: this happened at Lucca in carnival 1825, where the takings were minute but the government was generous, and at La Fenice in carnival–Lent 1851, where the Austrian authorities were topping up the municipal subsidy at a time of grave economic difficulty.[74] But subsidies on this scale were exceptional. A subsidy of about half the takings made for a loss at La Scala in 1819–20. According to the experienced Alessandro Lanari, an endowment of about two-thirds of the probable takings at La Fenice in the late 1830s – where, as he pointed out, owners and public alike were exacting – would still not be enough to avert loss.[75]

It looks as though, in a leading theatre, with leading soloists, and granted good luck and good management, an impresario in the 1830s and 40s could break even or make a profit if the endowment roughly equalled the takings. This was the situation at the Senigallia Fair season in 1823–45 and again in 1856–8; in the intervening years the subsidy exceeded the takings by about a quarter or a third, but that was largely because the takings fell in those years of slump (in 1855, of cholera) and, as we know, costs fell with them.[76] Fourteen seasons between 1830 and 1851 were run by Lanari. They were reckoned by and large to have been artistically successful; how many of them made a profit is not known, but this busy man would hardly have kept coming back if they had consistently made a loss.

Plainly, however, not all important seasons in the years of rising subsidy up to 1860 were on that footing. In the Turin royal theatres, where the subsidy in the early 1830s and again in 1851 seems to have been only a quarter or a third of the takings, the story in these years was one of mediocre results and repeated failures by impresari.[77] The subsidy in 1764–74 had been no higher as a proportion of the takings, but either costs were lower or the noble impresari of those years were better able to stand the loss; probably both.

The one theatre where we can catch something of the interplay of costs, takings, and endowment is La Fenice.[78] In the difficult early years of the Restoration, the boxholders at first (1820) voted to set a fixed limit on their contribution; the municipality began by wishing only to top that up, then stuck to a fixed sum until the Austrian government compelled it in 1828 to give more. By the early 1830s boxholders and municipality had both raised their contributions at more or less the same rate.

The years from the 1820s to the 1850s were the most brilliant in the theatre's history, with five new operas by Verdi alone; the board of directors was intent on 'splendour', to the length of insisting that even the druids' costumes in *Norma* should be embroidered.[79] Yet there are repeated signs of financial strain. We have seen that Lanari thought the endowment inadequate. Five carnival seasons (1823, 1831, 1843, 1844, 1847) had to be run by the board of directors because no impresario would take them on. It seems that even in relatively favourable conditions the chances of an impresario's making a profit ran along a knife-edge.

In Paris, by contrast, not only were prices of admission to the Opéra more than one-third higher than those of La Scala or the San Carlo; government subsidy between 1830 and 1860 ran at levels twice or three times the highest amounts ever granted to either of those theatres – and they were the best-endowed Italian opera houses.[80] Not that there could be any question in Italy of subsidy anywhere near the Paris scale. The same broad conditions made possible Paris subsidies and Paris prices. Italy remained a poor country. As it was, opera subsidies were paid for largely by municipal taxes on food.

This explains the outcry against subsidy after unification. The old eighteenth-century *opera seria* had been disliked by the republicans of the 1790s as a genre bound up with absolutist courts and sung by extravagantly rewarded castrati; it was still denounced in the

same terms by some Milanese democrats of 1848 who wanted to
keep La Scala closed as a place where 'lascivious harmonies' had
lulled the people to sleep.[81] Even an official had pointed out as far
back as 1788 the injustice of making the public at large subsidise
the enjoyment of the few.[82] The moment there were elected persons
in national and local government – even though elected on a
narrow franchise – opera subsidies came into question.

At the first major financial crisis of the new Kingdom of Italy,
in 1867, the Chamber of Deputies insisted on abolishing all central
government subsidies inherited from the old Italian states. It went
one better and imposed a tax of 10% on all theatre takings.[83]
Subsidies were at first mostly taken over by municipalities. But the
new middle class that was moving into power kept gunning for
them, and so, from the 1880s, did the new socialists. Figure 1 shows
the result: here and there a brief spurt after 1860, but then a general
decline – rapid in the former capitals Venice, Naples, and Parma (as
also in Florence and Modena), longer delayed in prosperous Milan
and Turin and in some smaller provincial towns like Mantua and
Voghera. Whether or not subsidies had fully bridged the 'income
gap' in the old despotic states, they were certainly now failing to
do so.

At the same time two other changes came together to damage the
opera industry. One was economic depression. It started in 1873,
partly because of international influences, chief among them the
opening up of rapid communications to and within the Americas,
which flooded Europe with cheap food. Depression recurred at
intervals to the end of the century. The other big change – also
helped along by the coming of fast steamships and railways – was
a decisive rise in the fees some singers could command abroad, not
now in European cities alone but in Cairo, Rio de Janeiro, or San
Francisco.

By the 1870s the Italian opera industry was going through a
phase of simultaneous expansion and disintegration. Within Italy
it was expanding through the appearance – from the 1840s and
especially the 1850s – of large new 'popular' theatres built often
by private individuals, as well as of new seasons in parts of the south
previously unregarded and in small towns everywhere. Yet the old
system of regular seasons was breaking down. In former capitals
now deprived of their courts it took a special financial effort to

attempt a short season with singers of the front rank: the San Carlo was closed for three seasons in the 1870s, La Fenice for eleven seasons between 1873 and 1897; after 1877 La Pergola, Florence, put on opera only fitfully.[84]

In the rest of the world the export of Italian opera had been a fast-growing business since the 1840s, but as with other exports volume had been achieved partly by expanding production at the cheaper end and by multiplying outlets. Thus Adelina Patti might earn over 20,000 francs per performance in the United States in 1882–3, but the second- or third-rank Italian principals who went out to Athens, Malta, and the Azores in the 1870s got 600, 800, or 900 francs a month – more or less what they might have got in Italy.[85]

Within Italy itself an even wider range of fees prevailed. Patti could get 10,000 francs for each of two Turin appearances in 1879, and the internationally famous tenor Roberto Stagno half as much for some performances, also in Turin, six years later. A principal tenor at Assisi in 1889, on the other hand, was being offered 6 francs a night – and that was in the carnival season when most singers were employed: in other seasons struggling artists in minor theatres might have to perform when driven 'to the confines of starvation'.[86]

Such evidence as there is suggests that a few artists with offers from two or three continents could command unprecedented fees – three, four, or five times, performance for performance, those of the 1830s – but that good singers without an international reputation did little better than before, and possibly worse: witness (Table 4) the fees offered in 1871 to the established baritone Aldighieri, and paid in 1872 to the bass Gaetano Monti, a noted singer though near the start of his career – decidedly less than equivalent San Carlo singers had got in the 1820s and 30s.[87] It may well be that the rise in singers' fees had less to do with bringing opera into crisis than had depression (which hit some of the boxholders), the end of the court hierarchies in former capital cities, and the cutting down or withdrawal of subsidy. In such conditions, Verdi wrote,

the unfortunate impresari can no longer meet the requirements of artist and public. Instead of worthily serving art they are often compelled, after having struggled in vain against a thousand odds, to flee, to go bankrupt, and, what is worse, to degrade that art with productions that certainly do no good either to its splendour or to public morals![88]

Verdi's answer was to call for renewed government subsidy – something that would come about only in the twentieth century when control of opera houses had passed to public bodies. In these, impresari had no place. They had depended economically on the privileged upper classes of the old Italian states which their seasons had so visibly served. The coming of a centralised state with liberal representative institutions and a growing middle class was not the only influence to strip the impresari of their creative role, and it needed a generation to take effect. Opera impresari and liberal individualism were, all the same, irreconcilable.

A spectacular staging: Pacini's *L'Ultimo giorno di Pompei*, Milan, La Scala, 1827. The set designer was Alessandro Sanquirico.

4 · *The strong arm of authority*

The royal orchestra – so one impresario's contract read in 1806 – would play in the opera season; the king would 'apply the strong arm' of authority to make sure it did.[1] The phrase was common. Impresari asked governments to bring the 'strong arm of the police' to bear on a prima donna who failed to turn up, on an undisciplined *corps de ballet*, on orchestral players who demanded higher wages or urinated in the backstage corridors.[2] What they meant was that the government should summarily arrest the culprits and force them to do their duty, as the impresario saw it, in accordance with their contracts or with the theatre regulations.

The Italian states before unification were all despotisms; the one exception was Piedmont after 1848. There were in practice gradations and differences. But the principle that the ruler (or, as in the eighteenth-century Venetian Republic, the ruling oligarchy) had the right to know everything and control everything was common to all; it held just as true in the kingdoms set up by Napoleon as in the traditional states that preceded and followed them. This was not just an abstract notion. It was a habit of mind, a structure of expectation among rulers and ruled. It went back at least to the coming of Spanish hegemony in the sixteenth century – in many former city states back to the emergence of despots in the fourteenth or fifteenth.

Despotism did not mean wholly arbitrary rule. There were laws and courts and entrenched privileges whose workings governments by and large allowed to take their course, and there were many things they could not in practice control. But a wide margin remained within which the 'strong arm' had free play – a margin defined not by law but by the willingness of rulers and ruled to enact dramas which reinforced authority. Humble petition on one side, paternal clemency on the other would – people understood – in all but the worst cases relax the strong arm's hold.

To Italian governments the opera house was an object of high policy. This had little to do with the ruler's personal tastes. King Charles III of Naples was bored by music; he none the less built and attended the San Carlo to keep his nobles under his eye.[3] By the Restoration period the Chief Minister of Lombardy–Venetia was anxious that La Scala should be kept open in the usual seasons because it 'attracts to a place open to observation during the hours of darkness a large part of the educated population'.[4] It was possible to see even wider advantages: mindful of the perils of liberalism and revolution, the government supervisory body in Rome advised the Pope that the theatre was the best means of keeping the people quiet and contented with the rulers set over them, hence 'the most salutary antidote to those plagues that have been growing almost throughout the world'.[5]

Governments are often taken to have interfered with opera above all by censoring the libretto. Censorship was one, but only one means of interference; it did not become an acute problem until the last decade before Italian unity, when governments severely shaken by the 1848 revolutions met the full tide of literary romanticism. Until then the colour of the ribbons worn by the chorus, or the behaviour of stage-hands and ticket collectors, mattered at least as much as the text. If one asks what aspects of opera the authorities interfered in, the answer must be that they – not only governments but institutions representative of the upper classes – interfered in everything.

Intervention worked through a three-tiered structure. At the top was the ruler, who, unlike Charles III, might take an intense interest in opera: besides screening the boxholders, King Charles Felix of Sardinia chose subjects, approved libretti, and even demanded fewer arias and more concerted pieces.[6] The ruler's Ministers were also likely to be involved in many decisions, especially the Ministers of the Interior, of Police, and of Finance. Below them there was usually in each city an official supervisory body known as the *Deputazione* (or *Soprintendenza* or *Direzione*) *degli Spettacoli* (or *dei Teatri*). This was in one sense a government body in that it was appointed by the ruler, in another sense an emanation of the local nobility who generally made it up. In Bologna, as compensation for the loss of certain aristocratic privileges in local government reforms of 1816, the supervisory board was by law made up wholly of nobles and was hence called the *Nobile Deputazione*;[7] but in other cities (with the usual exceptions of Trieste and Leghorn) nobles seem anyhow to have been dominant. Often the supervisory board would have one member assigned to each theatre, with under him a paid inspector of much lowlier status to do the day-to-day work; there might also be a small executive committee (*Direzione*), with a civil servant as secretary.

On the next tier down, a theatre owned or part-owned by boxholders was likely to have an association of proprietors. In Tuscany this was usually called an academy, even though it had been formed for the specific purpose of running a theatre. The association as a rule had an elected or appointed executive committee (sometimes also confusingly known as the *Deputazione* or *Direzione*, or else as the *Presidenza*); where the association fully owned the theatre this was in effect a board of directors. It too might have a professional secretary and other employees.

There were variations on this three-tier model of ruler, supervisory body, and owners' association. In a monarchical opera house like the Ducale, Parma, the ruler's Great Chamberlain at first supervised everything, with a noble inspector and plebeian sub-inspector under him but without a board; by the 1830s, however, he was flanked by a mixed body of government and boxholders' representatives. In Rome the cardinal–governor of the city had until 1801 been in charge of supervising theatres; even after a lay supervisory body was set up he often took a close interest in opera. So did the cardinal secretary of state in 1814–23, Consalvi – a passionate admirer of Cimarosa's music – and, at various dates, some of the cardinal-legates in other parts of the Papal States. In Tuscany there was no official supervisory board; the academies were allowed to supervise their own theatres under the general guidance of the Minister of Police.[8]

The seeming clarity of a three-tier model was further complicated by the intervention of parallel hierarchies. The Minister of Police and the officer commanding the garrison were involved through the presence in the theatre of their subordinates; at La Scala in 1802 responsibility for order was divided among the official supervisory board (in charge of the stage and backstage areas and of the licensing of cabs outside), the civil police (in charge of the auditorium and foyers and of traffic outside), and the military guard (in charge

of the approaches) – a fairly standard arrangement.[9] The municipality was also involved if it paid a subsidy or maintained the
orchestra.

The government might choose to be involved even when it owned
no part of the theatre. La Fenice was wholly owned by a boxholders'
association, but the mayor of Venice and a representative of the
government attended the association's meetings ex officio. The
government representative virtually imposed on the association the
expensive Rossini season of 1823 (at a bad time when nobody
wished to serve on the board of directors); successive mayors deleted
from the impresario's contract the name of a possible composer, tried
to insist on a particular singer (the expensive Giuditta Pasta, by then
in decline), and established a right to pass all productions down to
costume designs. On the other hand the owners' association resisted
all government efforts to make it open the theatre in the last period
of Austrian rule in 1860–6; it did so on economic grounds that were
afterwards explained as – and no doubt were in part – patriotic.[10]

The same largely aristocratic group staffed nearly all these
institutions. This could mean an extraordinary concentration of
functions in one man. The Marchese Bartolomeo Capranica was in
1826 virtual impresario of the Teatro Valle, Rome, owner of the
theatre, secretary-general of the supervisory board, and secretary-
general of the Ministry (*Direzione*) of Police. To keep a company of
actors in order he could threaten to appeal to himself.[11]

On the other hand it was common for institutions to differ. After
the taste of autonomy which Pius IX's early reforms had given
municipalities, the Bologna local government and supervisory body
carried on in the early 1850s a continual tug-of-war over the terms
of management contracts and the choice of singers; the municipality
seems to have won, since it came to approve theatre prices and
programmes and even to authorise the lighting of stoves in a cold
snap.[12] There might anyhow be factions within a single institution:
the Florence theatre academies were said in 1837 to be notoriously
riven.[13]

The impresario, then, had to deal with several authorities at once,
all of which might claim a right at least to be informed of what was
going on during the season, and possibly to dictate what ought to
go on. They accounted for a good deal of his incessant paperwork.

The business was most ponderous in monarchical theatres. At

Naples in the 1820s requests went usually from the impresario Barbaja to the supervisory board, then to the Minister of the Interior, then to the Council of Ministers, and finally to the king – on such questions as whether a dancer should be given his passport, whether to go on trying out a weak tenor, whether new seats should be wood or iron, whether artists should be fined or allowed benefits. When the king was in Vienna the government insisted on getting his consent to the slightest change in a gala programme which he had previously approved; it took fifteen days each way.[14] At Parma, Duchess Marie-Louise decided matters of this kind day by day, even the hour at which the performance was to start.[15] But even in a theatre away from capital cities a high-ranking official with a strong interest in opera would have his say: in an attempt to get the contract for the 1834 season at the Senigallia Fair, Alessandro Lanari had to correspond not only with the mayor whose municipality was subsidising it but with the cardinal-legate of Pesaro, who questioned his proposed choice of singers and objected to their singing less often than had been usual; Lanari tried to bring up another cardinal as reinforcement.[16]

Except in theatres directly dependent on the monarch, rulers and high-ranking officials were by and large concerned less with day-to-day running than with the terms of the impresario's contract; these they looked into and discussed in extraordinary detail, especially the provision made for a suitable level of 'splendour'. The Austrian authorities in Milan with their ponderous legalism tried again and again to achieve the terms they wanted by putting the concession up to auction, generally in vain: impresari either did not bid or set up collusive 'rings'. But auctions were required by the imperial government in Vienna, to whom everything of importance had to be referred. After the terms were settled the impresario dealt much more with the supervisory board and with the theatre owners.

A manual of 1823 set out the supervisory board's functions. It was to enforce discipline at rehearsals; settle from the start any questions of relative status among soloists (a frequent source of trouble); see that they were punctual; regulate access to the stage and behaviour on it; enforce fire precautions; ensure the cleanliness, decency, and historical accuracy of the costumes; require certificates for any absence on medical grounds; fight off sloppiness in performances; look out for immoral conduct; approve all posters and printed announcements; and call on the government's armed forces to arrest any theatre personnel who were insubordinate during the performance.[17]

There was nothing fanciful in this list drawn up by an experienced man. It was exactly what supervisory boards did. It was also what the more diligent executives of boxholders' associations did. One might then ask: what was there left for the impresario to do?

The system did make for duplication. Quite often supervisory authority, owners, and impresario seem to have all been dealing with the same matter and writing to one another about it. It also encouraged buck-passing. At one point in 1857 the Milan supervisory board, the two impresari of La Scala, and the chief *répétiteur* of the orchestra were all trying to get one of the other parties to decide which orchestral players should be got rid of for 'incapacity or negligence'.[18]

This suggests not mere poltroonery but a continuing ambiguity in the impresario's relation to his patrons. The supervisory authority and the owners, after all, provided an endowment, perhaps not quite enough to meet their demands, but enough to make the impresario something less than an independent risk-taking entrepreneur; and they insisted on taking a hand in the working out of the season. If things went wrong the impresario could hope (though often in vain) for extra endowment to make up the loss.

This ambiguity came out when Andrea Bandini made a great show of independence in negotiating a new contract for the Ducale, Parma. The supervisory authority wanted to insist on particular singers, to pass the set designs, to supervise the restoration of existing scenery, to see libretti and scores two months before the start of the season, to look at artists' contracts – all common requirements of official controlling bodies. Bandini objected that 'in every well-regulated theatre [the supervisory authority] has only the right to make the impresario carry out his contract, not on any account that of entering into his private business'; if these demands went through he would become a mere 'wretched paymaster'. Only a few months before, however, Bandini had successfully petitioned the duchess for an extra endowment to cover the loss on the opening seasons of the new Ducale. His declaration of independence was very likely no more than bluster, designed to get him out of signing a new nine-year contract in what had turned out to be a loss-making theatre, while allowing him to put the blame on unreasonable official demands.[19]

The supervisory bodies often saw themselves as upholding standards against the slackness of impresari, and fending off perilous discontent among operagoers. Unless the supervisory authority laid down requirements of the kind Bandini objected to – an official wrote – 'absurdities will never be got rid of which are now remarked all too often and with all too much scandal, such as seeing an American [Indian] dressed like a Turk, or a Parisian like a Roman'.[20] The members of the Bologna supervisory board thought that if they did not order an impresario to get rid of bad singers before the first night they would 'all expose [themselves] to the just animadversions of the public'.[21]

Impresari for their part were sometimes scornful of the 'ignorance' of supervisory authorities and owners, particularly of their insistence on established names[22] – the result, no doubt, of their wishing to play safe in an age when no one could know for sure what a singer sounded like until he or she turned up, and when bad singers could cause a riot. Supervisory boards generally asserted the right to dismiss singers who turned out badly when they opened their mouths at rehearsal; careful impresari put a clause into contracts exempting them from paying singers thus dismissed, and the clause was eventually (1861) upheld by the courts.[23] On similar grounds, supervisory boards at times required new works to be put on earlier than impresario and composer had planned (because intervening operas had failed and the public might grow impatient); and they could threaten to withhold part of the endowment if it was not done.[24] But they did not always have it their own way, even under the old governments: an impresario whose endowment had been cut because he was late with a new ballet successfully pleaded *force majeure* in the Parma courts.[25]

How arbitrarily a supervisory board might act seems to have varied with time and circumstance and no doubt also with persons. The authorities in the main Habsburg-ruled states, Lombardy–Venetia and Tuscany, before 1796 and again between 1814 and 1848 seem to have been rather more legalistic, those of the Papal States and Naples more arbitrary. As late as 1855 the Bologna supervisory board compelled the baritone Enrico Crivelli to appear in a benefit for the two Baucardè, a tenor and soprano couple, even though Augusta Baucardè's caprices had pushed the season beyond its expected term and Crivelli's contract had run out. It also undertook to make the impresario pay Crivelli a proper fee.[26] So much for the sanctity of contract.*

Probably the worst irritant was an episode like a deputy inspector's altering on his own authority the time the impresario had set for a rehearsal. The impresario in this particular case demanded that the man should be admonished; whether he was or not we do not know, but the system with its tiers of authority lent itself to petty annoyances of this kind.[27]

They were probably harder to take than were the effects of sexual intrigue between upper-class members of the supervisory authority or the boxholders and artists in the impresario's company. Domenico Barbaja and Alessandro Lanari at any rate felt strong enough to refuse to employ or promote an artist 'protected' by the head of the supervisory authority. This was a revealing test of how far the profession had moved towards independence: impresari of the early eighteenth century had been satirised as little better than pimps.[28] The question is of necessity ill-documented, but in a country where no singer could get by on a minimum of voice and a maximum of sexual attractiveness – there were famously ugly but successful prima donnas like Pisaroni and Barbieri Nini – it probably mattered little among leading soloists. Things were no doubt different among beginners and minor artists; here the impresario himself might be among the predators.

Similar variations can be found in the dealings between impresari and theatre owners. Lanari got some of the provincial Tuscan academies, and some town councils in neighbouring regions, to accept what would now be called 'package deals': one Leghorn academy complained only of not having been told about the programme for the coming season before it appeared in a newspaper. A generation later Lanari's son Antonio in effect told the Cesena town council 'take it or leave it'.[29] These minor authorities presumably took it because it was a way of securing better performances than they could have got from smaller, more amenable local impresari. On the other hand the executives of the academies in charge of the two main Florence theatres can be found pulling up

---

* The Baucardè also had a contractual right to a benefit, but the whole affair could have been left to make a pretty argument in court.

the impresario twice in one night for letting the stage remain too dark and the performance run too late,[30] or else going carefully – in the persons of two aristocrats bearing the fabled Renaissance names Guicciardini and Pazzi – through the costumes for a new ballet.[31]

At La Fenice the upper-class directors (*Presidenti*) were as a rule exceedingly active; from 1843 their secretary, Guglielmo Brenna, acted as a kind of resident manager. The line of least resistance in such a theatre was for the impresario to let the owners make most of the decisions and himself become a good deal of an executant. G. B. Lasina, nominal impresario of the 1851 and 1853 seasons that launched *Rigoletto* and *La Traviata*, seems to have done this systematically, not only there but in other seasons at Bologna and Parma: he wrote as if anxious to be told what to do, and congratulated himself on being treated by the Bologna supervisory board 'more like a son than like a concessionaire'.[32]

Tougher businessmen than Lasina had previously taken on the aristocrats of La Fenice. One of the directors' prime demands was that they should positively approve the soloists to be hired for the coming season, as a rule after the impresario had submitted a roster of three possible names for each part; that committed the impresario to securing the chosen artists, and hemmed in his bargaining power when he dealt with them over contracts. In the early 1820s, when the endowment was clearly inadequate, the old gambling concessionaires Balochino, Crivelli, and Barbaja probably got together to cut down the directors' claim. They all bid for the management concession or showed interest; Balochino offered the directors only the negative right to turn down certain names out of a list; when this was rejected, Crivelli got the contract, which allowed the directors positive approval of soloists but which was without the usual provision that they should be established names.[33]

'There's no trifling with those *illustrissimi* on the board of directors': so Alessandro Lanari concluded in the following decade.[34] He ran the 1832 and 1833 seasons under a five-year contract but grew more and more irritated at what he saw as the owners' unreasonable demands and their unhelpfulness: after they had exacted compensation for his failure to produce Giulia Grisi (who had run away), and had done nothing to meet the extra cost of a Pasta season, Lanari put in proposals for a third season that were clearly designed to provoke a break and let him off the rest of his contract. The owners then brought in the more accommodating local impresario Natale Fabrici. It had been a battle of wits between Lanari and the board of directors; indeed a former director of La Fenice thought that his office 'of itself involves a conflict with the interests of the impresario'.[35]

Lanari and the La Fenice owners came together again four years later. They both had their reasons. To the impresario one of the three most prestigious carnival seasons in Italy must have been tempting. To the owners Lanari held out – as was said on a later occasion by the Bologna supervisory board, which preferred his bid to another, superficially more attractive one – 'all the advantages of the moral and economic security afforded by his ability and solidity'.[36] But after three more seasons Lanari again lost patience with the directors' fussiness, which, as he claimed, made it very difficult to break even. He and Merelli colluded in an attempt to 'lay down the law to the board of directors' as Balochino and Crivelli had done in 1823, but this time their concerted bids failed: the owners once again fell back on Fabrici.[37]

A subtle annoyance to impresari in a theatre like La Fenice was that artists liked to deal direct with the gentlemen on the board of directors, who were well-educated, no doubt well-mannered, and might be generous. A leading choreographer asked the directors to press Lanari for more dancers – whereas, Lanari's man on the spot complained, he should have asked the directors to bear the extra cost: 'artists of merit must always prefer the interests of those leading impresari to whom they are contracted'.[38] One artist of merit who took no notice was Verdi: he made a point of concluding every one of his La Fenice contracts with the board of directors, thus bypassing the impresario.[39] In a theatre of this kind – and, so far as we can see, a theatre run by an ambitious academy like La Pergola in Florence was not very different – tension between owners and impresari seems to have been the norm.

Besides contending with the authorities over the terms of his contract and keeping them sweet in the day-to-day running of the season, the impresario faced his superiors on three main fronts: first, the make-up of the free list and the problem of bilkers in the theatre; then the censorship; finally, the maintenance of discipline during performances, perhaps through arbitrary arrest. In a hierarchical society run on despotic principles all these questions involved the role of the monarch and the use of his authority.

A free list was normal in eighteenth- and nineteenth-century theatres, not only in Italy. They were not expected to be full on other than special occasions. In most Italian theatres until the late nineteenth century there was a good deal of standing room: free entrance tickets given out to stage-hands and other theatre personnel might be a way of piecing out low wages without keeping out paying customers or taking up seats. The free list was none the less a problem to opera impresari, for three main reasons.

First, governments based on hierarchy and personal dependence used the free list to make a public show of their own dignity while at the same time rewarding their servants. Secondly, endowment gave them some sort of claim to a quid pro quo. Finally, part of the population in each town were straitened in their circumstances, keen to hear the opera, and persuaded that they were somehow entitled to get in free. These pressures could easily take up far more than the slack left in a half-full theatre; governments, besides, claimed not just entrance passes but boxes. Impresari had a constant battle to keep the earning capacity of the opera house from being eaten away.

Governments dictated free lists as they intervened in everything else. The only government we know of that tried to abolish free lists or whittle them down to almost nothing was the idealistic Roman Republic of 1798–9[40] – and it lasted only a few months; even then it is doubtful whether the officers of the French army of occupation took much notice. Other governments worked on one of two principles, the hierarchical and the functional.

The eighteenth century was the age of the hierarchical free list. This gave free entrance (and sometimes boxes) not only to high-ranking officials unconnected with the opera season but also to their 'families': this meant not so much their relatives, though some might be included, as their subordinates.

The papal territories, the most conservative of the Italian states, showed the hierarchical free list in full bloom. For the opening season of a fairly small opera house at Faenza in 1788 an official free list was drawn up of 105 people – exclusive of the cardinal-legate and vice-legate and their 'families' if they chose to come over from neighbouring Ravenna. On the list were, among others, the bishop's chancery (eleven people), the Holy Office (thirteen people, including four monks and a cook), and the governor's greengrocer. This was very like earlier lists at Bologna and Senigallia, which if anything had gone further in including a number of judges and their dependants. True, when the cardinal-legate saw the Faenza list he thought it 'exorbitant' and had it cut down to sixty-six; he also took steps to guard against people stockpiling free tickets.[41]

The cardinal-legate's action speaks for an enlightened rationalism common at that particular time. It heralded a change to a functional free list, that is, one limited to those officials who had a clear connection with the theatre. We can see this being applied at La Scala in 1790, under pressure from an impresario who had to do without the old gambling privilege.[42] From then on the shift seems to have taken place in the same scattered manner as the cutting down of free space for boxholders' servants. Even then the officials and soldiers involved in controlling a theatre were many; when a list included a monarch's train, as at Parma in 1829, it could reach 153 (plus an unknown number of the supervisory authority's 'families', down to an apothecary and a smith).[43]

Impresari who complained of excessive free lists were sometimes granted an extra subsidy.[44] Governments found it easier to do this than to curb their servants, many of whom considered either that they had a prescriptive right to free entry, or that if others had it so should they. This reinforced the impresario's character as a client of the great.

The problem abated somewhat after the early years of the nineteenth century. One no longer hears of riots such as those at Bologna in 1770–1, when government retainers forced their way into theatres without paying, or at Rimini in 1806, when some French dragoons tried to do the same; on that occasion several people were killed and wounded.[45] Associations of boxholder-proprietors, some of recent date, stood out as best they could against government interference and made even governors pay for their boxes. The owners of La Fenice boasted in 1854 that they had never allowed the chief of police a free box, though this was not strictly true: a French chief of police in Napoleonic times had truculently refused to pay for his box either there or, later, in Florence. In this he followed the example of some French generals, one of whose first acts on taking over an Italian town was to demand half-price entry for their soldiers and a number of free boxes for themselves.[46]

As municipalities came to subsidise opera they too wanted boxes, but, it seems, in discreet numbers. Things did not change much after unification: a potentially damaging provision at the San Carlo, Naples, late in the century allowed municipal employees designated by the mayor to pay half price.[47] This was in tune with a general Italian assumption that people connected, however indirectly, with government should pay less than others for public services, like railways. The hierarchical pomp was largely gone; the habit of privilege remained.

For the impresario faced with a large free list one of the problems was being sure of who was who. At the old Ducale, Parma, in 1794 – which was attached to the ducal palace – people would sail through the linking doors 'announcing titles before which the impresario had to bow' and failing to pay.[48] But this was only an aspect of a general problem. Impresari were always trying to fend off people who got in by pretending to be extras or journalists, using someone else's season ticket, or getting themselves smuggled in by a friendly usher:[49] phenomena of a poor country.

Preventive censorship was the norm in Italy. It went on before, during, and after the period of revolutionary and Napoleonic rule (but for a very short outburst of free expression in 1796–7), before and after unification, though the practice of censorship in united Italy was much more liberal.[50] Studies of the censorship have fastened on its political aspects – the ban on regicide, for instance, that gave Verdi such trouble over *Rigoletto* and *Un Ballo in maschera* – though recent work has shown how much it was concerned to uphold a timorous morality and avoid anything unpleasantly specific.[51] Impresari seem to have wanted above all to get libretti through the censorship as fast as possible: the schedule was tight enough as it was. Even then unsuspected dangers might spring up in performance.

Because the opera house was the centre of social life few things went down so well as local allusions – not, heaven forfend, allusions to the authorities but to a well-known noble cuckold or an eccentric literary man. For the same reason there were few things the paternal authorities of old Italy detested more. Allusions might cause murmurs, gossip, disorder; they must be stopped. So a comic opera by

Pacini making fun of the poet Monti was forbidden after the third performance. La Fenice refused *I due Foscari* as a new opera because the noble Venetian families of Loredan and Barbarigo might have been upset at seeing their fifteenth-century ancestors in a poor light; it did put on the work after a Rome theatre had taken responsibility for the first performance – a nice distinction.[52]

For the impresario the danger was that local allusions not in the text might be worked in by a singer, particularly in *opera buffa*. Severer vigilance after the Restoration may indeed go some way to explain the decay of comic opera: it killed improvisation. A kindred peril was that 'obscenities' might creep in. It is seldom easy to know what these were. Mostly they seem to have had to do with ballet dancers showing too much leg. The Imperial Royal Provincial Delegation at Padua was only one of several authorities to express indignation on this score (pointing to the number of university students in the audience); at such times the impresario might be ordered to have the dancers' skirts lengthened by the evening performance.[53]

Worse trouble hit the impresario of the Ducale, Parma, just before the opening of the carnival season of 1837. The director-general of police came backstage with the censor and the supervisory board to demand immediate changes in costumes: some for the ballet were 'indecent' and those of the female chorus in *Lucia di Lammermoor* had red and green ribbons on a white background – the tricolour of the Napoleonic Kingdom of Italy, an allusion quite unintended by the designer. 'He threatened like a madman that the fortress stood ready for anyone reported to have deviated in the slightest [from his orders].' The man in charge of the costumes had the green ribbons hurriedly taken off, but the impresario was so frightened that he insisted on substituting black ribbons at his own expense; the whole breakneck change cost over 1,000 francs.[54]

When the Parma chief of police threatened to send people to the fortress he meant business. To such men arrest came easy. The old Italian states nevertheless tried in the first place to control the people involved in the opera season by more bureaucratic means – the company through their passports and the audience through elaborate regulations published and posted at intervals.

Italy was a part of Europe where passports were always needed, not just to go from one petty state to another but to go from one town to another within the same state. This was in itself a problem for itinerant theatre people. When Verdi was in Venice preparing *Ernani* his passport had to be applied for before he could go to Verona (still within the province of Venetia) to hear a possible tenor.[55] In anxious times, as after the 1831 risings at Bologna and Modena, artists might need to produce documentary evidence of an engagement elsewhere if they were to leave town without going through 'infinite petitions and applications'.[56] Once they reached the *piazza* their passports were impounded as a matter of course until the end of the season. In Naples this happened even to artists who had no local engagement and were just passing through; they then had to get, and pay for, the supervisory board's permission before they could get away.[57] That seems to have been a local baroque elaboration. In general the point was to stop artists from bolting if they were offered a better engagement elsewhere. Since artists occasionally did this the system was, for the impresario, a convenience.

Regulations governing audience behaviour were largely uniform across the Italian states. It made little difference whether the government was republican or monarchical, Habsburg or Bourbon or Napoleonic, or was operating in the eighteenth century or the nineteenth. Their main points were: to forbid applause in the presence of the ruler (unless he gave the lead); to forbid curtain calls before the end of an act and encores at any time; to forbid whistling (hissing) and excessive noise, including excessive applause.[58]

Since most Italian audiences wished to applaud wildly when they approved, to whistle unrestrainedly when they disapproved, and to have artists take curtain calls in mid-act and give encores, we need to ask what led governments to persist with regulations that went so clearly against the grain. There seem to be two main explanations. Governments had a not unjustified fear of riot in the theatre; this shifted somewhat from fear of rowdiness in the eighteenth century to fear of political trouble after the French Revolution. At the same time, however, the rules look like another manifestation of the parent–child relationship so many Italians saw as the model for dealings between ruler and subject. Just as many eighteenth- and nineteenth-century parents thought children should for their own good be denied things they liked, so governments stood out against the self-indulgence of opera audiences.

95

This was shown by the way monarchs would deliberately refrain from applauding during a first performance – which was therefore heard in disconcerting silence – but would allow some applause at later performances: they displayed first their paternal power, then their indulgence.[59]

As in many parent–child relationships, however, it was not always clear that prohibitions would stick. A Padua audience in 1794 got the representative of the Venetian Republic to allow an encore of the overture in spite of large placards forbidding such things; when he refused them an encore of a duet they booed and whistled for half an hour, the performance was suspended, and soldiers were brought in.[60] It was not unknown for a Neapolitan audience to call out to the king in dialect 'If you don't applaud, we will,' and for a Milanese one to defeat an archduke's ban on applause or whistling by all coughing or blowing their noses at once.[61] We seem to be hearing about a repressed but still unruly school.

Faced with this kind of demonstration, governments might threaten: the papal government, which believed in old-fashioned remedies, in 1824 put up a flogging block outside the Teatro Valle as a warning against excessive applause by a prima donna's supporters.[62] Or they might retreat: the authorities at Parma changed their regulations in 1833 and 1850, those at Bologna in 1852, to allow some encores and curtain calls.[63] Either way the sense remained of a drama being enacted in the auditorium between authority and public as well as on stage. The impresario, who was caught between the two, might be found petitioning the government at one time to stop the audience from whistling, at another to permit applause or encores for the good of the performance.[64]

The authorities might also move in and arrest. This was a well-tried procedure. The best-known example of it was the arrest of a singer who had feigned illness or who was alleged to have otherwise broken his contract; the singer was then kept either in prison or under house arrest and was each night brought to the opera house under guard to perform. This happened from time to time to eminent singers and dancers all through the eighteenth century and right up to the 1850s; in a 'bad' case, as when the tenor Alberico Curioni – already arrested once for 'insults' to the public – at the end of the season whistled back at the Parma audience, the singer went to the fortress for eight days and was then expelled from the duchy.[65] But supervisory bodies also used arbitrary arrest to punish minor dancers for slanging each other backstage, orchestral players for refusing to play in certain intermezzi, stage-hands for arriving late or for allowing a backcloth to descend in mid-scene rather as at the climax of the Marx Brothers' *A Night at the Opera*.[66] Arrest was used as a means of labour discipline.

Yet this was not unmitigated oppression. The arrests lasted as a rule for a few days, sometimes for twenty-four hours or merely overnight. Those arrested were often released as an 'act of grace', or on their expressing contrition, or when their friends asked for mercy on their behalf. What was being displayed was, once again, a power relationship between superior and inferior; the superior used his margin of arbitrary power to exact obedience, the inferior was generally willing after a day or two to make submission. Nor was the strength all on one side, at least at the level of virtuoso singers and dancers rather than of stage-hands. Star performers were aware that their rarity value might more than counterbalance the ruler's will.

Clara Novello was singing at Modena in 1842 during the festivities that attended the marriage of the duke's heir. At one point she refused to sing on her rest day. 'They sent down two dragoons to take me off to prison, but I only laughed and said "You can put me into prison but who then will sing for the princess?"...Only fancy them trying to frighten me like that.'[67] Novello's being an Englishwoman in the age of Palmerston no doubt helped, and she may not have grasped the ritual element in such arrests. All the same, her position was different from that of a refractory dancer and first violinist at Faenza in 1788: they – it was pointed out to the authorities – could be dealt with by force because they were not irreplaceable.[68]

Arrest was also commonly used to keep order in the auditorium. It was a means used alongside rather than in place of institutional justice. Criminal prosecution still dealt with serious offences, and civil jurisdiction was not ignored: a singer who was made to perform under threat of arrest, like Luigia Boccabadati at Naples in 1831, could still take the issue under dispute before the courts and win.[69] The rule of status and the rule of contract went on side by side.

Impresari, as we have seen with Osea Francia, were not immune from arrest when a first night angered the audience, or occasionally when a company was left unpaid or a nobleman in authority thought he had been insulted. The examples we have all date from before 1820.[70] That is not conclusive evidence; but, as impresari began to look somewhat more like respectable businessmen, subjecting them to ritual arrest may have come to seem inappropriate.

Impresari were anyhow the first to ask the authorities for help in organising their seasons and sometimes in keeping discipline. Barbaja's and Lanari's notion of how to get defaulting singers and musicians to turn up or composers to finish their work on time was to go to the police.[71] Balochino, more subtly, hinted that a singer who did not honour his contract to sing in a government theatre might in future have trouble getting a passport.[72]

In doing this they acknowledged that the authorities were on their side. Governments, like impresari, wanted to see the best possible season and were prepared to exert themselves to get it. Opera was an affair of state. So the brother of the King of Naples interceded on Barbaja's behalf with the ruling Duke of Lucca to have a tenor released from his contract there, the papal nuncio in Vienna several times persuaded leading singers and dancers to appear at the Senigallia Fair, and the cardinal secretary of state – the nearest thing in Rome to a prime minister – was at one time trying to remedy a shortage of bassoon players.[73]

These were measures to fall back on when ordinary business correspondence failed. Diplomats or chiefs of police in other states could be asked to report on a new singer or inquire whether it was true that a dancer was pregnant.[74] The government might now and then harass an impresario, but it was his patron: he went on hoping that it could be induced to solve his problems, whether by largess or by the use of force.

Control of opera seasons and of discipline in the theatre was one matter where Italian unification made a difference. The prefect – the representative of central authority in each province – and the police still had wide powers to keep order; seasons could not begin without police permission. But it was no longer their business to enforce private obligations through arbitrary arrest, or to demand that impresari should provide financial guarantees. The army by 1870 no longer mounted a military guard in the theatre.[75] Liberal individualism had come to power, and with it the belief in the primacy of contract and the rule of law. It became easier for impresari and artists to default; disputes now ended more often in court.

For the opera world the change was at first disconcerting. The police in Bologna in the first months after unification were still being asked to compel a ballet dancer to perform or to make a financial guarantor pay up; they appear to have swung between trying informal persuasion and referring petitioners to the courts.[76] Storms of booing and whistling, of the kind that stopped performances or even cut short a season, seem in after years to have become more frequent in some of the towns of Emilia–Romagna, a region that combined political radicalism with headlong partisanship in operatic matters. This happened at Modena in 1862, 1866, and 1869, at Cesena in 1870. At Parma, where there had already been one suspension in 1857, serious trouble recurred in 1865, 1870, 1872, 1878, 1879, and 1882; in most of those years performances had to be stopped, sometimes before the end of the first act, and on two occasions the booing was such that prima donnas fainted on stage.[77]

Opera audiences of the region, those of Bologna included, already had the reputation of being hard to please, but it was in these years that Parma especially came to be known (it still is) as a place where a stentorian tenor might set off avalanches of applause but other singers might feel that they were lucky to get away unhurt. Declining standards in a former capital had something to do with it, but so had the withdrawal of the strong arm that had formerly kept the lid down on the passions the human voice can rouse.

Silhouette caricature of the impresario Domenico Barbaja, by Rossini.

5 · The impresario as businessman

Rossini had died; the committee that was promoting a new Requiem Mass for him hoped to get from the impresario at Bologna the use of his artists, orchestra, and chorus gratis. Alas, the impresario replied, he was not a patron of the arts but 'a businessman who has six children and is not well off'. They must think again.[1]

That was how professional impresari normally saw themselves. The commercial code of the new Kingdom of Italy likewise treated theatre management as a business: impresari must keep proper books and were theoretically liable to arrest for non-payment of business debts.[2] The impresario as feckless bohemian, concerned chiefly to scrape a living by pilfering from the box-office receipts,[3] is a superficial notion. It is not baseless, but it misses the dogged concern of most impresari with contracts, accounts, and bargaining in the hope of profit. Impresari were businessmen, though of a pre-industrial type whose methods and outlook changed only gradually through the eighteenth and nineteenth centuries.

In opera the unit of management, the firm, was essentially an individual, even though that individual might move about surrounded by a group of dependent relatives and assistants. Professional opera management seems not to have been compatible with a lasting partnership or joint-stock company: attempts were made to combine them, but they seem always to have failed.

The two main forms of collective management by and large excluded professional impresari. These were the joint-stock association of noblemen, and the management run collectively by the musicians and artists (on occasion by the stage staff) engaged for a particular season.

The noblemen's association was, as we have seen, an eighteenth-century form. Nineteenth-century revivals had a consciously anti-quarian air; attempts to praise it as more 'dignified' than professional management brought few imitators.[4] A variant that included some non-nobles worked to open a new opera house at Faenza in 1788. This season – an important event in the life of a small town, formerly a city state – was run by an association of forty-six shareholders, both nobles and citizens, who put up about 236 francs each, with an elected executive committee of two nobles and two citizens. Among the shareholders, Osea Francia was to run Faenza seasons for the succeeding ten years, while Vincenzo Caldesi – a non-noble member of the executive committee who acted as its nominee in contractual matters – went on to run seasons in Rome for six years around the turn of the century. It may well be that Francia and Caldesi were tradesmen who became professional impresari as a result of this experience; Caldesi was later said to have dissipated through his opera seasons 'a capital far from negligible'.[5] This kind of collective effort was to be found in the nineteenth century, generally in small towns and on special occasions; it was not the way opera management was normally carried on.

Collective management by artists, musicians, and perhaps stage staff was much more common. As many as fifty-one people might be shareholders, as at the Tor di Nona, Rome, in 1771.[6] Moralising commentaries on the ways of the lyric stage suggested that this was the ideal form of management. As Goldoni put it in *L'Impresario delle Smirne* (1761), a representative specimen of this kind of backstage comedy, 'under a single paymaster all are proud, bold, demanding. When the musicians run the *impresa* themselves, all are humble and work willingly.' This seeming general truth is however given away by Goldoni himself: his musicians come together only after their impresario has fled. Failure to attract a professional impresario, or an impresario's bankruptcy part way through his contract, was the usual reason for the setting up of collective management by artists: it was as a rule limited to one season and was intended to make the best of a bad job.

A variant of this type of management, in operation at the Teatro del Corso, Bologna, in 1853, was an association based on twenty-six shares of about 105 francs each, of which four were held jointly by members of the municipal orchestra, two by the lessee and sometime impresario of the Corso, and others by non-noble citizens of the town, with an agent as nominee. This too was said to be a means of keeping musicians and theatre people in work for a season, even though at an almost certain loss.[7] Collective management on something like this mixed pattern was to become common in the difficult last years of the century. It is best understood as a mixture of self-help and patronage, intended as a stopgap rather than as a substitute for commercial management.

Joint managements (*imprese sociali*) involving professional impresari seem to have been of two main types. One was the partnership or series of interlocking partnerships, with unlimited liability, at least for certain purposes. The other was the limited liability company (*società anonima*) whose shares might be promoted and sold to members of the public. Partnerships were fairly common; they sometimes went on for a number of years, but the examples that can be studied seem all to have been unstable. Limited liability companies had about them more than a touch of wishful thinking; two that were launched in Naples promptly fell apart.

A partnership might bring together a well-known singer, who invested his savings, and an impresario who needed capital for a deposit of caution money; a more disreputable form involved giving a young singer a share in the management instead of a fee.[8] Such a partnership ran for the season in which the singer appeared. Partnerships among impresari aimed at a run of several seasons, occasionally in more than one city. They were meant to unite complementary interests: one man's holding of costumes, another man's contracts with artists, a third man's local connections or expertise.

Such partnerships as are documented all involved Alessandro Lanari and at least one other impresario. They were all based on Lanari's costume workshop, and most if not all of them on his long-term contract artists as well. Their exact legal form is not known, but it involved unlimited liability within the limited purposes of the partnerships, which were all aimed at running specific seasons or series of seasons: the minor Florence impresario Pietro Somigli, who had a one-twelfth share in a partnership formed to run La Pergola, tried to get out of paying his share of the losses on the grounds that he was 'a poor father of twelve children without a penny in the world' – a common line of argument which did not avert the threat of a lawsuit if he failed to pay up.[9]

Some of the partnerships were short-lived because they were not meant to do more than enable Lanari to run a season in hidebound Rome by providing him with a local partner – first Paterni, then

Cartoni. The longest-lived partnership, that among Lanari, the choreographer Lorenzo Panzieri, and the semi-retired tenor Nicola Tacchinardi, went on from 1823 to 1828, the term of the partners' contract to run seasons at La Pergola and in other Tuscan theatres. Tacchinardi seems to have been a sleeping partner who was at times anxious for the safety of his investment. Panzieri was the anchor man in Florence; he and Lanari seem to have got on cordially, though there were disagreements over the valuation of Lanari's costumes and the cost of hiring them, and towards the end Panzieri, a sick man, was moved to wish that they could get through the rest of their contract in peace.[10]

Lanari's other main partnerships were, first, with Crivelli and Merelli for the management of La Scala and La Fenice in 1828–31, and secondly, a complex set of interlocking arrangements with Bandini and others for seasons at Florence, Parma, Bologna, and Venice in 1836–8. Both were cut short by quarrels; both seem to have been riven with mutual suspicion from the start. The trouble was each time that no partner could or would commit himself fully to the joint venture. Looking back on the first of them some years later, Lanari called it 'a business more than a little fearsome'.[11]

In that venture part of the problem was that Lanari and Merelli were not truly complementary: both had artists under contract, more than could be exploited by their joint management alone. When Merelli as agent placed Giuditta Pasta at Verona, outside the partnership area, rather than at La Fenice his partners immediately suspected a cheat. Running a partnership by post was difficult when complex decisions had to be taken: Merelli and Lanari each protested that the other had acted without consultation in matters that should have been decided jointly. After the partnership had been dissolved by Crivelli's death the two survivors quarrelled over a debt which Lanari maintained formed no part of the joint concern. Though the quarrel was patched up, similar disagreements ensured that later attempts by these two to revive the partnership came to nothing.[12]

This first venture was harmony itself compared with the extraordinary tangle of interlocking partnerships involving Lanari, Bandini, and others in 1836–8. The basic impulse seems to have been Lanari's ambition to spread his costume-hiring business to Parma, Bologna, and Venice besides maintaining it at La Pergola, Florence, even when he was no longer the chief impresario there.

That role now fell to Bandini, but he and Lanari suspected and disliked each other from the start; their partnership was really a truce sandwiched in between two Florentine 'wars' which Lanari conducted against the Bandini management of La Pergola from the smaller Teatro Alfieri. The exact arrangements cannot now be reconstructed; there seem to have been at least two partnerships, one of them involving Merelli as sleeping partner (but not Lanari), and several sets of working capital in different cities. Besides Lanari and Bandini, the Parma impresario Claudio Musi and the Florentine lawyer Niccola Tilli were partners, as well as the child-beset Somigli, perhaps along with one or two others.

The difficulties of running simultaneous seasons in four cities (besides Lanari's own separate network in Tuscany and Umbria) would have been great even if goodwill had prevailed. As it was, each partner maintained a comptroller to check the doings of the others: 'we spend all our time with the partnership contract in our hands', Lanari's man reported. Shortage of credit during the international financial crisis of 1837 made matters worse. Amid daily irritations a main cause of trouble was the other partners' refusal to pay for Lanari's costumes at the rates he thought suitable. Several of the partners had outside interests; all were short of capital and setting off their obligations to the various sets of working capital seems to have been an awkward business. Even allowing for personal animus, the venture shows the difficulties of running opera management on a large scale when the experience of impresari accustomed them to trust only in continuous personal control.[13]

Partnerships, even so, were a fairly normal way of running seasons; some of them may have worked more equably than the surviving evidence implies. Limited liability companies were, in opera management, a freak. Not that they differed greatly in this from other companies that were floated in Naples in the 1830s, often by the same mixed group of noble reformers, foreign merchants, and monopoly concessionaires. These companies set themselves high-minded goals of social and economic 'improvement' but, in the conditions of Naples, ended by doing such things as lending money to public servants whose pay was for ever in arrears.[14]

The problem of financing opera management through a limited liability company was that, although shareholders were protected from having to meet losses beyond the amount of their stake, there was little hope of attracting them through regular cash dividends. Promoters accordingly devised schemes whereby shareholders would be rewarded in free entry tickets to the opera house or free seats; what they proposed was a kind of opera consumer cooperative.

An early prospectus for such a 'new form of association' – intended to put on only one opera at the Teatro Comunale, Bologna, in 1780 – looked forward to recruiting 800 shareholders each of whom, on payment of about 69 francs, would have a right of free entry to the theatre and the stalls area. The project came to nothing.[15]

A much bigger venture was the Compagnia d'Industria e Belle Arti, which actually ran the 1834–5 season in the Naples royal theatres before foundering. It was launched with a proposed 9,000 shares (hierarchically divided into seven classes) and held out the prospect of cash dividends as well as of benefits in theatre seats, to be distributed daily. The nobles, merchants, and bankers who ran it enjoyed the services of the ubiquitous Alessandro Lanari, in the threefold capacity of shareholder, salaried manager, and provider of artists under contract; the company was also to have bought out his costume stock, but this did not go through. The season was lavish and by the summer of 1835 the company was in deep trouble; it just managed to put on the first performances of *Lucia di Lammermoor*, with Lanari's prize contract artist Duprez, before going out of business.[16]

The Compagnia d'Industria e Belle Arti had tried to run the Naples theatres as Barbaja had run them in the past but with a reduced government subsidy. The next attempt at company promotion involved Barbaja himself as well as the Prince of Ottajano, a central figure in Naples business ventures of these years, and the rising impresario Vincenzio Flauto. It seems to have been a more restricted affair, with no more than forty-five or fifty shares and without any attempt at a consumer cooperative. This company ran the Naples royal theatres from 1836 to 1840, but it lost money in the first two years (mainly because of a cholera epidemic), the shares sold slowly, and by 1839 Barbaja had quarrelled with the board of directors; the cause seems to have been in part his own brusque ways, but mostly a sustained campaign by Flauto and Ottajano aimed at putting him in the wrong.[17] In spite of this record, proposals for yet another limited liability company to run the theatres as a consumer cooperative were being put forward in 1850; by 1858 a joint venture by nobles and non-nobles was running them – under what arrangements is not clear – but was once again deeply divided.[18]

Why did these Naples companies run into such trouble? We do not know their affairs in enough detail to be sure. The principle of a consumer cooperative need not have been absurd; but it was fatally optimistic to link it with a hope of cash profits, all the more so when government subsidy was falling. The companies, besides, operated in an economy where capital was short, such trade as went on was often in the hands of foreigners, and even these depended largely on the government. They are best seen as an aspect of a short-lived 1830s boom. Illusions abounded: a lawyer who in 1837 thought the management of the royal theatres a sure road to ruin (unless the government paid out more) argued less than a year later, with the subsidy unchanged, that it could not fail to show a profit.[19]

We know of one other public company, technically a limited partnership (*società in accomandita*) rather than a limited liability company. This was the Società Impresaria Romandiolo-Picena, promoted by the Bologna theatrical agent Giacomo Servadio in 1855 and set up in the following year with, apparently, a minimum of 200 shares of about 529 francs each. Its headquarters were at Ancona, with branches in Florence and Bologna; it seems to have been designed chiefly as a means for Servadio to raise capital and hang on to it, for he was to have first call on any shares resold by other shareholders. It ran some seasons in Ancona (on the usual consumer cooperative principle) and elsewhere in east-central Italy, but not for long: by 1861 Servadio was leading an opera tour to Caracas and Cuba.[20]

In spite of these attempts at joint ventures the typical impresario remained the figure described in chapter 1, a mobile individual with about him a small group of relatives and hangers-on. One of these would act as his secretary – a useful lightning-rod as well as an amanuensis, for there was a convention of blaming on the secretary an unwelcome expression from a fellow impresario, even when that impresario had written in his own hand.[21] The etymology of 'secretary' was to the point: one of the drawbacks of collective management was supposed to be the impossibility of keeping secrets, and a leading impresario like Jacovacci did not like people to know even the date on which he was to set out on a journey.[22] For men with this kind of outlook a tight family enterprise was much the best.

This is not to say that individual impresari did not cooperate. They did, at arm's length. They sometimes cashed each other's bills of exchange and gave each other credit in a sort of miniature banking system, at least when they trusted each other enough. They exchanged information, within limits. They very occasionally divided Italy into spheres of influence: in the bad years 1848–9 Lanari, with his costume workshop based in Florence, and Pietro Camuri and Antonio Ghelli, owners of the leading Bologna workshop, agreed to divide Italy between Rome and the river Po and not to hire out costumes on each other's territory, or at least to do so only by consent and on payment of a commission – a far cry from the late 1830s when Lanari had tried to corner the whole of this area.[23] They formed rings when authorities in control of theatres sought to put the management up to auction, either sending in more or less identical bids or collectively staying away, though this probably did not happen quite so often as a Milan official thought: 'these people', he wrote, 'are generally united in their interests while pretending [to compete].'[24] Rings and cartels seem to have been formed most often when times were bad. When there was a hope of profit an outsider was likely to come in and spoil the game, as when Lanari and Merelli failed to 'lay down the law' to the owners of La Fenice.

The outlook that led to the formation of rings was at bottom monopolistic. It assumed that resources were limited and that the ideal arrangement was for a single impresario or group of impresari to deal with a single theatre controller. This assumption was probably sound, up to the mid nineteenth century at any rate. Not only did the hierarchical array of Italian society make opera a privileged genre; the restricted size of the upper-class opera audience in most Italian towns might well make competition ruinous.

The same assumption helps to explain the recurrent 'wars' between theatres giving opera seasons. These might occur even between neighbouring towns. For an opera season at Vicenza in 1787 to coincide with one at Padua was regarded by Paduans as an outrage. In 1791 and 1792 Padua itself was to be split between parties supporting rival theatres, until the government had to step in and force a compromise agreement to divide up the seasons.[25]

There the initiative came from noble theatre owners. Elsewhere the impresari carried on the struggle themselves. Lanari's Leghorn agent regarded it as self-evidently outrageous for another impresario to send a company there when he knew that Lanari was about to put on the opening season at a new opera house: such behaviour warranted taking steps to spoil the other man's business or force him out altogether, even though the seasons at the new and old theatres seemingly overlapped only in part. Another agent in Bologna, where the regulations allowed only two theatres to open during the spring season, advised contracting to put on a season of plays at a minor theatre alongside the opera season at the Comunale for the sole purpose of keeping out a rival opera season at a third house: it would pay to engage a theatre company and then keep it idle.[26] Even after the mid-century expansion of audiences and theatres the impresario of the Teatro del Corso, Bologna, claimed in 1879 to have been ruined because the rival Teatro Brunetti had unexpectedly prolonged its opera season into Lent.[27]

Some of these rivalries seem to have been dictated by spite. Barbaja, with his Naples contract about to run out, was said to have kept on the expensive Maria Malibran for longer than he had planned as a means of showing up his successors; Jacovacci was advised to sign up two promising young singers mostly so as to deny them to Lanari.[28] Cartoni's Rome wars against Paterni and Jacovacci owed something to personal rancour, though here again everyone aspired to monopoly as the norm.

All this suggests how far impresari kept to the outlook of pre-industrial tradesmen, used to working in an environment where resources were few and privileged access to them seemed essential, where secrecy, close-fistedness, perhaps deceit were prime commercial virtues.

Yet in other ways impresari were modern businessmen. This was shown, first, in their reliance on contract, and secondly, in their eagerness to work a free labour market, especially when it was likely to favour them.

The reliance of impresari on contract is beyond doubt. They might put forward sophistical interpretations of such documents as they had signed, but the very word used for a theatrical contract – *scrittura*, writing – suggests how ink on paper ruled their affairs.

Opera contracts went back to the Venetian public theatres of the early seventeenth century. At that time they were simple agreements by performers to appear at a certain theatre for a given fee. By the first half of the eighteenth century they had grown far more elaborate. By about 1800, if not earlier, such a wealth of practice had built up that printed forms began to come in; impresari went on revising them throughout the nineteenth century to keep up with court judgments and if possible to tighten them up in their own favour.[29]

The rule of contract, though, went hand in hand with the rule of custom. The many recognised customs governing theatrical affairs seem not have have been written down systematically until the appearance in 1823 of Giovanni Valle's manual – itself a sign that a more cashbound and impersonal outlook was coming in. Contracts, Valle wrote, should be as specific as possible, but various points were so well understood that they need not be spelt out: leading performers must not, in the season preceding the one they were contracted for, appear anywhere within sixty miles of the *piazza* (minor performers not within thirty miles); 'within the first days of the month' meant 'up to the 10th'; an obligation on singers to perform whatever they were given did not mean that they must undertake roles damaging to their voices; and so on.[30]

As the nineteenth century wore on these customs were increasingly written down in contracts; after unification the sixty-mile rule was simply turned into a sixty-kilometre rule. Points which Valle had thought well understood were tested in the courts. In the early years of the century the administrative office (*camerino*) of La Scala had by custom settled disputed points among impresari and artists throughout Italy, but by 1823 Valle thought its authority obsolete.[31] If this suggests an increased readiness to go to law – and there was plenty of litigation throughout the remainder of the century – that too points to a slow shift away from reliance on custom and personal ties and toward more strictly contractual relationships.

Such a shift took place in the contracts that gave impresari their seasonal concessions. A form still in use at the Comunale, Bologna, in 1782, but probably obsolescent, said nothing at all about the programme, the artists, or the seat prices, apart from stating that there would be two operas – presumably because the Bologna authorities intended to settle these matters themselves. What it did talk about was the theatre building, scenery and equipment, safety regulations, boxholders' rights, theatre employees to be kept on, the free list, and the impresario's rent payment and caution money.[32] At the other extreme, the form of contract for La Scala in 1887 took up seven closely printed pages, and dealt even with the material the *corps de ballet*'s shoes were to be made of (only the front two rows got satin). This was much more typical of late eighteenth- and nineteenth-century contracts. All the main headings of the Bologna contract were still in it except rent; it also provided elaborately for the number and kinds of operas and ballets to be given, the number and frequency of performances, and the dates by which every aspect of every production was to be submitted to the supervisory board for approval. One missing feature that had been common earlier in the century was the requirement in leading theatres that soloists should be already successful (*di cartello*). This had been resisted by impresari in bad times; it faded out in the 1860s and 70s with the general crisis of the old opera system, and was deliberately abolished in Naples in 1884.[33]

Impresari on the whole tried to carry out the terms of their contracts, or else asked the controlling authority to exempt them. Though charges of bad faith were common, only seldom do we find evidence of impresari deliberately flouting their obligations – and then not without some excuse. To meet the demand of the conservative Turin audience for both an opera and a separate ballet, even when the opera was as long as *Don Carlos* or *Aida* and already included a ballet, the late nineteenth-century impresario of the Regio faked an illness or an accident so as to cut out part of the programme. Turin society, it seems, preferred its ballet ration to *Aida* in full.[34]

What was much more common than a violation of the terms of the contract was a dispute over the arrangements for ending it prematurely. Since the early eighteenth century at least, contracts had provided that the season could be stopped because of fire, war, epidemics, the death of the ruler, or some other overriding government act (*fatto di principe*).

Were impresari to be made to pay for fire damage? Or should they on the contrary be compensated? In an age when theatres were made wholly or partly of wood, were heated (if at all) by wood-burning stoves, and were full of lighted candles and oil lamps, theatre owners tried to insert into contracts a clause making the impresario liable for fire damage, while impresari – especially after the San Carlo fire of 1816, which led to Barbaja's being sued for alleged breach of contract – at times successfully insisted on narrowing down their responsibility to matters of immediate and culpable negligence.[35]

Of the other causes that might stop a season, only government acts were thought to warrant compensation; after 1814, so as to cut short possible arguments over the terms, Milan contracts generally stated that when a season was stopped impresari should receive subsidy, endowment, or subscription money only in proportion to the number of performances already given. The contracts between impresari and artists dealt similarly with artists' fees; a weak impresario on occasion pressed the government to close the theatres when times were bad so that he in turn could stop paying his artists.[36]

The crucial question was what should happen if the season went badly, the audience was hostile, or the impresario ran out of money or was unable to carry out the advertised programme – all common situations.

The theatre owners could release the impresario from his contract – and impresari in a tight corner often pressed for this – but they did not necessarily choose to do so, particularly if they considered that the impresario was at fault or if he had found a pretext for claiming compensation. In such a case the owners might play a waiting game in the hope that the impresario would go bankrupt: this sort of struggle went on between Bandini and the academy that owned La Pergola.[37]

If the owners did agree to break the contract, and if they wished the season to go on, they had either to make a contract with someone else or to take over themselves. What happened depended a good deal on the will of a few upper-class personages.

Here too we see a movement toward greater contract-mindedness. When the ex-king of Sardinia died near the start of the carnival 1824 season, and the theatres were closed, the impresario and company of the Regio, Turin, implored the authorities to compensate them beyond the terms of their contracts, on the usual grounds that they were distressed heads of families. But by the 1850s and 60s the courts were ruling that a Genoa impresario whose season had been cut short must give the subscribers a refund, whatever the municipality might have decreed – the contractual tie with the subscribers overrode everything; also that when theatre owners took over an impresario's contract instead of cancelling it they must take over his contractual obligations to the artists.[38]

So far did this shift toward stressing contractual rather than personal ties go that in 1871 a lawyer with much theatrical experience gave his opinion that no composer or artist could back out of a contract made with one impresario if the seasonal concession was then transferred to another impresario: he or she still had to perform for the new man what had been promised the old, on the grounds that 'a change of impresario as a rule matters little to the conduct of performances'.[39] Such an opinion given a generation earlier would have startled the contemporaries of Barbaja and Lanari. It reflected not only a new legalism but the decline of the impresario as an individual creative force.

When an impresario could not meet his commitments the old governments were inclined to arrest him, seize his assets, and give the opera company and the theatre suppliers a preferential claim on them before other creditors could take their chance in the courts. Formal bankruptcies of impresari seem to have been rare. Jacovacci did go bankrupt in 1848 (paying off his creditors three years later at 6%); Antonio Lanari in 1862 reached a settlement with his creditors, apparently out of court.[40] But these were respectable men. Between 1858 and 1867 the Marzi brothers, the busiest impresari of the day, failed five times over in different cities without, so far as we know, going through the bankruptcy courts or paying off anybody. In the troubled 1870s and 80s we hear of impresari who fled without paying their companies and singers who demanded payment in instalments before every performance; the Rome impresario Costantino Boccacci was said to have given his creditors an appointment at the box-office after the last performance, stuffed the takings into his clothes, and made his escape over the roofs.[41] If such men did not land in court it was presumably because everyone knew there was nothing to be got out of them. But this, once again, showed how far the profession had declined.

Before the 1850s the relations between impresari and theatre controllers had tended to monopoly because both supply and demand were highly restricted. At most, impresari had been able to play on the political or social reasons that led governments and boxholders to wish to keep theatres open, while theatre owners tried to break the united front they sensed among impresari. Once they got a concession, however, impresari were keen market operators.

It was their business to commission new works, sign up performers and employees, and subcontract (as was the general practice) costume-making, scene-painting, lighting, the running of refreshment rooms, and, often, the gallery takings.

The humbler sections of the work force – orchestral players, chorus singers, production and front-of-house staff – were those where corporate privilege and customary rights were common, though generally at low levels of pay. From about 1820 in particular, impresari made repeated efforts to break down these pockets of privilege and to establish a free labour market. They met with resistance, often effective. In their dealings with soloists whose earnings were potentially far greater, the impresari enjoyed something closer to a free market, but one in which the other party was keenly aware of his or her own value.

'What must people do where so few professions are open? Can they all be physicians, priests or shopkeepers, where little physic is taken, and few goods bought?' Mrs Piozzi, Dr Johnson's former friend, was moved to this outburst after seeing an abbé play in the opera orchestra at Lucca 'for eighteenpence pay'.[42] Italian poverty meant that not only was the lyric theatre one of the few means to a living; people who managed to get a job in the opera house did their best to hang on to it for themselves and for their families. Governments before unification (and some elected municipalities after it) tended to protect these jobs and keep 'foreigners' from out of town at bay, though the old governments also wished to put down 'insubordination'.

For an orchestra player or theatre employee the ideal was to work for a royal or municipal theatre with a fixed roll of salaried staff who must be taken on by the impresario. We can see this system at work in Bologna. There Napoleonic rule shook the old corporate order when the famous Accademia Filarmonica lost its control of orchestras; this allowed impresari, as hostile witnesses complained, to hire cheap incompetent players. At the Restoration, however, the best musicians banded together in what has been described as a trade union but was probably more like a labour monopoly run by a permanent contractor. At any rate the municipal orchestra by the 1850s was paid and run by the leader of the orchestra (*maestro direttore*) under regulations enforced by the supervisory board. It consisted of an inner core of officially appointed lifetime members (some of whom also taught in the well-known music school), a surrounding ring of officially temporary but often long-serving players who hoped to be taken on one day as permanent, and an outer ring of students who played for nothing. There was an intricate system of officially approved substitutes: a permanent member could hire out his instrument and make over part of his salary to a deputy of his own choice while he himself took leave, with the permission of the supervisory board, sometimes for years at a time. A home-made pension system allowed a member too old or ill to go on playing to draw half his salary till his death while his replacement drew the other half. There were also customs 'practised from time immemorial', whereby established players could get extra payment for attending certain rehearsals or else could send deputies to them. Players in theatres other than the Comunale keenly aspired to join the municipal orchestra, and meanwhile tried to establish similar rights in other jobs even though without official sanction.[43]

This system shows exactly the kind of entrenched group whose privileges impresari wished to break down. True, at an unprotected minor theatre where the leader of the orchestra was a full-blown labour contractor and attempted to cut wages the impresario could appear as the players' friend, urging the *maestro direttore* to 'let everyone live': apparently he paid the man a flat rate for the orchestra's services and it made no material difference to him what individual players were paid.[44] But at the Comunale the impresario Mauro Corticelli's attempt to do away with 'immemorial' abuses brought a threat of a strike which had to be settled by a compromise.[45]

'Arrange to get me an excellent orchestra...for little money': that was the impresario's watchword when he had the chance.[46] The opera season at the Senigallia Fair, in contrast with those at royal or municipal theatres, shows the free market in musicians fully at work. Here was a brief but important season held during a generally slack season (July–August) in a town where otherwise there was no permanent orchestra. The local agent who recruited Lanari's orchestra for the 1836 season has left us full documentation of the bargaining and beating down he undertook to fulfil Lanari's request. At least once he openly recruited a second-best player for the sake of cheapness, but in general he asserted that he had got some of the best available; he even claimed to have found a bassoonist better than the one who had played the year before but costing little more than half as much.

The labour market he drew on spread as far as Bologna, Perugia, and Ascoli – a good slice of east-central Italy, presumably over-stocked with musicians at that time of year. Since the impresario did want a good orchestra, however, the bargaining power was not all on one side. Some players refused to come down below a certain figure. Some took engagements still farther afield, in Padua or Viterbo or even Cadiz, rather than accept Lanari's terms.[47] The players' readiness to move about did something to counter the impresario's ability to tap a wide pool of labour. By the 1850s some Bologna musicians were able to get regular engagements in Athens and even Constantinople and then get back home for the important autumn season. But players of no more than average skill clearly had a thin time.

'How is one to wring another penny from these wretched people?'[48] This cry from another of Lanari's agents after a bargaining session with orchestral players for a minor theatre suggests how close we are to the sweated trades of early Victorian London. The basic conditions were much the same. Certain skills were widely held by people some of whom worked in a traditional, protected environment, while far more were enabled by expanding demand to get some kind of work but were unprotected. Yet we also have to recognise that when impresari tried to crack down on the use of deputies, or to get rid of mediocre players from protected orchestras, they were acting not unlike the Toscanini of the early 1890s, who so upset the custom-bound opera orchestras of Genoa and Pisa by his insistence on using only the best musicians that he caused a strike.[49]

What was true of orchestra players was true of many theatre staff: the head of stage staff (*macchinista*) and the stage-hands, the scene painter, the stage manager, the box-office manager (*bollet-tinaro*), and their staffs. In each department the man in charge was often a labour contractor, and in each there was the same contrast between protected and unprotected theatres, the same official reservation of only certain jobs, and the same general expectation of tenure.

Cosimo Canovetti, head of stage staff at La Pergola, Florence, had dealings with Lanari over two decades, and so did his son Cesare. Father and son complained several times that Lanari was 'assassinating' them by seeking to cut estimates, or was failing to advance money they needed to build sets; Cosimo once threatened to take his grievance to the Grand Duke and Grand Duchess of Tuscany, whose subsidy was intended to keep theatre people in work and whom he claimed to know better than Lanari did. Yet on another occasion Cosimo tried to borrow money from Lanari for six months or so. The Canovetti father and son, it seems clear, had no officially fixed post; but, in a theatre patronised by the Grand Duke and by a leading academy, custom was nine-tenths of the law. They and the leading Florence impresario were bound in uneasy symbiosis.[50]

In the second-rank Teatro del Corso, Bologna, on the other hand, the supervisory board, faced with similar disputes between impresario and head of stage staff over a bill, and between impresario and stage manager over a 25% wage cut, could do no more than attempt conciliation. The impresario Corticelli's retort to the stage manager – 'he answered that I might do whatever I pleased and we would be friends none the less' – shows the confidence of a man aware of working a free labour market.[51]

Such a free market was most likely to be found in short seasons like the Senigallia Fair and in minor theatres like the Corso. It could also be encouraged by the spread of economic liberalism and by the financial weakness of governments and other theatre controllers. In the Grand Duchy of Tuscany, a European pioneer of economic liberalism, the owners of the Cocomero, Florence, shifted between 1764 and 1775 from making the impresario keep on a permanent company of actors at fixed salaries to allowing him full freedom to get rid of them.[52] In the other Italian states – even in Tuscany itself once the heady days of the reforming Grand Duke Peter Leopold had passed – such uninhibited freedom of contract would have to wait until unification, and even then would meet with constraints from newly elective municipal authorities.

What happened in the Naples royal theatres is revealing. There the government first gave way in the 1820s, after the highly lucrative gambling monopoly had been abolished. In an attempt at compensation it allowed the impresario in 1822 to dismiss any theatre employee, in 1824 to bargain with orchestral players and members of the *corps de ballet* over wages; this in practice meant that he could get rid of them if they refused to take a wage cut. Free bargaining, however, seems to have been thought troublesome: later contracts went back to a fixed wage scale. But in 1843, after the impresario had endured a cut in subsidy, he was allowed to take on at fixed salaries only half the *masse* (orchestra, chorus, *corps de ballet*); the other half were to be offered contracts, but at much lower pay. In 1848, under a (briefly) constitutional government, the impresario had once again to take everyone on at a fixed tariff, and this arrangement was still in force in the early 1860s.

With the removal of the strong arm of Bourbon authority the chief problem came to be the defaulting impresario who left the *masse* unpaid: the Naples municipality therefore started holding back over half the subsidy, to be either paid to the *masse* direct or kept in reserve for them and for the theatre staff. The impresario kept a right to turn down individual members as too old or unfit, but one who tried to do this in 1892 got into a dispute with most of the orchestra and had to go back on nearly all his demands.[53]

As the Naples story suggests, low-paid members of an opera company were not wholly defenceless, at least at certain times. Chorus singers appear to have been, as one official put it with some exaggeration, 'always troublesome in all seasons and in all theatres'.[54]

Italian chorus singers were notoriously cooks, street vendors, minor artisans, and the like who sang part-time; few could read music. Their inability to look like ladies and gentlemen was given by the directors of La Fenice as the reason for putting *La Traviata* into the fashions of about 1700 – beneath which their low origins 'disappeared'. They were paid labourers' wages, were apt to smoke, drink, and gamble in the dressing-rooms, and were altogether 'the pariahs of art'.[55]

Yet chorus strikes recurred throughout the nineteenth century, and so did strike-breaking by impresari. Like orchestral players, many chorus members were mobile; it was not difficult to import them. Under the old governments entire choruses that had gone on strike were arrested at Lucca in 1836 and at Piacenza in 1844; a

Parma chorus rioted in 1829 and its self-proclaimed leader was arrested by an officer who feared that any more trouble might lead the impresario to bring in 'foreigners'.[56] Methods of discipline might be crude: Lanari's deputy, faced with an unruly chorus, slapped one member of it; he later threatened to have them all arrested and ostentatiously posted several policemen backstage.[57]

Choruses took advantage of periods when the old despotic governments had been overthrown and no new order had as yet firmly taken their place, notably the 1848–9 revolutions and the turbulent period of unification in 1859–60. A Lucca impresario in carnival 1849 doubted whether he could stand out against the chorus if they used 'force'; the issue, a recurrent one, was a convention that sometimes allowed chorus members to wear their stage costumes in the street during masquerades.[58] No question in Lucca just then of carting everyone off to jail. At Bologna the chorus of the Comunale won a wage increase in 1859. The following year they demanded not only a further increase of 31% overall (including payment for rehearsal time) but a tenure system on a par with the orchestra and the right to choose their own chorus master; they referred to themselves as 'this corps which has given honourable service for 28 years'. The impresario Ercole Tinti protested against 'mutinies unheard of in the theatre world'. He offered to break the strike by bringing in outsiders if the municipality would pay him an extra subsidy, but clearly the moment was not right and the dispute was settled by a compromise – Tinti paid 23% more overall while the chorus dropped their other demands, that for rehearsal pay included.[59]

The impresario Luigi Piontelli, however, had no difficulty in breaking a chorus strike for higher pay at the Carlo Felice, Genoa, in 1891. By then the state was firmly re-established and if anything was on the employer's side.[60]

In a highly seasonal business like opera not only revolution but the rush of the carnival season could give lowly employees a chance to assert themselves. That was the time when music copyists went on strike if they were not paid daily.[61] It was also the time when tailors and seamstresses employed in costume workshops – among the worst-paid of urban craftsmen – formed shadowy 'combinations' ('*leghe*') and employers dared not sack anybody; the right time to sack was late spring.

Lanari's costume workshop next to La Pergola in Florence had begun around 1820. Its expansion into a large-scale hiring business intended to cover the whole area between Parma and Rome came after the failure in 1834 of Lanari's plan to sell his stock to the Compagnia d'Industria e Belle Arti in Naples. By the late 1830s it was employing at peak periods forty, fifty, or sixty men and women, some in the workshop, some outside, among them women specialised in embroidery, braid-making, and dyeing. This was not a negligible figure in a pre-industrial economy.

By carnival 1837 the workshop was producing costumes for three operas and two ballets at La Pergola, two operas at La Fenice, Venice, two operas and a ballet at Parma, and two operas at Pisa; most of these were new and the two main ballets at Florence and Parma (one Chinese, one Turkish) required 255 and 211 costumes. Everyone was working fifteen to seventeen hours a day, Sundays and holidays included. Carnival 1839 was much the same; by 1840 costumes were being made for Havana. 'All we need', Lanari's deputy wrote, 'is one more order...and we can all go and jump in the Arno'.[62]

The labour force was for the most part casual and flexible. All we know about their pay is that a man and four women were paid, over two days, an average of 0·84 francs a day each – but the women almost certainly got a little less; the average was itself a little less than women sailmakers were then getting at Leghorn, and that was one of the lowest Leghorn wages.[63] Some of the workers insisted on part-payment in advance, but others did not: their pay was sometimes in arrears and they might have to pawn their household goods to keep going.

This was a sweatshop. Its owner Lanari behaved like a villainous employer in a melodrama; melodramas about villainous employers had some basis in the reality of societies where commercial expansion had taken place in a rush. His workshop depended heavily on the chief tailor, Vincenzo Battistini, a semi-literate man who was paid about 170 francs a month. When Lanari was trying to sell his stock and workshop to Naples he cracked up Battistini as the finest tailor in Italy, and highly economical besides. But Battistini was caught stealing. Lanari took him back, on condition that he repaid what he had stolen; for this, he told Battistini, 'I deserve your eternal gratitude'.[64] His real reason was that he needed Battistini to carry out his plan for an extended Florence workshop: 'I have to think', he wrote to his cashier, 'of keeping this capital of mine at work.' In an oddly blasphemous strain he added 'I am the father of mercy, and sometimes in order to do good to my fellow men I become three times better than I ought to be'; later, when Battistini was accused of overspending, he sent word 'that I must be his first God because I feed him, and he had better beware of putting me off for good'. Battistini appears to have been finally dismissed in 1848.[65]

Yet Battistini was not just a victim. He was an awkward customer. Lanari's assistants suspected that he was not only stealing but taking bribes from singers (to make their costumes more splendid) and perhaps egging on the work force to go slow at peak periods. His skill and knowledge, however, were such that they could not do without him.

Lanari's costume business was at once complex and precarious. Designs had to be sent for approval to other towns, many kinds of material bought, costumes cleaned, adjusted, checked, and despatched in good time to get through customs, all this to a famously high standard and to the tightest of schedules. Yet money was often short; an under-capitalised business was being run from hand to mouth. Hence Lanari's angry complaints at every setback that it was leading to his 'total ruin', and his attempts to control everything from a distance. Tension ran high; Lanari's sister and his two assistants, left to run the place without a clear management hierarchy, burst out now and then into open quarrels.

With all its troubles, this was a business that went on for over forty years until Antonio Lanari's failure in 1862. Relentless personal management was what kept it going for so long. Alessandro Lanari's deputy complained of his 'systematic distrust' and unending reproaches: 'when you use the whip no postilion can come up to you'. Yet Lanari must have had some kind of personal ascendancy if his long-serving musical director, right-hand man, and boon companion Pietro Romani could write to him emotionally 'you are now to me a necessary being', and again: 'do with me what you will'.[66] An impresario of this calibre must have had about him a touch of the ringmaster or hypnotist.

A career like Lanari's puts an ambiguous gloss on Verdi's well-known charge that he had found impresari 'always harsh, inflexible, inexorable, if need be with the code and law-books in their hands. Always good words and exceedingly bad deeds...I have never been considered as other than...a tool'.[67] Verdi was well able to look after himself; he too could at times be harsh. What he did not say (because everyone knew it) was that composers like himself, and leading singers too, operated alongside impresari in a free market where, by the time he was writing, he could pretty well dictate terms.

What made this section of the market so open was the eagerness of nearly all concerned to move – not just within Italy but abroad as well. To the end of the nineteenth century, it is true, we find here and there a minor singer who sang secondary parts in the same theatre year after year, no doubt giving lessons on the side. Composers whose operatic careers were failing or were only moderately successful settled down as cathedral organists or heads of music colleges. Others failed altogether and vanished from sight. But the goal was, first, the circuit of leading Italian opera houses, then Madrid, Paris, London and ultimately, from the 1840s, New York.

'Do you suppose I am practising this profession for fun?' the veteran composer Pacini once demanded of Jacovacci.[68] By the late eighteenth century cash payment was the standard that measured achievement and status. There was still some payment in kind – up to the 1830s leading singers and composers were sometimes found lodgings, sometimes in the impresario's house – but it was dying out fast and anyhow no longer counted for much. Cash was, in Lanari's words, 'the thermometer'. Those who were paid the same were reckoned to enjoy the same standing.

Bellini was intensely aware of having achieved a marked differential between his fee and that of any other Italian composer; he had no mind to give it up. Mercadante, on hearing that Donizetti was to get nearly twice his fee in the same season, demanded parity – in vain.[69] Leading singers frequently refused to sing for less than had been paid to a rival. These pretensions were often ridiculed, as were singers' demands for elaborate and steadily inflated titles indicating status. *Altra prima donna* ('other leading lady') came to be a euphemism for *seconda donna*; *assoluto*, originally applicable to one person only, came to be demanded by all leading performers; two performers' names sometimes had to be printed diagonally across each other to avoid giving one of them precedence.[70] Comic operas of the eighteenth and early nineteenth centuries throve on backstage stories in which (like Cecil B. DeMille in *Sunset Boulevard* and for much the same reasons) the impresario as a rule cut a benign figure, while absurdly vain singers strutted about demanding their *convenienze*, an untranslatable term conveying the requirements both of status and of individual vocal aptitudes.[71]

The act of singing, it is true, can bring the ego into riotous efflorescence. But the fuss about parity of fees and *convenienze*, again like disputes about star billing in the Hollywood of the thirties – a world in some ways not unlike the one we are dealing with – is best understood as a means of establishing a market quotation.

We can see this by looking at what happened to two men who failed to make their quotations stick. Nicola Vaccaj achieved some success as an opera composer in 1824–7; although his fee was never more than two-thirds of Bellini's the publisher Giovanni Ricordi was begging him for songs 'with joined hands'. Vaccaj's career then faltered and he made a living chiefly as a fashionable singing teacher in Paris and London. When a late opera had a moderate success in 1845 Ricordi found excuses for not paying him any kind of fee to publish it. He could have free copies – that was all.[72]

Stefano Pavesi was a prolific opera composer who by 1830 was aged sixty-one, out of fashion, and knew it; he had withdrawn to the cathedral organ in a small town. Merelli got him to write an opera for a second-rank Milan theatre at a low fee. Pavesi was irked to begin with, then agreed on condition the fee was kept secret. He came to Milan, but Merelli kept him waiting, then 'said "You're an honest man and you won't fail me on account of the fee. If you like, you can take advantage of the moment, you can make your own terms" – well, by dint of telling me I was an honest man he got me to sign the contract for 2,400 Austrian lire [2,088 francs]' – over 300 francs less than Pavesi had expected to settle for.[73]

If Bellini, Donizetti, and Verdi dealt at times sharply, even fiercely with impresari, that was because they did not want to suffer the fate of Vaccaj and Pavesi. If singers fussed about dressing-rooms, lodgings, and the order in which the impresario's carriages picked them up, that was partly because they did not want to end like the *seconda donna* who railed and wept when she found that she was not, after all, to get a modest engagement, or the minor bass who was willing to do anything, even sing in the chorus, for the mere cost of his food.[74]

In a profession that depended on public favour, anxiety could strike even the great Giuditta Pasta: so worked up was she during rehearsals of the first *Norma* that she declared that if her performance did not go down well she would leave the stage.[75] And if Pasta and other leading soloists demanded extravagantly high fees, their motives differed little from those that impel modern captains of industry to exact a high salary even when much of it goes in tax.

From the impresario's point of view the ideal market was one overstocked with good performers. Goldoni, once again, put it in a nutshell when he made his noble impresario play off one singer against another, saying each time 'take it or leave it – there are ten more who are begging me to take them on'.[76] Reality was often like that among minor singers and in minor theatres, particularly outside the carnival season. The baritone Charles Santley, who started in Italy in the 1850s, remembered it as a deadly struggle for survival.[77] But things were different when the impresario had to mount a season of some importance. There he had to engage in prolonged, intricate sessions of bazaar bargaining.

Singers mattered most. The impresario might approach a number and ask them to state their demands. This opening demand was often referred to as the singer's *sparata* (opening shot) or *cannonata*, and was by and large turned down as impossibly high. Sometimes the impresario made an opening offer and it was for the singer to reject it as absurdly low. Then, often though not always, the parties edged toward agreement in a series of steps.

Singers and impresari became expert in devising elegant formulae for talking fees up or down, for expressing agreements that must not be allowed to set a precedent, and for breaking off negotiations. When the Genoa impresario Francesco Sanguineti asked Marianna Barbieri Nini to appear at his theatre she said she would 'restrict' her fee to 20,000 francs 'for the sake of the pleasure of singing at the Teatro Carlo Felice, and also in order to enjoy the beautiful views of Genoa'. He answered that he could not meet her request but would be delighted to send her a postcard of the view.[78] Terminology was important: a singer who for one reason or another agreed to take less than the usual fee was said to be getting a 'present' (*regalo*) rather than a fee (*paga* or *compenso*); an impresario might even coax a singer to take, as an intermediate arrangement, a 'little fee' (*paghetta*).[79]

Because bargains generally had to be sealed in a hurry, intricate points arose of professional ethics and of law. A common Italian arrangement was to make a pre-contract (*compromesso*) which was binding for a time, perhaps only for a few days, but which either party could get out of on certain conditions. An impresario and a singer often made a pre-contract while each still carried on a criss-cross of negotiations with other singers and impresari. When, as happened to an Italian tenor at Barcelona in 1830, the singer was negotiating with two Spanish impresari and one Italian, while the Italian impresario to whom he was pre-contracted was himself negotiating with another tenor – all this by slow post – the singer could end up without an engagement even though no one was legally at fault. In this case the Italian impresario may have felt a moral obligation to help the singer to find an engagement elsewhere.[80] On the other had, a letter of acceptance or an oral undertaking from a singer – without a legal contract or even a pre-contract – was sometimes asserted by impresari to be binding; one claim based on an oral undertaking was thrown out by the courts, but only because the witnesses were interested parties.[81]

Like much else in the dealings between singers and impresari, how far this kind of claim could be pressed depended on their relative power in the market. Balochino in Vienna tried to make out that Fanny Tacchinardi Persiani – the leading light soprano of the day – was 'in some way contracted' to his official employers, but she kept him pleading for another eight years before consenting to turn up.[82]

Now and then a singer signed contracts whose dates clashed – because a more appetising contract had come along. In such a case the impresario who had been ditched could not compel the singer to perform, but he could sue for damages or try to reach an agreed settlement.[83] Telegraphs and railways speeded up negotiations but did not quite do away with all these hazards.

Apart from the amount of the fee, the questions uppermost in singers' minds were whether they could be sure of collecting it, how often they could be required to sing, and how well particular roles would suit their voices. There were also more indefinite questions of mood and confidence.

The most successful impresari, like Merelli, seem to have had a gift for jollying singers along, flattering and teasing them; Barbaja, for all his loud bark, showed real humanity in his dealings with

Adolphe Nourrit, a leading French lyric tenor who made the deadly mistake of trying to turn himself into a fashionable *tenore di forza* in unaccustomed Italian conditions, suffered a paranoid breakdown, and eventually killed himself.[84] Even Lanari could be understanding on occasion, and his musical director Pietro Romani, according to his own account, could lick even Giorgio Ronconi – a gifted baritone but a lazy unreliable man – into shape: 'I've needled him, I've threatened him, I've caressed him, I've kissed him, I've embraced him, I've begged him, I've counselled him, I've played all kinds of tricks and I've managed against his will to make him sing this part exceedingly well and word-perfect.'[85]

These, however, were impresari who scarcely ever failed to pay on time. When working for minor impresari, singers might reasonably fear that they would be paid late, perhaps not at all. Some got round this by demanding a guaranteed fee: this usually meant that they would have first call on the endowment, a device frowned upon by many supervisory authorities because it was unfair to lesser artists and stage staff who had no such assurance. Leading artists got it none the less; the tenor Luigi Mari, knowing that the Modena impresario in 1826 was running out of money, successfully held out for a guarantee even at the cost of a spell in jail. Nothing, however, exempted artists from performing if they were left unpaid part way through the season – unless, exceptionally, they had a clause in their contracts to that effect. Sing first, sue later was the rule.[86]

Another hazard was that a singer, on first being heard at rehearsal, might be turned down by the impresario or by the supervisory board as unfit; or he or she might rouse such hostility in the first-night audience as to have to be speedily replaced. This problem seems to have got worse as the nineteenth century went on and seasons multiplied. Law and custom were unclear, except on one point – beginners could have their contracts cancelled if they did badly at the first performance. Among experienced singers it was a fertile source of dispute; a court did however rule in 1859 that those rejected at the start of the season were entitled to the first quarter of their fee.[87]

How many performances a singer would give each week was a matter to be settled by contract, but also open to pressure or to friendly agreement in an emergency.

It is now unheard of for opera singers to sing leading parts four or five times a week, but in Italy it was the norm until the late nineteenth century – and six times a week was not unknown. Most opera companies gave four or five performances a week; unless there was a 'double company' (meaning two lots of soloists) all the leading singers would have to appear at each performance. Double companies were rare outside La Scala and the San Carlo, and could not always be afforded even there.

Impresari accordingly tried to get even the best-known singers to agree to five or at least four performances a week – on top of rehearsals which went on through at least half the season. Until the early nineteenth century this seems to have been regarded as normal. The tenor Nozzari was described in 1809 as 'capricious' because he refused to sing more than three or four times a week.[88] But by the 1820s and 30s the most successful singers were imposing the same limitation. Others no less successful, however, can be found doing things that would now be thought crazy: Giuseppina Strepponi, Verdi's future companion and wife, sang Norma, of all parts, five times in six days when in the early stages of pregnancy (and at one point six times in one week); the tenor Duprez sang in *Lucia* five times a week, at one point six times; as late as 1866 Antonietta Fricci, one of the foremost singers of the day, sang five times a week at La Scala in *Norma* and *La Juive* (another heavy part).[89]

This was exploitation – but not just exploitation of singers by heartless impresari. Singers exploited themselves. The reasons why they came to prefer three or at most four performances a week are clear: heavier vocal writing by composers, heavier instrumentation, the withering away of recitative.[90] What needs explaining is why they so often agreed to give four, five, or six.

To do so was, within the 'single company' system, genuinely helpful, and to some extent they were helping the impresario. They were also pressing forward their careers: Teresa Brambilla, the first Gilda, 'played havoc' – as she wrote – with her voice 'to make a name', but once she had achieved it she was determined never again to sing more than four times a week.[91] Finally, they were making money, or balancing money against status. Eugenia Tadolini wanted to sing only three times a week at La Fenice in 1847 but was prepared to sing four times a week for more money; Erminia

Frezzolini, shortly afterwards, was also prepared to sing four times a week 'on her word of honour' provided her contract read 'three times a week'.⁹² Strepponi's and Duprez's self-exploitation (which wrecked her voice but launched his) came of a mixture of these motives.

Impresari and supervisory boards were well aware of the risks to voices and health. Duprez's six *Lucias* in one week were made possible only by faking an illness of the baritone so that Duprez could cut the Act IV duet. But the reason for the six *Lucias* in one week was that the management was contractually obliged to give thirty-six performances that season, had missed two earlier ones because of Duprez's own illness, and was bound by the calendar: if it fell short it would have to pay compensation. To paraphrase a noted account of early factory life, men and women – artists and impresari both – were yoked to timetables and cash.

When time pressed as it did in Italian opera seasons, illness was a troublesome matter. Custom said that leading singers were entitled to up to eight consecutive days' illness without loss of pay; this was generally embodied in contracts, especially after the Milan and Rome courts in 1826-9 had given perverse and contradictory rulings. An illness or pregnancy that developed between signature of a contract and the start of the season could cancel the contract (but if it had been concealed at the time of signing it could mean an action for damages). Medical certificates were essential; impresari who – as we have just seen – could do a bit of faking of their own when it suited them were frequently suspicious. A blusterer like Bandini could threaten to sue Eugenia Tadolini for heavy damages on the grounds that she was pregnant 'without a husband', but he is unlikely to have got anywhere. Barbaja in a fit of irritation claimed that he need not pay Luigia Boccabadati because she had missed eleven performances over eighteen months, but the Naples courts found against him.

A more normal cause of dispute was a singer's feeling off colour without being clinically ill. The impresario would then plead, coax, and press; star singers made a big difference to the box-office takings, and it looks as though – at a time when replacements of equal standing could not be quickly found – they were often induced to perform below their best. At the same time a singer in a strong position on the opera market could get away with occasional caprice.[93]

The logic of the market indeed ruled here as in most things. Leading singers could defend themselves. Minor artists who appeared in places like Malta or Bari in the 1870s, or in a third-rank Milan theatre, not only had to perform five times a week as a matter of course; some of them were allowed no sick pay at all, could have their contracts revoked at any time on vague grounds of 'imperfect performance' or on no grounds at all, and had to pay heavy damages in circumstances (such as failure to turn up on time) which for a leading performer would have led to no more than cancellation.[94]

Though impresari had often begun as singers or dancers they were apt among themselves to speak contemptuously of 'the performing rabble' ('*la virtuosa canaglia*') or, as Barbaja called them, 'these scoundrels and ingrates'. One side or the other, it seemed, must 'lay down the law': from time to time there was talk of a managers' cartel to keep down 'exorbitant' fees, but then as now such talk got nowhere – impresari were aware that with London and Paris as well as Italian cities eager to hear the best singers there was no real hope of drawing a line.[95]

What was true of singers was largely true of composers as well. The one novelty was the emergence of the composer who could not only dictate terms but could impose himself as an autonomous artist, entitled to his privacy and able to create away from the world of the theatre. That was the difference between the young Rossini, who stayed at his impresario's house and composed with the opera company laughing, talking, singing around him, and Verdi, who insisted on staying at an hotel[96] and kept the impresario at arm's length.

Composers who had made a decided hit could pretty well control the choice of singers for their later operas. It was Verdi who was first able also to demand that his works should be performed as written, without the transpositions and interpolations that had been common form; even then he remained willing to make changes so long as he could control them. Verdi made this demand as early as 1846, seven years after his début; he set out to enforce it after *Rigoletto* (1851),[97] and, after *Un Ballo in maschera* (1859), virtually stopped dealing with impresari direct. His unchallengeable position, backed as it was by a publisher who could enforce his copyright, was by then a sign that the old helter-skelter opera business with its journalistic methods was drawing to an end.

Not that the young Verdi had been as alien to that old opera world as he made out in his denunciation of his 'years in the galleys'. In the 1840s he had advanced his career and fortune by writing two operas a year, just as his future wife had tried to advance hers by singing five times a week. For both it meant inner strain; compulsion came not just from outside – Bellini had managed to write only one opera a year – but from an inner need to make one's mark as fast as possible in a poor society where there were few other openings and in an art where success might not last.

On the opera market as it worked in the late eighteenth century and for much of the nineteenth, composers were placed by their current fees in the same way as singers. But it was more common for a composer than for a singer to make a début unpaid or even to pay for the privilege of having his work put on. None of the best-known composers ever had to do this except the visiting German Otto Nicolai (he wrote a cantata unpaid, but then entered the normal round of an Italian career, being paid for writing operas in different cities by this impresario and that).[98] Sometimes an opera put on for nothing, or on payment of a sweetener, was the work of a young local composer with friends in high places. But the best impresari did not necessarily accept any and every opera that came along with a private subsidy attached. Lanari in such circumstances turned down an opera by the young Abramo Basevi – who later wrote a pioneer critical work on Verdi – on the grounds that the libretto was bad and it would be a flop.[99]

An unusual figure, disconcerting to impresari, was Meyerbeer. His early Italian operas (1817–25) were successful, but as a rich banker's son he refused a fee. At the same time he made unusual demands for control of the production and, after his earliest experiences, for sole ownership of the score. 'Total deference' – which the Trieste impresario Adolfo Bassi professed – seems to have been the normal attitude to such a combination of talent and munificence. But Crivelli to begin with jibbed at letting Meyerbeer have sole rights to the score of *Il Crociato in Egitto* (La Fenice, Venice, 1824), his most successful work.[100]

He had a point. Meyerbeer's work by then was saleable. In the days before effective copyright, but when opera houses no longer insisted on all putting on new works – roughly from the late eighteenth century to the 1850s – composer and impresario were in some circumstances able to make money from letting out the score of a successful work and from allowing publishers to print a vocal score. The change in temper that this brought can be seen by comparing Mayr's gentle complaint in 1808 about an unauthorised vocal score[101] with the angry denunciations of Bellini and Donizetti twenty years later. Mayr seemed unprepared to do anything; Bellini was all for setting the police to work.

In the first half of the nineteenth century the usual arrangement was for the impresario either to buy the full score outright or to divide the rights in it with the composer. Either way this meant an iron watch on copyists and, if possible, on fellow impresari to whom the score was hired out. These safeguards generally failed and the correspondence of the time is full of complaints about pirated scores, often orchestrated by a hack composer from the printed vocal score, but sometimes stolen.

Double standards prevailed. Impresari complained bitterly about others' piracy, but even Barbaja and Lanari were willing on occasion to buy a pirated score cheap. Even Bellini, so indignant on his own behalf, tried to make a secret deal for the Naples rights in *I Puritani* so as to cheat the Paris impresari who had first staged it of their legal share. A common negotiating ploy was for one impresario to write to another that he could get a score locally very cheap but that he would hire the other man's authentic version if the price was reasonable.[102] Occasionally a vigilant impresario managed to do good business out of secondary rights in scores, as Lanari did out of some of 'his' Donizetti and Mercadante operas, but this meant generally either putting on the works himself in one city after another or else a straight exchange with an impresario who had an equally valuable score to offer.

Hiring out rights could afford scope for bazaar bargaining on an impressive scale. In negotiations with singers and composers, after all, time generally pressed. Dealings between impresari over rights could be stretched out, one is tempted to say luxuriously, over many months. Barbaja and Lanari carried on one such set of negotiations – over a proposed hiring out to Naples of Donizetti's *Pia de' Tolomei* –

from August 1837 to September 1838; even then they came to an agreement only because the Naples censorship had unexpectedly forbidden Donizetti's newest opera, *Poliuto*, and Barbaja had to find a substitute in a hurry. The details of the bargaining we need not go into; it was complex and involved the rights in two other Donizetti works as well. To thrash out this and other questions outstanding between them the two leading impresari wrote to each other every few days, long and often repetitive letters. In the end Lanari took 725 francs instead of the 1,000 francs he had originally asked. Probably both men considered the time well spent.[103]

The step-by-step procedure followed in these bazaar bargains can best be observed in a relatively simple and amiable exchange between Lanari and Sanguineti. This Genoa impresario wished to hire the tenor Musich for the spring season of 1843, but did not wish to pay more than he had the previous year: Musich, he wrote, could not have made such progress in a year as to deserve more. Lanari (who had Musich under long-term contract) replied that he had in fact progressed a lot but as a concession the fee would be unchanged. Sanguineti then objected to providing lodgings – it was an expensive nuisance – and proposed to pay an extra 200 francs instead. Lanari pointed out that he was normally obliged to provide lodgings but, as another concession, was willing to settle for 270 francs plus Musich's travelling expenses. Sanguineti then brought up as reinforcement the fact that this year, unlike last, Lanari was not having to pay commission to a local agent and was therefore saving 250 francs: let him therefore bear the cost of travel while, to show that he was not stubborn, he, Sanguineti, would after all provide lodgings. Lanari agreed but added that, since he now had to pay travelling costs, Musich would not travel by post and would therefore arrive a little later than planned. It is this last stroke (in which Sanguineti acquiesced) that reveals the master bargainer.[104]

The principle underlying nearly all these negotiations was that either party should at all times put forward his or her maximum merits and grievances, and should use the areas of uncertainty in existing or proposed contracts as a means of manoeuvre to get the upper hand, sometimes beyond the obvious needs of the case. What was at stake was not just money: either party sought to achieve dominance by imputing obligation.

How strong was the ritual element in these dealings may be seen from the language used by members of the opera world in their business correspondence. It was so stereotyped that the letters of this singer or that, this or that impresario, often seem almost interchangeable. Certain key terms recurred. The most important were 'friendship', 'condescension' (in the sense of 'helpfulness'), 'interest', 'sacrifice', and 'self-esteem'.

'If you are my friend, as I believe, you will find a way.' Later: 'Never would I have believed that you could act like that toward a friend.' That was Barbaja, first coaxing Pacini to come to Naples and see his new opera on to the stage, then upbraiding him for being late with the score. 'You [are] not returning the friendship I profess for you': that meant that Donizetti was demanding of Lanari 10,000 francs for a new opera.[105] Passages like these could be duplicated from many other people's letters.

'Friendship' had something to do with the feeling between two people, but not much: it could be attributed to someone you had not even met.[106] A 'friend' was someone who did what you wanted ('condescended'); hence the many calls on the other party in a bargain to 'prove his friendship', for instance by putting business in your way or by knocking something off the hire of costumes. Contrariwise, for the other party to refuse your offer showed a lack of friendship or esteem. The ritual answer to such charges was to stress your own disinterested friendship and the 'sacrifices' you had made – now so ill-requited – point out all the ways the other party was in the wrong, but assert that friendship between you nevertheless remained unchanged. Lanari, after having accused Somigli of bad faith and threatened him with a lawsuit, added that none of this would affect their friendship, 'since that has nothing to do with interest'.[107]

'Interest' meant financial interest. It could be opposed to friendship: 'you are looking after your interest and I praise you for it', a minor Florence impresario wrote to Lanari (who was refusing him a discount on costume hire); but by so doing Lanari was failing to show himself a 'great friend' ('*amicone*'). Another line of argument was that the other party was neglecting both friendship and true interest: this might well go with a dispassionate-sounding remark that, after all, both parties could do each other a bit of good. A minor Naples impresario who had just been angrily denounced by a baritone as a 'trader in human flesh' (another cliché) offered a financial compromise and added that if the baritone refused this it would mean 'not only...that you are not my friend, but that you are not at all good at looking after your own interest, since...I could later on propose to you some better deals'.[108] This reciprocity was often stressed: a man who had just said that he would make a 'sacrifice' in favour of the other party would then spell out that he expected similar favourable treatment at some future date.

Bargaining involved a good deal of self-praise: 'I am an honest man' ('*galantuomo*'), 'I never go back on my word', and so on. This need not imply excessive vanity. A capacity for seeing oneself in a flatteringly dramatic light and putting the picture into words was often met with in Italian culture. Here it was heightened by the need to put oneself at an advantage. What was perhaps more deeply felt was the need to safeguard one's 'self-esteem', and to avoid cutting a bad figure (*sfigurare*). This was bound up with status. Merelli declared that his self-esteem had suffered because the prima donna Carolina Ungher had demanded more money from him than she had been content to get from Lanari. Ungher for her part said she had raised her demand because she wanted to be paid as much as Giulia Grisi had been; so her self-esteem (and status) were also involved.[109]

So ritualised was this language that one may read a string of letters exchanged between Merelli and Lanari, full of reproaches for unfair usage mingled with declarations of unshakeable affection, and be left little the wiser about the relations between the two. On the whole, the plainer the correspondence the greater the chance that there existed a genuine friendship; the more elaborate the protestations, the likelier it seems that we are hearing the conventional exchanges of business life.

Verdi called the Paris Opéra '*la grande boutique*', 'the big shop'. The Italian opera world was a great bazaar, an older form of commercial organisation, centuries old, in fact, where chaffering and jockeying for dominance were the stuff of trade.

An art that dealt in utmost contrivance was grounded in a poor society's understanding of the need to scrabble for every penny. In such a world, not even the impresario, according to the famous baritone Achille De Bassini, should think himself the necessary man: 'the only necessary man I know is the cashier'.[110]

6 · Agents and journalists

Is the agent's commission legitimate? The feeling that it probably is not – that the agent is an expensive parasite – goes back a long way; as late as 1978 several respected administrators of Italian opera houses were sent to jail for a short while on charges of having used the services of theatrical agents. This happened under a twentieth-century law – till then disregarded. In the late eighteenth and nineteenth centuries many Italians were already hostile to a go-between who seemed to assert a right to earn a living without producing anything. That was the period when there came to be probably more professional agents than at any time before or since, while their role in the lyric theatre was probably at its most equivocal. Agents' conduct of their business showed many of the social and economic tensions within the world of opera, often taken to an extreme.

In a poor, overpopulated country like eighteenth-century Italy it was normal for many town-dwellers to earn part or all of their living as go-betweens. Some drew irregular incomes from performing small services, not just as porters or hawkers but as touts for shops or inns or prostitutes. Others held modest but privileged jobs – steward to a nobleman, clerk to a revenue farmer – that allowed them to grant favours in exchange for a tip, a discount, a commission.

Since the late seventeenth century most of the opera world had been perpetually on the move, with singers, composers, sometimes impresari flitting from one town to another: this too helped to make the business of theatrical agents an amorphous one. On the one hand almost anyone might draw a modest commission – say a flautist or a chief stage-hand or a prompter – from having put someone in the way of earning money. On the other hand rich or powerful amateurs did much to forward the opera seasons that provided their class with a focus of social life; they did it for nothing and went on doing it well into the nineteenth century. The papal

The impresario Bartolomeo Merelli (1794–1879).

nuncio in Vienna who in 1847 exerted himself to get Eugenia Tadolini to sing at the Senigallia Fair, or the French deputy entrusted by Cavour with reporting on the talents of another soprano, were only two of many.[1]

Just how many shapes agency – or 'mediation', as it was often called – could take may be seen from the work that went to prepare the opening season in 1788 of the new Teatro Comunale at Faenza. Theatre building and opening season alike meant a considerable financial undertaking for a small city – though one whose nobles were just then launching a brisk neo-classical revival in the arts. The management of the inaugural season, a combination of the nobility and the bourgeoisie, was first of all concerned to secure a new *opera seria* and a male soprano. This was done in Rome through its emissary, an abbé, with the help of a 'mediator'; the mediator's name is not known and he was said to be content with whatever reward the Faenza management thought fit. At the same time other singers were recruited through a dense correspondence with Bologna. There the Faenza management could count on two amateurs – one a doctor, the other a friend of a well-known prima donna – and two professional men of the theatre: Antonio Tamburini, a well-known agent,[2] and Luigi Becchetti, owner of a costume workshop and sometime impresario of the main Bologna opera house. Becchetti sent to Faenza a stream of news and advice about singers – where they were, how they had been singing of late, how much they were likely to want. He behaved like a classic 'theatrical correspondent' – another term for 'agent' – and though the evidence is missing the chances are that he got a regular commission or fee.[3]

Another owner–impresario who behaved much like the Faenza management was Duke Sforza Cesarini of the Teatro Argentina in Rome: he too had an abbé for his amateur representative, but at the same time he dealt with professionals such as Angelo Bentivoglio, a Bologna agent and impresario of the Teatro Ducale at Parma, whom his enemies liked to call 'Bentinbroglio' ('Swindlewell').[4]

Though amateur mediation never quite died out, professional agency came into its own around the turn of the eighteenth century. It had its own clearly understood functions and its own geography.

What a professional agency might be expected to do was well set out in a circular advertising the setting up of a new firm in 1827.

The agency saw its own main purpose as twofold: on the one hand to provide artists with contracts; on the other to secure for impresari and supervisory bodies the 'quality and quantity of artists' they required. To this end its office would contain 'many highly competent people' who could provide managements with accurate information. Finally, the agency would advance money on behalf of managements to theatre personnel and suppliers, and would dispatch any material managements might need. On all these operations the firm's commission would be 5% within Italy and 6% abroad.[5]

This advertisement would have fitted many other agencies. An agent was a man of all work, ready to engage not just solo singers and dancers but chorus singers, orchestral players, stage-hands, prompters – any theatre employee however humble; he was also a forwarding agent – an essential task at a time when scores and costumes had to go through customs in the various Italian states – and he provided an information service.

One kind of agent shaded off into an impresario; another kind shaded off into a journalist. Many a nineteenth-century agent ran a theatrical journal, with himself most likely as proprietor, editor, reporter, and layout man rolled into one. The 'many highly competent people' mentioned in circulars should not be taken too seriously; the trade was highly individualistic and ran at most to short-lived partnerships among a few people, with perhaps a secretary. But the impresario type of agent and the journalist type were two ends of a spectrum.

Another occupation that sometimes went together with that of agent was the running of a shop selling music and musical instruments, with a copying business attached. For some agents, running such a shop may have been no more than a second string, while for Giovanni Ricordi, founder of the well-known publishing firm but originally a shopkeeper, agency was a sideline.[6]

In the eighteenth century Bologna was the theatrical exchange for Italy from Naples to the Alps, and hence the place where most agents were to be found. In the early nineteenth century the exchange began to shift to Milan (because of Milan's position as capital of the Napoleonic kingdom of Italy and the 'splendour' La Scala attained through the gambling monopoly). Bologna in 1821 was described (by a Milan impresario) as 'no more than a skeleton in this respect'; he was exaggerating a real decline that went on gradually until, in 1863, an elderly Bologna agent had to admit his city was no longer the market-place for 'resting' artists.[7]

Agents could also be found in Venice, Florence, Rome,and Naples, but always far fewer than in Milan. There an elaborate theatrical exchange was carried on in the streets around La Scala. The best-known agents had offices there, but much business was done in a café across the street from the theatre – frequented by pretty well the whole of the opera world – and, from 1878, under the soaring roof of the new gallery. There were also humbler agents who had no office: the publisher Giulio Ricordi denounced them in 1889 as 'the so-called freewheeling agents [*agenti volanti*] who infest the gallery'.[8] When these men put pen to paper the paper must have rested on a café table. But we know little about them and they may have been mere touts.

Even when professional agents had become commonplace they bore a stamp of dubiousness. This ran deep. It came, first, of agents' being widely seen as parasitical, and secondly of the ease with which people close to the theatre world could set up as agents: this meant constant oversupply and cut-throat competition.

Impresari and supervisory bodies liked to do without agents if they could, for the simple reason set out by Crivelli. He wished to engage the famous soprano Violante Camporesi, but 'if we go through an agent we'll have to pay her two or three thousand francs more'.[9] Besides, there was the further benefit of avoiding, according to a member of the association of nobles that ran the Regio, Turin, 'the usual sordid intrigues, the obstructiveness, the deliberate procrastination of Milan agents'.[10] If agents were to do business they had to make themselves indispensable. For the most part what made them indispensable was the relentless rhythm of the seasons and the multiplication of theatres: through increased home and foreign demand in the Restoration period, the business of arranging a season became at once so complex and so hurried as to require their help.

But if demand went up, supply went up faster still. In the latter half of the nineteenth century a baritone whose career lasted for more than three decades dealt with at least forty-four theatrical agencies; most of these were active at any one time throughout this period.[11] Agents proliferated; there were probably more of them in these years, roughly between 1850 and 1890, than ever before, though as early as the 1820s the situation had not been fundamentally different. Already in those years two or more agents may be seen fighting over the same contract while impresari and theatre owners played them off against one another.

There was an accepted convention: 'in theatrical affairs the first person to send in a [signed] contract is the one who gets the commission'.[12] But this rule was more easily stated than enforced. One of the commonest happenings in the opera world was for two or three agents to approach a singer, each of them claiming that the same management had asked him to engage the singer for a particular season.[13]

Often the agent was simply trying it on: if he could bring singer and impresario together he might earn a commission even though neither party had had it in mind to employ him.[14] Often enough, though, an impresario or theatre owner had in truth given two or three agents grounds for thinking that they had been instructed to approach particular singers.

The Marchese Bartolomeo Capranica, owner of the Valle, Rome, in the 1820s systematically got two or three agents at once to try to recruit artists for one of his seasons; a refinement was that he and his nominee impresario sometimes passed that particular buck from one to the other, Spenlow and Jorkins fashion, when there was any trouble. The point undoubtedly was to see which agent could secure an artist on the most favourable terms.

Thus the well-known agent G. B. Benelli was asked in August 1825 to try to sign up for the coming carnival season at the Valle the soprano Virginia Blasis, the tenor Sirletti, and the bass Cosselli. He soon realised that two other agents were approaching those same artists: 'These men are perfectly incapable of planning a season, even at Roccacannuccia [the byword for a provincial backwater]. I should be sorry if they were to profit from the trouble I have taken and from my plain and honest proceeding.' By mid-September, after some haggling, he managed to get Sirletti to agree a pre-contract on the terms Capranica wanted, but on the very same day Capranica wrote to tell him that he had signed up a different tenor through another agent; three weeks later the nominal Valle impresario signed up Blasis and Cosselli through yet another agent.

The notable thing is that Benelli merely complained of having cut a poor figure: 'Your honour and mine', he wrote to Capranica when he heard about the new tenor, 'are compromised'. When the impresario told him of the Blasis and Cosselli contracts and, by way of solace, thanked him, adding that he might use Benelli's services sometime in the future, the agent exploded. He had been insulted; 'If we were in Turkey or Africa this might be the handsomest way to deal, but here in Italy I hardly know how to describe such a proceeding. What a world! And what people are to be found in it!'

Yet – after further charges and counter-charges – Benelli remained willing to deal with artists for the Valle season provided the management sent him contracts for them to sign. By December 1825 he had written no fewer than twenty-eight letters to Rome (not to mention others to other destinations) without earning a penny; but he was still corresponding with the impresario as though all was well. Two other agents, Tommaso Marchesi and Gustavo Galeotti, came in for the same treatment during 1828–30: not only were theatre owner and impresario using competitors of theirs but Capranica was writing direct to a few singers in an attempt to bypass agents altogether. Marchesi and Galeotti too complained, but without ever suggesting that the Valle management had incurred any obligation to them.[15]

These agents were making the best of a bad job. In the face of a management backed by a noble theatre owner their relative economic position was weak – even that of noted and none too scrupulous agents such as Benelli and Galeotti. They had to put up with many humiliations in the hope of one day bringing off a coup.

Agents working in such conditions were unlikely ever to achieve the exclusive right to deal on behalf of any one theatre, though various agents from time to time claimed it. Even the respectable proprietors of La Fenice were not always above taking to the methods of the Marchese Capranica, partly because the three directors, not to mention their secretary and the impresario of the season, were all liable to have their own ideas.[16] Alessandro Lanari, when he worked as an agent only, tried to enforce the principle that 'it is not fitting for a reputable agency to be treated as an alternative source by the same commissioning management for the same *piazza* and for the same artists'; but in the bad year 1849 he soon dropped it and asked to be kept in mind without making any such condition.[17]

Lanari himself, in his great days as impresario, had tried at least twice to channel all his contracts exclusively through two agents, one in Milan and one at Bologna (first Merelli and Antonio Magotti in 1828, then Filippo Burcardi and Magotti in 1833). The two were supposed to divide between them all commissions received by either on account of Lanari's business, but each time the arrangement lasted only a few months and the agents ended by quarrelling over the commissions.[18]

One agent would readily describe another as a 'scoundrel', 'intriguer', or (in loose translation) 'bastard'. Merelli had four of his competitors and 'enemies' – Pietro Camuri, Gioanni Rossi, Raffaele Maffei, and Gustavo Galeotti – sentenced to a few months' imprisonment for criminal libel; they petitioned for an official pardon and may not have gone to jail. Burcardi, for his part, wrote of Merelli: 'He is eaten up with rage...because I have taken a couple of good theatres away from him, and if God grants me life I want to show him a thing or two.'[19] An 'alliance' formed in 1826 by four agents in Milan, Bologna, Rome, and Naples fell apart within a month.[20] Competition was too fierce to allow agents to work together; most of them were too hard-pressed.

Rivalry among agents could turn piratical. Two impresari from Constantinople landed at Venice in 1850; they were described as Turks but were almost certainly Italians or Levantine Jews. Their plan was to go to Florence to arrange the recruitment of an entire company for the Constantinople opera house. But the Milan agent Alberto Torri got wind of their coming, dashed to Padua, intercepted them, and bore them off in triumph to Milan.[21]

A 'solid' impresario or theatre owner was economically stronger than almost any agent: this helps to explain why agents, though they drew their commission as a rule from the employee, gave the impression of siding with the employer.

Burcardi offered to bring down a tenor's fee by showing him an ostensible letter from the impresario instructing him to sign up another singer; the impresario's real intentions were to be conveyed on a separate sheet. Ercole Marzi, in his capacity as impresario, gave away one of Lanari's clients who was trying to bypass the agent and work out a contract direct. Galeotti, the day after an opera by the ageing Pietro Generali had flopped at La Scala, urged the owners of La Fenice – where Generali was due to bring out another opera three months later – to repudiate the composer on grounds of 'mental decay' and commission a replacement opera from the young Luigi Ricci; needless to say, the new contract would be arranged by Galeotti.[22] Artists were many; employers – those who could put an agent in the way of securing many contracts over several seasons – were few.

For most of the nineteenth century, agents earned most of their income from the usual commission of 5% or 6% on soloists' fees (or on the wages paid to other employees). This percentage – low by present-day standards – remained unchanged to the 1870s, when some agents began to ask 8% or 10% on contracts for the bountiful Americas; in the 1880s we find some commissions at 7% in Italy and 8% abroad.[23] Where so much else came under government regulation agents' fees were left for the market to determine: under a law of 1865 agents had to register – something few of them had bothered to do before, unlike brokers handling commercial contracts – but registration was open to anyone who paid a small fee and had no criminal record.[24]

At some point in the eighteenth century it had been the practice for half the agent's commission to be paid by the artist and half by the impresario; this arrangement had not quite vanished in the nineteenth.[25] But it happened more frequently that the artist paid the whole of the commission and the agent and impresario split it between them. This was the norm at the Teatro Carolino, Palermo; at La Fenice the secretary to the directors, Guglielmo Brenna – who in practice did much of the impresario's job – split at least some of the commissions with the agent G. B. Bonola. At one point the directors wished to make Bonola a present of 900 Austrian lire (783 francs) as a reward for all the work he had put in on the carnival 1851 season (the one that launched *Rigoletto*); Bonola offered Brenna a cut of 100 lire, but Brenna demanded and got 200.[26]

When there was a straight split the agent's commission of course came down to $2\frac{1}{2}$%. This might happen not only when an impresario demanded a share but when one agent passed a singer on to another.[27] The cake, however, might be divided up into even thinner slices. When several partners had the management of La Pergola in 1836–8 the agency commission was divided three ways among some of their subordinates: no one got more than $1\frac{2}{3}$%.[28] On the other hand agents could sometimes earn payment from both sides. The well-known agent Antonio Magotti at one time acted as representative of the management that ran the Teatro del Corso, Bologna, while his son and partner collected the commission on the chief stage-hand's pay – and no doubt on the contracts of other members of the company as well.[29]

If an artist had not paid the commission on his fee by the start of the season an early nineteenth-century agent could ask the impresario to deduct it. This later became so much the general practice that the printed contract forms drawn up by one impresario allowed the agent's commission to be deducted automatically.[30] Other printed contracts (drawn up by an agent) stated that if an artist whose contract had been arranged by the agency made a fresh contract with the same management, the agency would automatically earn commission on the new contract even though it had had nothing to do with setting it up.[31] These changes seem to show agents and impresari drawing closer together.

Agents could do with a little help in collecting what was owed to them. Even some well-known singers such as Giuditta Grisi and Catherine Hayes at times declined to pay until the agent had brought a suit, or else went abroad and failed to answer letters; one singer tried to get out of paying on the grounds that his contract did not bear the agency's stamp.[32] In this competitive world an agent on occasion claimed a percentage to which he had no obvious title; or else two agents both demanded a commission on the same contract, after negotiations so tortuous as to give both of them some sort of claim. When this happened, the impresario Jacovacci, Solomon-like, could think of no better solution than to have the contract drawn up by yet a third agent.[33]

Besides his commission, the agent's other main source of income (unless he was also a more than occasional impresario) was journalism.

Italy from the 1820s saw an explosion of musical journals, most of them taken up almost wholly with opera. Up to 1848 they held a central place in the life of the educated classes. Opera was one of the few subjects you could write about without getting into trouble with the Restoration governments; it was also, as the librettist of *Aida* was to recall later, 'the subject of greatest concern among polite society; and therefore the *Pirata*, the *Figaro*, and the *Fama* were eagerly awaited and read by all literate persons'.[34]

Nearly all musical journals belonged to a publishing house or an agency; many agents were journalists. There were nevertheless a few journalists who, so far as we know, were not agents: Carlo Tenca, a Mazzinian republican, edited *L'Italia musicale* up to 1848 – this was a journal owned by the publisher Francesco Lucca; a very different character, Pietro Dolce (real name Gaetano Barbieri), had been a corrupt police officer in Venice, then a spy sending in fanciful reports on secret societies, before editing the Milan journal *I Teatri*.[35]

By and large, though, musical journals in the years 1820–80 were mouthpieces for agents. This raises problems for anyone who tries to use them as evidence for the history of opera or of music criticism. Many such journals were venal in the most literal sense: they printed what they were paid to print.

In a country without a large educated public these journals scraped along by getting a notable share of their subscriptions from members of the opera world themselves: from impresari, composers, dancers, above all from singers. The point of taking out subscriptions to a number of journals was to pay for favourable mentions: 'journals' – so Lanari explained to the noble but inexperienced 'protector' of a young woman singer – 'do not readily mention those who are not subscribers'.[36]

Not all journals spoke as plainly as *L'Arpa* of Bologna – the organ of the Raffaele Vitali agency – whose masthead informed readers: 'Articles for insertion must be paid for in advance' and 'Kindly indicate contracts already concluded, seasons available, and repertoire of operas.'[37] *L'Arpa* did not specify the cost of 'insertions', but we know that a Florence journal a little earlier charged 5 francs each.[38]

Were all musical journals mere advertising sheets? Probably not. While it was naïve of one agent–journalist to draw a distinction between paid advertising and 'the system I have adopted of asking no more than the cost of a subscription in exchange for all services, thereby leaving artists and impresari freer scope to grow rich',[39] we do get a glimpse of a wider ideal of journalism in what the leading agent–journalist Francesco Regli, editor of *Il Pirata*, had to say of a somewhat earlier figure, Luigi Prividali, 'one of the founders of the theatrical journalism of today'. Prividali, he wrote, had been well-informed but 'eccentric, contrary, partial, and exceedingly stubborn, all the more when his opinions were ill-founded or were dictated by private passions and motives'; besides, the news and gossip he had served up had too often been stale. It had fallen to *Il Pirata* to meet the needs of the time and to transform journalism.[40] We in turn need not take this last claim too seriously. All the same, Regli – author of a biographical dictionary that showed the opera world taking stock of its own past just as it was going into decline – was something more than the usual blackmailing journalist.

'Blackmailing' may seem a strong term, but it fits journalists who demanded a full year's subscription at about 30 francs (then a substantial sum) after a singer had received three complimentary copies without sending them back; the young baritone Charles Santley got rid of one such by threatening to throw him downstairs. Other journalists demanded arrears on subscriptions by threatening 'unpleasantness and distasteful publicity': subscribers who failed to pay up would, in other words, face lawsuits and their names would appear in the list of defaulting debtors.[41]

Musical journalists appear to have been thought mean in two senses – at once mediocre and nasty. Bellini's reaction tells us a good deal. A forged letter purporting to be his had been paraphrased in *L'Omnibus*, a Naples journal edited by Vincenzo Torelli; the point of it was to feed an attack on the soprano Giulia Grisi, a friend and colleague of Bellini's in Paris. Bellini was furious; but for the sake of getting a denial he made a show of thinking Torelli had been innocently bamboozled.[42] It is all too clear why Verdi suspected a trick whenever the journal owned by his publisher gave him anything short of a straightforward favourable mention, and why the critic Filippo d'Arcais in 1879 denounced the kind of journalism agents engaged in as an aspect of the *camorra* – the newly fashionable term for organised corruption.[43]

Agents' journalism shows them in the worst possible light – though Italy was not the only country where such practices were common: when Donizetti went to Paris to launch himself on the French lyric stage he found that there too a flock of journalists touted for subscriptions and would have to be appeased.[44] Some agents, however – none of them a journalist – played a more positive role. They were a small group, and were most of them impresari as much as agents.

The main figures, already familiar to us, were Merelli, Lanari, and Barbaja (with his Milan representative G. B. Villa). Other agent-impresari – Ercole Tinti at Bologna and Jacovacci in Rome – acted in much the same way as those three leading impresari but probably on a smaller scale. Merelli and Lanari were at all times agents as well as impresari, and sometimes concentrated on agency; Barbaja was an agent only in that the custom, prevalent at the Naples royal theatres, of putting artists under contract for a year or for several months rather than for a season enabled him to transfer some artists to other managements and make a profit.

Merelli and Lanari seem to have launched in Italy (perhaps in Europe) two notable new arrangements. One was the long-term contract under which the agency paid an artist a regular salary and hired him out. The other would now be called a package deal: the agency supplied an entire opera or ballet company as well as the works it was to perform. The impresario of the Naples royal theatres – which from 1809 to 1840 nearly always meant Barbaja – had had the benefit of long-term contracts earlier than Merelli or Lanari, but Merelli and Lanari were probably the first to exploit them systematically.

In their agency work these men were not desperate go-betweens so much as respectable merchants. They talked of artists as 'stock in trade' that would have to be 'sold' or 'marketed'.[45] Having to pay a group of artists a large salary was a considerable commitment: Lanari's nightmare – which now and then came true – was that he might have four or five artists whom he had failed to 'market' and would therefore have to pay them 'to keep them gallivanting around Florence'.[46] On the other hand a long-term contract made on favourable terms with a young singer could be highly profitable; so could a more expensive contract with an established artist, if the artist was carefully placed.

At one time, probably in late 1833, Lanari had under contract ten leading singers (among them Duprez, Carolina Ungher, and Giorgio Ronconi), six minor singers, and eighteen dancers, among them the choreographer Antonio Monticini and the ballerina Carlotta Grisi: a good-sized and expensive troupe. Most of the contracts ran for about one or two years.[47] Though that is the only precise information we have, we do know that commitments on this scale often induced Lanari to take on the management of a season

147

so as to exploit his contract artists. Sending them on tour with the minimum of idle periods was the main point of the circuits he and his collaborators set up in central Italy, and towards the end of his career he joined the agent Lorini in sending companies abroad, particularly to Havana and other American cities. Merelli's business is ill-documented, but his many north Italian managements can probably be explained by his need to place his contract artists. In the 1820s Barbaja, for the same reasons, ran a kind of operatic shuttle service among Naples, Milan, and Vienna.

The danger of long-term contracts was that the agent's commitments might force him to run unwelcome risks. This happened to Lanari's son during the war with Austria in 1859. His contract artist, the famous soprano Antonietta Fricci, was due to sing at Verona, but the town was now cut off; to keep Fricci occupied Antonio Lanari had to take on the management of the Teatro Pagliano, Florence, though acting as impresario just then was about the last thing he wished to do.[48] Another danger was that an artist hired out to a theatre management for a season – like Giorgio Ronconi, hired out to Jacovacci for carnival 1842 – might repudiate the contract and flee abroad; the agent might then be sued and have to pay compensation.[49]

Ronconi was a shady character. On the other hand, young artists could innocently land in an unfortunate situation still known today to popular singers in their early days – to Frank Sinatra, for instance, after his wartime breakthrough. They might become stars almost overnight but remain bound by contracts that left the agent the lion's share of the profit. In such circumstances Giulia Grisi fled from Lanari to make a career in Paris. Later the young Marchisio sisters got the better of Merelli in the courts – on a perhaps dubious legal point; he had wished to 'market' them in Rio for two years and would have pocketed 30,000 francs of the 80,000 francs fee.[50] Italian unification in 1859–60 gave free play to the economic liberalism that was already beginning to inform judicial rulings in the 1850s. The courts threw out as illegal a contract which another agent had made with one of the Marchisio sisters to last for the whole of her life. They ended by ruling against even an exclusive contract for a fixed term of the kind that had made Merelli's and Lanari's fortunes: the artist's own freedom to contract for his services could not thus be curtailed.[51]

To promising young singers such contracts had not necessarily been harmful. True, Giuseppina Strepponi, Verdi's future wife, did declare 'I will no longer sell myself by the year': by controlling her own engagements she would not have to work quite so hard and above all she would not have to endure 'continual reproofs like an unwilling schoolgirl'. On the other hand the tenors Duprez and Moriani considered that their long-term contracts had served to launch them: the system, Duprez recorded, 'preserved me for a fixed term from all business worries, and handed me over to a man capable of directing and supporting a young artist with all the resources at his command' – a handsome and, by the time it was given, disinterested testimonial.[52] It is not surprising that, just after his début, the young baritone Achille De Bassini should have wished to engage himself to Lanari for two or three years 'in the hope of thus advancing his career'.[53]

For a contract of this kind to work, the artist probably needed to hold his own by means of a good deal of shrewdness and cool judgment – qualities which Giuseppina Strepponi could scarcely cultivate amid the hectic emotional upheavals of her years on the stage.

From the 1840s, as the opera market expanded, agents developed a new line of business: the operatic package deal. Merelli and Lanari might send whole opera companies to Como or Siena; other agents, working on a more modest scale, sent companies year in year out to yet smaller or remoter towns. From Bologna the Magotti, father and son, would send companies (often including orchestra and chorus) to small towns such as Adria, Medicina, or Spoleto, to towns of south-east Italy such as Bari or Martina Franca, to Greek towns like Corfu and Patras which in practice formed part of the Italian market. They combined this with management work: representing an outside management for a Bologna season, or following a company to Bari and taking the few rehearsals allowed for, or putting on a miniature summer season of opera in the little town of Castel San Pietro, near Bologna, as a busman's holiday. They must have acquired a solid reputation, more solid than that of many impresari: when the Corfu opera house in 1879 wanted a guarantee that impresario, company, music, and costumes would arrive on time it was Alessandro Magotti who supplied it.[54]

This business of providing on operatic package deal depended, in the second half of the nineteenth century, on singers and audiences being familiar with a standard repertoire. An agent could then rustle up for Corfu or Malta a whole *Trovatore* company without too much difficulty. What were the resulting performances like? There must have been, to say the least, ups and downs.

Another solid and long-lived agency was that of G. B. Bonola (?–1867), carried on after his death by his son Giuseppe (1828–91). The father, a contemporary of Rossini, was by the mid-century the leading agent in Milan; already in 1834 he had described himself as 'the least *scoundrelly* of all [the agents]'.[55] This seems justified. Bonola must have come to be fairly well off by 1851, when he gave his daughter in marriage to one of the D'Adda, a leading Milanese noble family.[56] How did he get there? In part by unremitting work, whether at his desk or at the café table. To Lanari alone he wrote, between 1836 and 1850, an average of twelve or thirteen letters a year, most of them involving further correspondence with others – and Lanari was only one impresario among many, though a leading one.

Agents who got anywhere at all worked hard: of that there can be no doubt. Benelli sometimes wrote replies without leaving the post office where he had just collected his correspondence. Merelli, at the peak of his career as agent, in 1828, appears to have written letters at the rate of about 8,000 a year, or about twenty-two a day (Sundays and holidays included), many of them in his own hand.[57]

At one point in 1829, while his wife was mortally ill, Merelli wrote to Lanari on 14 and 18 May, then twice on 20 May; on the 27th he wrote 'You must have been annoyed at my silence' and gave his wife's illness as his excuse.[58] It was a mercantile world, a stock exchange or bazaar where in July 1861 there were in Milan 427 solo singers available (among them seventy-eight *prime donne soprano*),[59] and where even the heads of the profession had to engage in niggling repetitive correspondence to make their pile.

What was the agent's share in the creation of nineteenth-century Italian opera? Little enough, especially where the work of Rossini, Bellini, Donizetti, and Verdi is concerned. At most the impresario type of agent played some part – as impresario rather than as agent. Merelli as agent arranged for Bellini's early work *Bianca e Fernando* to have a second production at Genoa (partly rewritten) and duly collected his 5%;[60] but this mattered less to Bellini's development than Merelli's work as the impresario who put *Norma* on the stage. By the time Bellini had taken the first few steps in his career he could do without agents – unlike most performing artists; but he still needed a manager to put on his operas.

To nearly all singers, on the other hand, agents were indispensable. Few besides Lanari had the means of 'supporting and directing a young artist'. A young man or woman setting out on a singing career generally took pot-luck.

Take the young baritone Charles Santley: after his studies in Milan, a minor agent (unnamed) found him an engagement at Pavia for the carnival season. At the end of the season the agent declined the commission he was entitled to (about 13 francs) because he could see Santley was still hard up; instead he offered him another engagement at Padua. It was characteristic of the ever-shifting opera bazaar that Santley should not have stayed with this agent (who had shown tact or a nose for talent, or both) but went on to deal with others.[61]

At almost the same time, Adele Salvi Speck, once a well-known prima donna but now an agent, was writing to another young baritone who was singing at Rovigo. She reproached him for having asked too high a fee to sing in Spain: as 'artist and friend' she pointed out that 'you are only a beginner, and however much talent you may have you cannot demand what you could demand if you had a *name*'. Life in Spain was cheap; she had already sent moderately well-known singers there for fees no higher than he had refused. She had singled him out because she liked him and appreciated his voice, but she did have two other baritones pre-contracted to her who would be willing to go for the same fee: 'do as your heart tells you, but think over the mistake you're making, this I tell you on my *most sacred honour*'.

She then added that according to report the young man hadn't after all sung so well at Rovigo; it turned out, apropos of nothing, that 'while I am trying to get your fee increased I've had an offer of a baritone in the Marches whose voice I am assured is *unique*'.[62]

Agents were indispensable because, on a growing and hurried market like that of nineteenth-century Italian opera, there was a need for a crowd of intermediaries. Some agents were more honest and reputable than others. All of them, however – unlike other members of the opera world – were creatures of the market and no more: they did not depend on closed guild-like groups or (except so far as they took on the work of management) on local hierarchies; they had no fixed employment; they produced nothing that could be heard or seen or touched. In their anxieties and their frequent meanness that largely pre-industrial market found its fullest expression.

7 · *The impresario and the public*

Every small town, every village has a theatre…The poor may lack food, the rivers may lack bridges, the countryside may be undrained, the sick unprovided with hospitals, and no measures may have been taken to deal with public disasters, but we may be sure that the idle will not want for a Colosseum of a kind.[1]

This satirical picture painted by an intellectual of the 1780s was exaggerated; by no means every village had a theatre. But it suggested both the passion for opera and ballet that ruled many Italian townspeople and the social boundaries beyond which that passion was unlikely to spread. By harking back to the Roman circus it also suggested the element in Italian opera of athletic display.

Berlioz meant to be disparaging when he called Italian operagoers '*routiniers et fanatiques*', untouched by the poetic aspect of art and eager to swallow a new opera like a plate of macaroni.[2] It was not a bad description of a sporting audience who wanted no change in the game but who could be fired to intense enthusiasm by displays of skill. In this sense there is no conflict between Berlioz's saying that the Italian audience hated the least innovation and Verdi's later saying that it was impatient and soon tired even of the finest singers.[3] Football audiences want no change in the rules, but they may tire even of Pelé.

Though the old Italy was fragmented into petty states the opera audience seems to have struck foreign visitors as much the same from one town to another. Italians themselves, especially members of the opera world, saw differences. Rome audiences were supposed to need something out of the ordinary to rouse them; failing that, they would not bother to turn up. Until the early nineteenth century they were largely made up of clerics: Stendhal describes these fanatical abbés holding rushlights to make out the libretto and trading insults with the composer whenever they disliked the music.[4] Florence operagoers, in contrast – those who went to the most

A memento of a special occasion: artists who sang and danced at Faenza during the fair season of 1837, run by the impresario Alessandro Lanari. The soprano Strepponi (Verdi's future wife), the tenor Moriani, the baritone Varesi, the bass Cosselli, and the ballerina Brugnoli-Samengo were all artists of the very front rank: a small town like Faenza could secure them all at once only thanks to a package deal with Lanari, who had them under contract and sent them to several towns in succession.

fashionable theatre, La Pergola – were supposed to be restrained and highly cultivated.[5] Yet a little further north, in the Emilia–Romagna triangle between the Apennines, the river Po, and the Adriatic, audiences in such towns as Bologna, Modena, Reggio, and Parma were feared as the most partisan and unpredictable.[6] These towns do seem to have had a high incidence of riot in the theatre. Yet, just as Italian opera spoke the same musical language from Palermo and Naples to Turin and Trieste, so its audiences seem to have shared much the same expectations and to have behaved in much the same way.

In any Italian city before the 1848 revolutions the opera impresario who was about to put on a season at a leading theatre was an important figure. His arrival at the start of rehearsals was news on the street corners, and the season was likely to keep the town in gossip. With luck it might rouse '*furore, fanatismo, entusiasmo*' and that might well attain a pitch seldom known elsewhere. A letter of the dead Bellini could be cut up in 1849 and sold piece by piece like a saint's relic. Three years earlier a living performer's memento had suffered a like fate in Venice when an invading crowd broke the chamberpot in the hotel room just vacated by the dancer Fanny Elssler and fought over the pieces; the winners displayed their trophies in the cafés.[7] On the other hand the failure of a season could mean danger to life and limb. At the Pagliano, a Florence theatre of a more popular kind than La Pergola – it flourished in the latter half of the century – a bench thrown from the fifth tier once narrowly missed the impresario; after that a dried cod's head thrown at the baritone was a trifle.[8]

The impresario's relationship to this audience was a personal one. Until at least the last third of the nineteenth century, when Milan, Turin, and Rome grew into modern cities with business districts, tram services, large apartment blocks, and other tokens of urban anonymity, Italian towns were compact and the educated population generally knew one another. When impresari talked of serving the audience they had in mind people many of whom they had dealt with personally. Tourists excepted, the potential audience was not an anonymous mass. In the boxes especially, the people who might take up seats were most of them known in advance; the question might be, up to the first night or even beyond, whether they would choose to take the plunge and subscribe.[9]

In these conditions an impresario could hope for a personal reward: not just profit but a curtain call and a round of applause for himself.[10] Sonnets might be addressed to him, the mordant topical sonnets which the great dialect poet Belli addressed to various impresari of Rome theatres – not the adulatory kind that poetasters addressed to prima donnas but not hostile either. The sonnets joked about rather than against the show; Belli wrote them because opera was news and the impresario was a man in the news.

When things went wrong the punishment was just as concrete, even if it fell short of physical mayhem. A bad performance of *L'Elisir d'amore* at the Teatro Valle, Rome – it was the start of the 1834 spring season – had crowds chanting 'send the impresario to jail'; as we have seen, governments might do just that, though on this occasion Paterni got off. There was a touch of special pleading in Lanari's statement to the great Maria Malibran that if the people of Lucca thought he had prevented her from coming 'such a revolution would break out as to put my life in danger'.[11] So too, a later impresario may have been laying it on thick (to avoid putting on a doubtful opera) when he wrote to the composer Pacini that the Genoa public 'is the sworn enemy of all impresari, [and] is always waiting for the management to leave a weak flank uncovered so that it may plunge into it the dagger of malice and calumny'.[12] But this gladiatorial view of the impresario as a figure always on guard against a potentially hostile public must have had some truth in it if it was to convince veterans like Malibran and Pacini.

The humble servant of the public was the figure implied in announcements by impresari. A minor impresario ran into trouble in 1829 with the audience at a second-rank Venice theatre and had to replace the prima donna and the comic bass. But then the new prima donna fell seriously ill:

The unfortunate impresario, after having made so many sacrifices, is unable to remedy this unforeseen new mishap. He begs of you Venetians, his patrons, that you should not impute to him the ending of the season through any lack of the regard he owes you on so many counts, but rather to a fatal consequence of that destiny which sometimes persecutes those who are most respectful toward you and most intent upon doing you good service.

The impresario was able to add that he would give subscribers their money back in proportion to the number of performances missed, and that he had reached an accommodation with the singers over their fees.[13] By this means he presumably put himself in the clear, and could hope to get away undisturbed and perhaps come back to a good reception one or two seasons later.

There were several things an impresario could do to forestall a battle with the audience. One was to avoid any seeming offence to local patriotism. When we keep in mind how split up Italy was, and how intense the 'bell-tower loyalty' (*campanilismo*) in each town, the surprising thing is how few impresari got into trouble through being outsiders. This is true of composers and singers as well: though audiences here and there had a touch of prejudice – Neapolitan audiences were said to be prejudiced against composers such as Mozart who were not Naples-trained[14] – cultural unity at the level of the opera audience generally worked.

On occasion, though, an impresario got across local feeling. A Bologna impresario putting on a season at Reggio Emilia in 1791 was rumoured to have spoken ill of the townspeople: this led to such riot in and out of the theatre that soldiers were brought in, the officer in command (another 'outsider' – from Modena) was murdered, the government arrested the impresario and promised to put him on trial, singers and dancers had to be escorted to the theatre under armed guard through a city in a virtual state of siege. The same circumstance – an impresario's supposed insults to civic pride – caused disturbances at Piacenza in 1846 that were less serious but still led the government to close the theatre. Both these episodes took place in times of general political tension; but yet another episode at Modena – well-known singers were stoned for being reluctant to appear in a work by a local composer – suggests that injured civic pride was explanation enough.[15]

Another danger the impresario had to watch for before the season opened was overselling of tickets. The combination of unnumbered seats and tickets giving entry to the theatre meant, on those rare occasions when the house was full, a recipe for a scramble when the doors were opened, with hats and scarves lost in the crush and some people squeezing in ticketless.[16] It probably happened all the time on the gallery stairs without anyone's noticing; the mad rush up to the unnumbered gallery was still going on at La Pergola in 1949. But when it happened in the nineteenth century to the ladies and gentlemen who frequented the lower parts of the house the trouble was much more serious. It was worse still if more tickets had been sold than there were places: on a notorious occasion, the first night of Donizetti's *Adelia* at the Apollo, Rome, in 1841, the performance came to a halt and the impresario Jacovacci was arrested and heavily fined.[17]

Jacovacci was almost certainly not the culprit. All through the eighteenth and early nineteenth centuries, governments and impresari tried to guard against the sale of tickets at inflated prices away from the theatre box-office, the resale of used tickets part way through the performance, and the printing of fake tickets. The crucial figures were the *bollettinaro*, a kind of box-office manager, usually a native of the town, and the porters and ushers (*maschere*, for in the eighteenth century they were sometimes masked, to give them some clout in their dealings with their social superiors in the audience). Manuals of theatre management warned impresari to watch these men closely and ward off their tricks by marking and checking tickets daily.[18] Impresari took these lessons to heart without always managing to apply them any more successfully than the producers of modern Broadway musicals or the directors of football clubs. The problem may have become easier to cope with in the late nineteenth century with the spread of numbered seats; we hear less about it.

Another thing that made the job of the *bollettinaro* and his subordinates particular tricky was the habit among operagoers of asking for and expecting credit. Most announcements of opera seasons stated that no credit would be given; but it is clear that in the poverty-stricken Italy of the eighteenth century credit had to be given to some boxholders and townspeople as they bought subscription tickets, and even to some members of the audience at the doors. The practice went on into the nineteenth century but was probably on the wane; a woman of the Jewish merchant class at Leghorn was still pledging her wedding ring in exchange for a box in 1823.[19] Credit meant troublesome extra bookkeeping and repeated applications for payment; but clerical labour was cheap.

Other employees who made a difference to the impresario's relations with the public were the secretary who dealt with boxholders, the stage manager (*buttafuori* or *butta in scena*, literally 'thrower on to the stage' – thought-provoking title), the porter who defended the stage door against intruders, and the call-boy whose manifold duties might include finding lodgings for the company, bringing them to the theatre in hierarchical order, and acting as go-between or pimp; a famous one in Rome called Carletta (Carlo De' Giuli, 1769–1848) had a sideline in stealing dogs, painting them a new colour, and offering them for sale, sometimes to their former owners.[20]

Of these people, the most important to the impresario was probably the stage manager: he might have to face the audience when there was an awkward announcement to be made, unless the impresario did it himself. Even he might be borne down by the sheer noise from an unruly audience or, as once happened at the Regio, Turin, by a voice calling out in Piedmontese dialect (and quite gratuitously) 'Button your flies!'[21]

It seems odd that Italy should have done without the claque, that well-known means of ensuring at least the appearance of success in the opera house. The most notorious of claques flourished in Paris, where it hired itself out on set terms. No such professional body existed in Italy: we have Verdi's word for it, and that of the tenor Adolphe Nourrit, with experience of both Paris and Naples; they should have known.[22] The nearest thing we hear about is a group of '15 or 20 hired people' at Modena in 1798, but not even that seems to have been a permanent institution.[23]

For the rest, we have evidence of groups of students and the like organised by a singer to support him, but much more often of what might be called an anti-claque – a group organised to hiss and to bring about the failure of an opera, usually inspired by a rival impresario or singer or by their supporters in the town. The Italian opera house with its passionate clientele was subject to cabal and faction rather than to the straightforward commercial performance of the claque.[24]

Still, even if it was not easy to lay on a commercially inspired ovation within the opera house, there are signs that so-called spontaneous demonstrations of enthusiasm could be rigged in advance by the impresario or by the friends of the composer or singer.

A refrain of Italian opera chronicles is the torchlight procession after the triumphal first performance, ending beneath the composer's windows, sometimes with a serenade by the theatre orchestra, all to tremendous cheers. On one occasion at least this torchlight procession had been planned in advance; we know this because the place was Rome in the troubled period just ahead of the 1848 revolutions and a friend of the composer who was to be honoured advised him to call it off for fear of getting mixed up with low-class radicals.[25] How many more such demonstrations were similarly arranged? At least it can be said, once again, that partisanship rather than sheer commercial promotion was likely to be the motive. Certainly this was true of the young Bolognese supporters who accompanied their fellow citizen Gobatti to neighbouring towns and organised curtain calls and yet more torchlight processions: Gobatti was a composer whose *I Goti* had a flash-in-the-pan success in the 1870s, but the enthusiasm of the Bolognese, though misplaced, was real.[26]

Who organised hostile demonstrations? A man of much experience has left us a list:

A tenor or a ballerina without a contract, a hanger-on of an unemployed prima donna, an author who has been hissed and who longs to ensure for a brother artist successes similar to his own, impresari or would-be impresari who aspire to the theatre concession in the following year and who begin by bringing down the current impresario, journalists in search of subscribers who want to punish an artist for having dared to return their paper, now and then ill-advised champions among the public who seek to make themselves arbiters of domestic and private questions, avenging on the stage a betrayed lover or a disappointed hope.

All these might set up a deliberate barrage of whistling and overbear the general feeling even of a well-disposed audience.[27]

Sometimes a rival management might do this; at least the management of the Teatro Carcano, Milan, in carnival 1831 (an ambitious season that launched Bellini's *La Sonnambula*) was accused of having planted troublemakers at La Scala.[28] At other times we hear more vaguely about 'individuals well known for their restless temper', or 'an ill-disposed party' from a rival theatre, doing their best to make a new opera fail. This was alleged of the first nights of Rossini's *Barbiere di Siviglia* (1816) and Bellini's *Beatrice di Tenda* (1833);[29] something of the kind was to happen much later, in 1904, at the notorious first night of *Madama Butterfly*. We cannot now make out how far these theatrical storms were organised or how far they were the work of people who were genuinely disaffected (because a promised new work had been delayed or a composer's success had made others envious).

More often, disorders in the opera house centred on factions that supported rival prima donnas or dancers, on occasion actresses or orchestra leaders. Here too it is not always clear whether these factions were riotous fan clubs or whether they reflected pre-existing divisions among local notables and their families, with the two singers or dancers affording a pretext.

Such divisions might well be political. In the Napoleonic period opera factions at Turin and Parma reflected struggles between radicals and moderates, or between followers of the military governor-general of Parma (who supported Freemasonry) and those of the civilian prefect (who seems to have been a Catholic conservative).[30] Conflicts between anti-clerical liberals and clerical conservatives lay at the back of the extraordinarily bitter struggles in the small town of Busseto over the appointment of a music master – struggles involving first the young Verdi and then, nearly twenty years later, his pupil Emanuele Muzio – though no doubt personal animosities within a little group of notables came into it too.[31] These struggles are known to us only because Verdi was involved: how many other towns did they go on in? At Lucca in 1841 fights in the two main theatres had something to do with resentment among local democrats of a lavish opera performance put on by rich amateurs, members of the princely Poniatowski family; they countered by supporting an opera by a local peasant–poet.[32]

No such explanation has come down to us for the violence of other struggles over rival performers – at Padua in 1788, 1825, and 1829, at Piacenza in 1824, at Parma in 1843 and 1866, at Voghera in 1820, 1851, and 1867, at Palermo in 1838, 1839, 1840 and 1844. But their intensity is not in doubt. At Reggio Emilia in 1841 tempers ran so high that the authorities temporarily expelled some of the nobles, local people beat up a prima donna's lover, and demonstrations in the theatre were such that a performance had to be stopped and the season cut short.[33] At Cesena in 1858 the prima donna had to be changed four times in twenty performances: 'not one evening went by without hissing or without the various factions throwing aubergines, tomatoes, and the like at each other'.[34]

Passionate partisanship on behalf of one artist against another may have been the sole cause of these disturbances. But one is again left wondering when a leading figure in recurrent faction fights between supporters of rival prima donnas at the Carolino, Palermo, turns out to have been the Mazzinian democrat Rosalino Pilo: in 1844, as a gesture of derision at once heavily symbolic and in poor taste, he threw at the singer he opposed a wreath of esparto grass with a live owl attached.[35] Such gestures were to have a long history (in the 1950s a supporter of Renata Tebaldi threw a bunch of radishes and leeks at Maria Callas) but in the smouldering political atmosphere of the 1840s they may have provided an outlet for conflicts that could not be openly expressed.

Impresari by and large clung to the authorities; most of them seem to have taken no part in these semi-political faction fights. One impresario did go too far in his reliance on authority and paid the price. Pietro Rovaglia, owner of a Milan costume workshop, ran seasons at the two main Modena theatres from 1842 to 1846. He was so firmly backed by Count Riccini, the all-powerful Minister of the ageing Duke Francis IV, that he thought he could safely economise on production costs and on singers (Modena was one of those towns where the public expected performances worthy of a capital city at rock-bottom prices). By 1844 he was said to have earned in Modena a 'diabolical hatred'. On the opening night of the carnival 1846 season an overheard remark by the heir to the throne spread round the house: 'Really, with the amount the municipality pays out in subsidy it seems to me we could expect the management to put on a better show.' The audience felt authorised to hiss – so loudly that the police dared not interfere. Rovaglia stole away before the end; the crowd pursued him to his lodging, shouting 'down with Rovaglia' – a slogan directed largely at the Minister. The government suspended the season for a fortnight; a few days later Francis IV died and the Minister fell shortly afterwards.[36] Although the heir to the throne had no clear political line the chances are that at the end of a long autocratic reign he served as a focus for discontent: Rovaglia may have failed to recognise that what looked like a stable authority was a faction that divided the audience and might turn out to be a losing one.

After unification, as we have seen from the example of Parma, riots became more frequent and more unmanageable, but perhaps less political now that most opinions could be freely expressed. From then on impresari needed keener wits and good lawyers.

Just before the proclamation of the short-lived Roman Republic of 1849, at a time when a revolutionary situation already prevailed, 'the people' broke into the dress rehearsal of Verdi's patriotic opera *La Battaglia di Legnano* and filled the house from top to bottom.[37] The event might have been symbolic. It might have heralded a united Italy where opera houses would be opened to a new audience. The half-century from the 1860s to the First World War did see operatic music diffused more and more widely among the people, even among peasants some of whom named their children Otello or Norma. This process of diffusion seems to have come about largely outside the opera house, through workers' choral societies and amateur bands and even through itinerant puppeteers, some of whom in the 1890s would give puppet *Aida*s in the farmyards of Emilia–Romagna with a Socialist, anti-colonial slant.[38] But impresari had little to do with it.

Here is a paradox. Already in the second and third decades of the nineteenth century composers, even on occasion impresari, liked to say that 'everyone' in a particular city was singing the tunes from the new opera. Yet composer and impresario both had every reason to keep the score under lock and key – certainly until effective copyright came in around mid-century. The most successful numbers did become known quickly through a variety of means, but theatre people may have overestimated the effect.

Clara Novello, writing from Milan in 1840, reported that in the area around La Scala you could hear the sound of music being rehearsed: 'add to this the street organs and instruments, men and women servants whistling or carolling the airs from the last opera'. But she went on to say that 'the babel...pervades this part of Milan'[39] – and not, perhaps, other parts? Her words suggest an opera district with its specialised activities, rather like the leather-workers' or the jewellers' districts.

A year after Pacini had composed a new opera for Naples (*Stella di Napoli*, 1845) its tunes were still to be heard there – played by military bands in the park or on the barrack square, by barrel organs on the main street, by organists in church (for Italian musicians, to the scandal of foreign visitors throughout most of the nineteenth century, made no more distinction than Vivaldi had between secular and religious tunes), even at a funeral. They were also being played and sung at home by people, no doubt of the middle and upper classes, who had bought the many transcriptions published for piano, cornet, violin, and other instruments.[40] This was an impressive catalogue, gratifying to the composer (but for the thought that most of these performances brought him in no money); still, it probably left out a large part of the population in the back alleys of Naples who did not frequent the park or the fashionable main street, to say nothing of the thickly peopled rural hinterland. What a composer or impresario called 'everyone' was almost certainly not everyone.

Opera in the first two-thirds of the century, the period when *Il Barbiere* and *Lucia* and *Rigoletto* were first performed, can scarcely be called a popular art within the opera house, a building most of which was taken up by the well-off (*benestanti*), with perhaps a gallery occupied by artisans. Here it was a minority affair: this was well understood by contemporaries, who took it as a matter of course.[41] How far it was a popular art outside the opera house, through the kind of diffusion we have just glanced at, is a more open question though hard to answer precisely. What is clear is that as opera did spread more widely in the last decades of the century, establishing Verdi by the 1890s as a national figure recognised and cheered by railway workers and porters,[42] the impresari were unable to bring more than a section of this potential new audience into the theatre. The reasons for this failure, which was bound up with their general failure as a group of businessmen, are discussed in the next chapter.

8 · The end of the impresari

Through large parts of continental Europe the failure of the 1848 revolutions marked a turning-point. Romantic ideals of spontaneous regeneration were seen to be illusory: new nations or new democracies would not spring to life through the joyous coming together of liberated men. Tougher action would be needed; determined leaders would have to get their hands on the levers of power; manipulation, perhaps deceit would have a place. It is not at once clear why 1848 should have marked a deep change in the world of Italian opera as well; and yet it did.

To the impresari and to many other members of that world revolution was unwelcome. Not only were their fortunes bound up with those of existing ruling groups; revolution was bad for business. Seasons collapsed; fees came down; some weaker impresari went bankrupt and even 'Napoleons' like Merelli and Lanari were badly shaken. The industry did not recover fully until the mid-1850s.

This is worth recalling because one of the most enduring and least examined assumptions about Italian opera in the nineteenth century is that it was almost throughout a carrier of nationalist feeling. Only in recent years have Italian writers come to admit that Rossini favoured the old régime, that Bellini and Donizetti were non-political but eager to please the authorities, and that even Verdi was not quite the full-time nationalist he was once made out to be.

A closer look shows that the nationalist implications of opera – even of a single opera – changed with time as political circumstances changed and as nationalist feeling among the audience hardened.

A perfect example is what happened at two performances of *Norma* in the same town, Cremona, ten years apart. *Norma* is often described as a nationalist opera because its Gaulish rebels are thought to have conveyed a summons to rise against Austrian domination. Yet the first of these performances, in 1838 (with Verdi's future wife Giuseppina Strepponi in the title part), was given

The Teatro La Fenice, Venice, destroyed by fire, 13 December 1836, less than a fortnight before the start of the carnival season. Though a fire like this one was the impresario's worst nightmare the season went forward in another theatre.

in honour of the Austrian Emperor Ferdinand, who was visiting the town. A cantata opened the performance, with the singers in medieval Cremonese costumes – a reminder, clearly innocuous, of the city's past as an independent commune. 'Then the popular hymn "Viva Ferdinando" was sung, with the people joining in and giving continuous signs of joy.' There were no further incidents.

In January–February 1848, on the other hand – just ahead of the revolution – *Norma* had to be taken off and the theatre closed by the authorities because of patriotic demonstrations at the line 'Sgombre saran le Gallie' ('Gaul will be freed from the foreigner').[1] The line had had its inflammatory significance read into it during the ten-year interval.

Until sometime in the 1840s even outright expressions of love for an oppressed or distant fatherland could be taken in a very general sense, as a spur to improvement or to awareness of Italian culture; they could be reconciled with allegiance to the old Italian states. This is true even of the celebrated exiles' choruses in *Nabucco* (1842) and *I Lombardi* (1843): Verdi dedicated both operas to Austrian archduchesses, the first to the daughter of the Viceroy of Lombardy–Venetia (who was shortly to bring out the ambiguities of the situation by marrying the future King Victor Emmanuel II), the other to Verdi's own sovereign, Marie-Louise, Duchess of Parma.[2]

Nor was this mere opportunism. The second of these choruses, heard in a church full of Austrian soldiers, prompted the nationalist poet Giusti to overcome his hatred of the foreign occupier and to feel instead a sense of brotherhood with oppressed conscripts from Bohemia or Croatia: a true reading, this, of the sense of human community that informs Verdi's music, wider than any single nationalism.[3]

Tempers began to change about the early 1840s, even among the people on either side of the opera house footlights, who – according to an eyewitness in Milan – until then had had little nationalist consciousness.[4] Yet, even during the two-year period of enthusiasm that ran from the election of the 'liberal Pope' Pius IX in 1846 to the 1848 revolutions, many people believed that an Italian federation could be easily shaped from the existing states. Demonstrations in the opera house were generally nationalist: throwing of tricolour bouquets at the exiles' chorus in *Macbeth*, wild applause at the word *pio*, taken, however speciously, to refer to the Pope (Pio Nono in

Italian). Yet the audience was at times divided: 'many gentlemen' of Venice gave the chief of police a standing ovation at La Fenice in January 1848.[5]

After the failure of the revolutions and of Charles Albert's war against Austria, the 1850s were a decade of repression, far more vigilant in the opera house than ever before. This was not just a matter of censoring texts or preventing demonstrations. The police can be found interfering behind the scenes with a high hand – threatening the directors and impresari of La Fenice with 'energetic measures' if they dismissed a certain bass and warning them 'not to exhaust the patience of the authorities'.[6] The relative innocence of pre-1848 days was gone.

The course of revolution and war in 1848–9 was complex. There were many disturbances; the upheaval came after an economic slump; it was accompanied by higher taxes, forced loans, and the issue of paper currency which soon lost part of its face value.

Revolution or war going on within or near a town had always been disastrous for the theatre, for instance between 1796 and 1801, though wars going on at a distance could mean prosperity thanks to the presence of large garrisons with money to spend, as in Milan after 1802. In 1848–9 everyone did badly. With occasional shots fired in the streets no one would go out after nightfall; there was so little money about that Malibran or Pasta herself could have made no difference to the takings; in such times not even a new score by God Himself would be worth paying for – so ran the correspondence of impresari and publishers.[7]

In the opera world a few people identified themselves with democratic revolution. In Venice a minor impresario (unnamed) is said to have paraded as an officer of the civic guard wearing gilt epaulettes from the costume workshop and dragging on the pavement Almaviva's sword;[8] the agent–journalists Pietro Cominazzi (a strong nationalist), Francesco Regli, and Luigi Romani fled from Milan to Switzerland as the Austrians returned in August 1848.[9] But the commonest attitude seems to have been that expressed by the agent G. B. Benelli: 'if they would only get it over at last, and let poor artists breathe'.[10]

Many performers took engagements abroad, in countries like Spain and Cuba that were on a different revolutionary timetable. In Florence the composer Teodulo Mabellini wrote a cantata, *L'Italia risorta* (*Italy Resurgent*), to celebrate the granting of a civic guard – the prelude to a liberal constitution – in September 1847. He then wrote another cantata in 1849 to mark the Grand-Duke's return on the back of the Austrian army. On neither occasion did he necessarily mean much more than 'the show must go on'.[11]

But the strength of the reaction itself showed that the 1848 upheaval had shaken beyond repair the old local hierarchies and the unquestioning loyalty to the old governments. In every city some notables had taken part in revolution; some were now waiting in exile for Piedmont to give a lead towards unity, this time a decisive one. In the world of opera this questioning of old assumptions coincided with other changes that had been under way even before 1848. The result was to undermine the old opera industry even as it seemed to be entering its period of greatest expansion.

First, opera ceased to be the focus of social life for the upper classes. This was a slow process. In the 1880s there were still people in Parma who spent the carnival season in the opera house for the sake of conversation and cared little about the music.[12] But already in 1850 the owners of La Pergola in Florence were complaining that politics was taking young people away from the opera.[13] In the 1850s such political interests could not be openly expressed outside Piedmont. But there were newspapers, journals, scientific clubs, and the like; the habit of novel-reading was taking root; from 1859 on there were plenty of opportunities to get involved in parliamentary or municipal politics.

The old masked balls that had been the high spot of the social year gradually faded away. By 1869 the author of a popular work of moral uplift found it necessary to say that 'no one who has not lived in Italy before 1848 can realise what the theatre meant in those days...The success of a new opera was a capital event that stirred to its depths the city lucky enough to have witnessed it, and word of it ran all over Italy.'[14] Even if we allow for exaggeration – the author as usual claimed that 'everyone' had taken part – opera was losing its central place in town life.

The opera industry was also becoming less creative. It was producing more and more performances of fewer and fewer works. The modern notion of opera as a museum art was wholly foreign to Italy up to the late eighteenth century: operas were by definition new. It remained largely foreign until the 1830s, though the habit began to spread of putting on operas that had had their first performance in another town, usually no more than a few years back. The whole outlook of the people who created operas was still much more akin to that of Hollywood in the 1930s than to anything that goes on in opera houses today: so many new works were constantly being turned out that Meyerbeer, for instance, feared his librettist might let a rival composer get in first with some striking 'situations' he was counting on for his own new opera.[15]

The notion of repertory opera began to come in during the 1840s. The term itself was used in correspondence of 1845 between the impresario Balochino and the soprano Tacchinardi Persiani: she was to start a Vienna season in 'a repertory opera best suited to her and to the company'. It came in at the Regio, Turin, from 1849, and was officially embodied in the contract for the management of the Naples royal theatres from 1851.[16]

This was the time when the rhythm of production of new works began to slacken. If we allow for comic operas, one-act *farse*, and *pasticci* (operas cobbled together from bits of existing works) it seems likely that more new works were produced in some of the years between 1750 and 1814 than at any time before or after. But comic opera in the Restoration period was a fading genre. At La Scala (founded in 1778) the decade with the highest number of new creations was 1831–40, with thirty-eight. By the 1860s new creations were down to one or two a year. The San Carlo in the late 1830s was still expected to put on five operas a year that had not previously been heard there, three of them expressly written for Naples, but in the 1840s no more than one or two of these bespoke jobs were asked for each year.[17]

By the mid-1850s, when the industry had fully recovered from the upheaval of 1848–9, repertory opera was becoming established. By the 1870s it was the norm.

Leading singers had each his or her repertory of perhaps twenty parts, could ask for the right to choose which operas they would appear in, and could in turn be asked to appear in 'their' parts at short notice. This made for frequent disputes and for scamped productions. Even at La Scala, to judge from Santley's account of the 1866 season in which he took part, the singers almost made up the programme as they went along: if the public had had enough of *Il Trovatore* then something else was pulled out of store. One hardly likes to imagine what the Constantinople season of that same year can have been like: the leading bass was expected, though under protest, to sing up to eighteen parts.[18]

The reasons why creativity falls off in an art or a form of entertainment are hard to fathom. Slackening creativity in Italian opera probably had to do in part with the changes already mentioned – with the new opportunities for political oratory or novel-writing or journalism, all of which could absorb talent and attract a following. While these new forms developed, practitioners of opera other than Verdi failed to renew their long artistic tradition.[19] But the slackening also had to do with the spread of a new kind of opera house, large, unsubsidised, bringing opera and ballet at low prices to a wider public.

Though such houses could in theory have supplied yet more new operas (and some did), in practice their development paralleled that of repertory opera, depended on it, and in turn helped to make it possible. The coming of these theatres meant, in the words of a recent historian, a new commercialisation of opera through private investment on an 'epic and adventurous' scale, but also a 'hardening of models and formulae' and therefore an impoverishment.[20]

Large theatres offering some kind of entertainment at low prices were not new. In the early nineteenth century several open-air arenas were built to give daytime as well as evening performances. Performances in the daytime or early evening were generally understood to appeal to a lower social class than late evening performances: the Naples authorities more than once forbade matinées at the San Carlo to avoid cheapening the leading royal theatre.[21] The arenas, however, seem at first not to have given opera, though some were run by impresari who at the same time put on opera in fashionable indoor theatres. The Anfiteatro Corea, Rome (built 1803), did well enough out of bull-baiting, bareback riding, and firework displays to be contended for over several decades by Paterni and the Cartoni family.[22] There were also minor theatres of no great size where cheap opera performances were given: in Naples the Teatro La Fenice as early as 1817 was putting on daytime and evening performances, with two companies singing alternately, and by 1839 it was giving twice-daily *Normas*, no less.[23]

Around mid-century, the new style of theatre building and the new repertory opera came together. Very large theatres were now built for the specific purpose of giving opera, though they might also put on equestrian or acrobatic displays or, from the 1870s, the new French- or German-inspired operetta.

Of a number of such theatres built in the 1850s, two (at Bari and Salerno) were in the South, a region where, until then, theatres outside the capital cities had been few and had in the main been used fitfully by comic opera companies touring a southern circuit.[24] From the 1830s on, the habits of north-central Italy spread gradually to the southern provinces. Other theatres like the Pagliano in Florence (built in 1853 by an eccentric who had made a fortune out of a herbal elixir), the Vittorio Emanuele in Turin (1857), and the Dal Verme in Milan (1864) were at times to play an important part in the operatic life of those cities. New theatres were also built in small towns some of which had never had one before: the baritone Felice Varesi, the original Rigoletto, was astonished and gratified in 1852 to find an enthusiastic audience at Ascoli Piceno, a remote town with scarcely a road leading to it.[25]

Unfortunately, just because these theatres were built by private enterprise and were unsubsidised, we know far less about the way they were run than we do about those older theatres with which governments concerned themselves. The Pagliano was said to enjoy a subsidy from the founder's elixir,[26] but most of the others were expected to pay their way, and some in consequence did not last long. The Marzi brothers, the busiest impresari of the 1850s and 60s, ran a number of seasons in these new theatres as well as in more fashionable ones; they were financially unreliable and, according to Verdi, thoughtless and inept.[27] They seem to have behaved no worse in the cheap new theatres than at La Scala: if anything, the pretensions of the old leading theatres may have brought disaster closer once resources failed and governments ceased to care. Half a century later Arnold Bennett, attending the Pagliano (by then renamed the Verdi), caught the tail end of what sounds like a tradition of competent opera production on a large scale.[28]

Prices – to judge from the little we know of them – were lower than those of leading theatres, by about half or two-thirds in the cheaper parts of the house. It says something about the audience that the Pagliano in 1868 gave commercial travellers a discount, while in 1885 a large new opera house at Lecce, in the heel of the Italian boot, had a special price for children under seven.[29] Audiences like these, with a strong contingent of shopkeepers, minor civil servants and other clerical employees, and artisans and their families, had existed since the mid eighteenth century. But until the mid nineteenth they had not been expected to appear (elsewhere than in the gallery) at the *opera seria*, especially not in the fashionable season: if they did, that was because the upper-class audience was at another theatre.[30]

Now the hierarchical array shifted somewhat. *Opera seria* invaded far more theatres; the shopkeeping, clerical, artisan audience no doubt expanded, but chiefly into the better parts of the large new 'popular' theatres. In the old leading theatres, generally dominated by the boxholders, the traditional hierarchy died hard. This we may deduce from the way they closed down when times were bad and subsidies were cut, presumably rather than put on something cheaper, and from the near-boycott with which the Rome aristocracy greeted the Teatro Costanzi in 1880: the new opera house had two open galleries and only three tiers of boxes – proof in their eyes that it was a 'popular' theatre.[31] Some change overtook even these theatres – after the first few years the Costanzi established itself as the leading Rome opera house – but it was slow.

The nominal impresario of the first season at the Costanzi was old Vincenzo Jacovacci, then at the end of a forty year career; he died immediately afterwards. In practice he had done little beyond supplying a company, as we saw Bologna agents doing for other new theatres. Whether in new popular theatres or old royal ones, the initiative by the 1870s had slipped out of the hands of impresari.

Barbaja had made a difference to the career of the young Rossini, and Merelli and Lanari to that of the young Verdi. But the composers whose first works appeared in these decades – Ponchielli, Catalani, Puccini – were launched by publishers. Not only that: publishers decided where operas were to be done, controlled casting, supplied set and costume designs, and often directed the production, if not in person then through the issue of production books.

This change too had come about gradually. Italian music publishers developed from music copying, engraving, and printing, much helped by the spread of the piano. The firms of Artaria and Ricordi – both founded in Milan by Italians with previous German experience – made a modest start in 1805 and 1808; the firm of Lucca was a breakaway from Ricordi in 1825. There were other music publishers, especially in Naples, but those who mattered by the 1870s were Ricordi, Lucca (to be merged with Ricordi again at the end of the eighties), and Sonzogno, an existing firm of publisher–printers who branched out into opera.[32]

What brought the publishers into opera production was, first, the gradual trend towards repertory opera, which meant an increasing demand for the hire of orchestral scores; and, secondly, the establishment of copyright protection through the Austro-Sardinian treaty of 1840, which in the end suppressed piracy and made exclusive rights in a score worth paying for.

In 1836 a publisher could still be described by a rival as eccentric and mad for wanting to know where a score let out on hire was to be performed and by which singers.[33] Within a few years not only were publishers beginning to exercise this kind of 'quality control'; they were beginning to commission scores and act as go-betweens to composers and impresari.

Francesco Lucca was something of a pioneer in this. In 1845 he commissioned Verdi to write *Il Corsaro* without having at that time any particular theatre or group of singers in mind. At the same time he was trying to commission a libretto for another composer to set in Madrid, and in the following year he dealt on Verdi's behalf with the London manager who was to put on the first production of *I Masnadieri*. In 1853 he influenced Mercadante's choice of subject for an opera for Naples, and seems to have been determinant in working out the contract with the impresario.[34] Verdi, meanwhile – who had taken a dislike to Lucca – had signed in 1847 his first long-term contract with Ricordi.[35] From then on, Ricordi too acted on Verdi's behalf in dealings with impresari – exclusively after *Un Ballo in maschera* (1859), the last opera over which Verdi dealt with an impresario direct.

During the 1850s publishers began to supply designs and sometimes production books.[36] The key influence here was the example of the Paris Opéra with its elaborate and historically accurate productions; it worked on Italy through Verdi – by then a Paris composer some of the time – and through the requirements of Meyerbeer's Paris operas. At about the same time publishers started insisting that scores should not be altered without their consent, and that any changes should be made by the composer – a break with long-standing Italian practice.[37]

When publishers started dictating casting is not clear. In 1865 Lucca laid down who should sing in *L'Africaine* at La Scala; by the 1870s it was the general practice for the publisher 'to propose, accept, or refuse artists'.[38]

The publisher, then, by the last third of the century controlled the composer and much of the production and casting: so much so that the Turin impresario who had successfully introduced Massenet to Italy in 1878, and to whom the composer had promised his next opera, could not get it because of disagreements with the publisher over casting; while in the next decade Catalani would not contemplate dealing with an impresario direct even when the publisher was too busy to attend to him or when he had other grounds for dissatisfaction.[39]

What then was left for the impresario to do? Logically the next step would have been for the publishers to manage opera seasons themselves, either in their own name or through a nominee. Ricordi and Sonzogno, deadly rivals, alternated as, in effect, managers of La Scala through most of the 1890s.[40] In Milan this put them in a position akin to that of the old noble proprietors of Venice and Rome theatres who had virtually run their own opera seasons, though with an impresario nominally in charge. What was new was their ability to dictate to impresari in all kinds of theatres up and down the country. These local impresari might still put on opera seasons, in some places up to the First World War, but they were little more than executants. The only area where Italian opera impresari kept a good deal of initiative was Latin America.

Verdi made the point in his usual downright fashion. 'Suppose', he wrote in 1889, 'that...some Piontelli or other should become impresario of La Scala...' Luigi Piontelli was one of the best-known impresari of the day; but Verdi clearly regarded him and his fellows as interchangeable. Verdi's immediate point was that such an impresario might influence the appointment of a conductor, though he himself wished to see a conductor at La Scala independent of any impresario (as Toscanini was to be a few years later). Verdi's collaborator Boito did express some preference for one impresario over another. Plainly, however, for both men the important managerial figure in the making of *Otello* and *Falstaff* was the publisher Giulio Ricordi.[41] In running opera seasons of any note the impresari had had their day.

They had always been dubious figures. New business and professional opportunities in the latter part of the century perhaps drew
away such entrepreneurial types as might earlier have taken to
opera management. Those who tried to run *imprese* through the
crises of the 1870s and 80s tended to seem still more disreputable.
The rise of the publishers made them seem unimportant as well.

How far had impresari influenced the quality of the operas they
put on? With a few exceptions such as Barbaja and Lanari, little
enough. The musical tastes of impresari are hard to make out. They
seldom wrote about quality, and then what they discussed was
nearly always success with the public or singers' technical pro-
ficiency, as when Crivelli urged a composer to build up the arias
introducing star singers so that these could produce a 'grandiose'
effect.[42] When impresari did give an opinion of a work's musical
quality it was anyhow suspect, because as a rule they were either
trying to hire out a score or to talk down its price. The impression
one gets is that either they had no aesthetic opinions or they liked
what had succeeded in the recent past.[43] In this too they remind us
of 1930s Hollywood producers.

Unlike Hollywood producers, however, they served a hierarchically
dominant group and went down with it. In an art that needed a
subsidy this was no doubt inevitable once electorates had a say:
public finance meant public control.

Even the big unsubsidised opera houses of the late nineteenth
century seem to have done little beyond keeping up with the
expansion of petty commercial and artisan groups. Efforts to bring
in industrial workers were left to twentieth-century activists of the
political Left; and by then, after the flowering of the 'young school'
of Puccini and Mascagni, no new Italian opera could strike root in
a large public.

Back in 1838, when the fortunes of Italian opera were at their
height, an employee of one impresario drew a caricature of another,
rival impresario that inadvertently fixed a type. The rival thought,
mistakenly, that he was about to become the kingpin of a new
management at La Pergola, still at that time a leading theatre:

He, who already thinks himself enthroned, is already reckoning up the immense
profits he is bound to make on the costumes, on the agents' commissions, pilfering,
thievery &c &c &c &c &c &c. He's already haggling over horses, making promises
to this man, issuing threats to that, extending his patronage to others, he's swelling,

chuckling, smiling sardonically, and he hasn't an inkling of the fate that lies in wait for him.[44]

It was an unfriendly portrait; but it conveyed the resilient hopefulness of men who, like so many of their countrymen through the centuries in which Italian opera flourished, had to live on their wits.

Problems of evidence for the economic history of Italian opera

Any attempt to understand the economic history of Italian opera must mean collating and comparing data within a category. Such an attempt is bound to be in some way artificial. Not only was opera part of a hierarchy of genres. Impresari were not necessarily confined to one genre; nor were theatres; nor did all impresari keep to one city or state.

The category best suited to this kind of comparison is the major opera season (often, though not always, the carnival season) held in a leading theatre of an important city. It has two advantages: it provides continuity (such seasons were going on from the early eighteenth century at least); and it shows the problem of costs at its most acute. On similar grounds we should compare the fees paid to leading singers, and occasionally to less famous singers engaged by leading theatres.

Even then there remain problems of comparability. These, though real, should not be exaggerated. Just as no two singers are alike, no two theatres are exactly alike in size, reputation, money-making capacity, or involvement with local society. Yet there was, especially up to the 1850s, a well-understood group of leading theatres (*primari teatri d'Italia*) which enjoyed something like 'parity of esteem' even though their financial resources were not uniform. This category (which appears over and over again in contracts) was codified in united Italy as the first of three classes into which 940 Italian theatres in 699 towns were divided for tax purposes.[1] It then (1871) included the leading theatres of Turin, Milan, Genoa, Venice, Florence, Rome (two theatres), Naples, and Palermo, and, at certain seasons only, those of Reggio Emilia and Bologna. Other theatres that had been regarded as important in pre-unification Italy were the leading theatres of Parma, Modena, Lucca, and Trieste (at least in certain seasons), and, during annual trade fairs, those of Bergamo, Padua, and Senigallia.

To have successfully sung a leading part in a leading theatre made one an *artista di cartello*: singers thus certificated did not all command the same fees, but they were thought of as a category generally suited to the same group of theatres. If we keep in mind the standing – at any one time and over a period of time – of both theatres and artists, which is well documented in contemporary evidence, we should be able to make meaningful comparisons.

Again, carnival seasons – extended at various dates into carnival-Lent seasons – were not of uniform length. But in engaging artists mostly paid by the season, as against humbler employees paid for each performance, impresari seem to have used a short carnival as an argument to extract minor concessions rather than as serious grounds for proportionately cutting fees. So long as we are making rough rather than minutely exact comparisons it is not unreasonable to treat carnival seasons (or other leading seasons) as a category.[2] Table 1 is accordingly based on such seasons, with the exception of the Teatro Valle, Rome; in this case an unusual amount of evidence over a number of years makes it worth while to include all available seasons. Tables 3 and 4 are entirely based on carnival fees.

There are, finally, problems of finding reliable evidence, and technical problems of dealing with the many currencies of pre-unification Italy.

Few subjects lent themselves better to rumour and exaggeration than the costs of opera production. But there is no need to rely on gossip. We have plenty of correspondence between impresari and the authorities who gave them their concession, between artists, impresari, and agents, occasionally between impresari and their underlings. We have a good many contracts naming fees. We have information arising from lawsuits. We have rather few complete accounts of receipts and expenditure for a whole opera season.

Some of this evidence needs to be treated with caution. Shaw wrote in the 1890s that no member of the theatrical profession dreamt of believing a public statement made by another: though the shaft was, as usual, exaggerated there was some truth in it. Certainly we should not take for gospel, any more than people did at the time, what an artist wrote to one impresario about the high fees and splendid conditions she had been offered by another.

Even contracts were thought sometimes to name fictitiously high sums to bolster an artist's ego or to help an impresario to extract a high subsidy. The earliest mention I have found of this is in the anonymous libretto of a comic opera, *L'Impresario burlato*, dating from the very end of the eighteenth century[3] – a suspect source, for it was a convention in such works to make fun of singers' pretensions, one of the few safe subjects in the old despotic Italian states. The one clear case is that of Maria Malibran; for two performances at the Teatro Valle, Rome, in Spring 1832 she was given a fictitious contract doubling her actual fee, which was named in a separate document; the fee was also doubled in the accounts which the impresario prepared for the theatre owner.[4]

Among impresari, Merelli was suspected in Vienna in the mid nineteenth century of drawing up two different sets of contracts, one for the artists and one for his official employers.[5] But the suspicion seems arbitrary – it may have had to do with the general impression of shiftiness Merelli often gave – and the correspondence of his Vienna partner Balochino does not support it. An impresario who did offer to draw up a fictitious contract (to save a singer's face at a time when fees were unusually low) was the busy but somewhat disreputable Ercole Marzi. He also wanted Lanari – then an agent – to name a fictitious high fee in a letter which Marzi could show to the authorities. Lanari, a canny as well as a more reputable person, worded his letter so as to avoid naming a figure.[6]

These instances suggest no more than a sporadic practice. In a profession where people went to law over contractual matters as readily as did Italian impresari and artists it seems unlikely to have been common: the risk of having a fake contract enforced would have been too great. On the whole, contracts may be taken to tell the truth.

Again, if one impresario was doing business with another they were unlikely in their private correspondence to misstate sums of money, if only because the chances of being found out were high. From these sources one can gather a good deal of reliable information. The problem is rather that of putting together a significant series.

This problem becomes still more acute when we come to accounts. The main (and voluminous) sources are the papers of governments and other controllers of theatres. But because the impresario was a concessionaire he took his detailed accounts away with him – and very few archives of impresari's papers seem to have survived.[7] We can do something to work out a series by collating archival documents with accounts reproduced by a number of late nineteenth-century theatre historians, some of whom had access to papers no longer available. One or two recent theatre histories are also helpful. Table I draws in part on such sources.

Currencies have to be coped with by reducing their diversity to a common unit. Not only did the various Italian states have each their own coinage and currency of account; payments were often made in Spanish, French, Bavarian, or Austrian coin. Rates of exchange varied. Sums named might be *effettive* (to be paid in the actual coin named) or payable in some equivalent currency at a discount. I have reduced all sums to francs, a currency that circulated in Italy during the revolutionary and Napoleonic period and that was often used later on for payments to opera artists; after 1814 the Piedmontese (ultimately Italian) lira was officially at par with the franc, though in practice there were very minor fluctuations. Where actual exchange rates are known I have used those. Otherwise I have used the tables of exchange rates drawn up by various Italian economic historians.[8] Sums paid in the pre-revolutionary period (usually in a variety of gold coins, sometimes recorded in a local currency of account) I have somewhat arbitrarily reduced to francs by using a combination of the rates set in the 1790s and the recorded exchange value of the gold coins at the relevant point in the eighteenth century. The result does not pretend to total accuracy, but it should allow comparisons of orders of magnitude.

In studying costs, takings, and endowments I have not tried to allow for fluctuations in the general price level. The difficulties involved in doing this in any detail seem too great. It is one thing to measure a farm labourer's wage against a basic subsistence budget, quite another to measure singers' fees or prices of admission against opera consumers' total expenditure, governed as that was by an array of prices not all of them necessarily moving the same way. Not even so thorough and scrupulous a work as De Maddalena, *Prezzi e mercedi a Milano*, goes beyond working out a general index of basic food prices.

What can be said in a general way is that, like other parts of Europe, Italy went through the Napoleonic inflation and the immediate post-war slump. After 1823, price rises were far from uniform, and there seems no way of relating the rise in opera costs to them.

Notes

1   A season in the life of an impresario

1   See S. J. Woolf, *A History of Italy 1700–1860*, London, 1979, chs. 2, 12.

2   C. De Nicola, *Diario napoletano*, 21 Feb. 1819, in *Archivio Storico per le Provincie Napoletane*, xxx, 1905, app. p. 162. See F. Clementi, *Il carnevale romano nelle cronache contemporanee, secoli XVIII–XIX*, Città di Castello, 1938.

3   M. Lessona, *Volere è potere*, Florence, 1869, p. 298.

4   V. Bellini, *Epistolario*, ed. L. Cambi, Milan, 1943, p. 136; F. Abbiati, *Giuseppe Verdi*, 4 vols., Milan, 1959, I, p. 737.

5   Archduke Rainer, Viceroy of Lombardy–Venetia, to the Emperor Francis II, 4 Dec. 1822, ASCM Sp. P. 56 (about Giuseppe Crivelli).

6   Lorenza Correa, quoted in M. Rinaldi, *Due secoli di musica al Teatro Argentina*, 3 vols., Florence, 1978, I, p. 374.

7   Bellini, *Epistolario*, pp. 157, 177–8, 228–40, 252, 265–7.

8   Pacini to his wife, Dec. 1852, Fondo Pacini, Biblioteca Comunale, Pescia (the opera was *Il Cid*, La Scala, C1853).

9   G. Radiciotti, *Gioacchino Rossini*, 3 vols., Tivoli, 1927–9, I, pp. 186, 265–72, 413–17; W. Ashbrook, *Donizetti*, London, 1963, pp. 126–7, 138; G. Pacini, *Le mie memorie artistiche*, Florence, 1875, pp. 13–14, 20, 83; Rinaldi, *Argentina*, I, pp. 432–3.

10 E. Verzino, *Contributo ad una biografia di Gaetano Donizetti*, Bergamo, 1896, pp. 68–74 (the opera was *Lucrezia Borgia*, La Scala, C1833).

11 G. Valle, *Cenni teorici-pratici sulle aziende teatrali*, Milan, 1823, pp. 85–8.

12 A. Basso, ed. *Storia del Teatro Regio di Torino*, 3 vols., Turin, 1976–80, I, pp. 217–19.

13 Deliberations of the Società Proprietaria del Gran Teatro La Fenice, 1820–2, ATLaF Processi verbali convocazioni b. 3.

14 Correspondence between the Marchese Bartolomeo Capranica and Domenico Barbaja, July 1828, BTBR Fondo Capranica.

15 Performances at the Teatro Ducale, Parma, C1828 (Mercadante, *Donna Caritea*) and the Teatro Alfieri, Florence, C1839 (*La Sonnambula*): P. E. Ferrari, *Spettacoli drammatico-musicali e coreografici in Parma*, Parma, 1884, p. 144; Gazzuoli to Lanari, BNF CV 365/86.

16 Rinaldi, *Argentina*, I, pp. 492–501.

17 Donizetti to Mayr, 15 May 1828, in G. Zavadini, *Donizetti*, Bergamo, 1948, pp. 259–60 (*Alina regina di Golconda*, Teatro Carlo Felice, Genoa, P1828); Duke Carlo Visconti to (?), MTS CA 5641 (*L'Elisir d'amore*, Como, c. 1834–6).

18 J. Ebers, *Seven Years of the King's Theatre*, London, 1828, p. xxvii.

19 Gaetano Rossi to Meyerbeer, 22 Aug. 1826, in G. Meyerbeer, *B, iefwechsel und Tagebücher*, ed. H. and G. Becker, Berlin, 1960–75, II, pp. 32–3 (about Giovanni Perottini, Vicenza F1826).

20 De Nicola, *Diario napoletano*, 17 Feb. 1817; F. Walker, *The Man Verdi*, London, 1962, p. 178.
21 Appuntamenti presi coll'appaltatore Maldonati per l'interna pulizia del Teatro alla Scala, 27 Dec. 1789, ASCM Sp. P. 28; J. d'Espinchal, *Journal d'émigration*, ed. E. Hauterive, Paris, 1912, pp. 75, 92–3.
22 M. Nani-Mocenigo, *La Fenice*, Venice, 1926, p. 18.
23 Stendhal, *Life of Rossini*, ed. R. N. Coe, London, 1956, pp. 428–9; L. Spohr, *Autobiography*, 2 vols., London, 1865, I, p. 259; [J.-J. Le François de Lalande], *Voyage d'un françois en Italie*, 8 vols., Venice, 1769, I, p. 114.
24 O. Nicolai, *Briefe an seinen Vater*, ed. W. Altmann, Regensburg, 1924, pp. 58–61, 185. See also F. Milizia, *Del teatro*, Venice, 1794 (1st edn. 1771), p. 40: H. Berlioz, *Correspondance générale*, ed. P. Citron, 3 vols., Paris, 1972–8, I, p. 554, and *Voyage musical en Allemagne et en Italie*, Paris, 1844, pp. 216–17; M. F. Robinson, *Naples and Neapolitan Opera*, Oxford, 1972, pp. 63–4.
25 L. Quicherat, *Adolphe Nourrit*, 3 vols., Paris, 1867, I, p. 417.
26 Nicolai, *Briefe*, pp. 185–6.
27 C. Santley, *Student and Singer*, London, 1892, pp. 83–4.
28 Broadsheet announcing Pisaroni's benefit at the Teatro del Corso, Bologna, 8 Aug. 1818, Biblioteca dell'Archiginnasio, Bologna, Avvisi di teatro.
29 Valle, *Cenni teorici-pratici*, pp. 63–73; announcement of Maria Marcolini's benefit, Rome, 9 Nov. 1808, Biblioteca dell'Istituto di Storia dell'Arte e Archeologia, Rome, Manifesti teatrali. The *bacile* (bowl) collection was abolished in 1832 by the leading company giving straight plays, the Compagnia Reale Sarda, but was still in force until 1870 in opera seasons in the small town of Voghera: C. L. Curiel, *Il Teatro San Pietro di Trieste*, Milan, 1937, p. 28; A. Maragliano, *I Teatri di Voghera*, Casteggio, 1901.
30 G. Radiciotti, *Contributi alla storia del teatro e della musica in Urbino*, Pesaro, 1899, p. 10.
31 Pecori to Lanari, Dec. 1848–Feb. 1849, BNF CV 400/161 *et seq.*
32 R. Bonini to Lanari, March 1837, BNF CV 348/159.
33 ATRP carteggi 1819, correspondence of Neipperg, Sanvitale, Osea Francia, petitions.
34 For Osea Francia's career, see Piancastelli 130, 207, 215–16; Ferrari, *Spettacoli in Parma*; A. Gandini, *Cronistoria dei teatri di Modena*, Modena, 1873; G. Radiciotti, *Teatro, musica e musicisti in Sinigaglia*, Milan, 1893, pp. 24, 60; U. Morini, *La R. Accademia degli Immobili ed il suo teatro 'La Pergola'*, Pisa, 1926, p. 99. For Pecori: Ferrari; Gandini (A1859); E. Santoro, *Il Teatro di Cremona*, Cremona, 1969–72.
35 S. Dalla Libera, 'Cronologia del Teatro La Fenice', ATLaF: N. Mangini, *I Teatri di Venezia*, Milan, 1974, p. 173.

2 A profession of sorts

1 Deputazione degli Spettacoli to Minister of the Interior, ASN Min. Interno II inv. f. 4356.
2 F. Regli, *Dizionario biografico dei più illustri poeti e artisti melodrammatici...in Italia dal 1800 al 1860*, Turin, 1860, s. v. Verger; O. Tiby, *Il Real Teatro Carolino e l'ottocento musicale palermitano*, Florence, 1957, pp. 231–2; F. De Filippis, ed., *Il Teatro di San Carlo*, Naples, 1951, p. 27.
3 BNF CV 351 s. v. Cambiaggio, 364/153, 365/35; *Enciclopedia dello Spettacolo*.

4 Basso, ed., *Teatro Regio*, II, p. 285 n.; Gandini, *Modena*, II, pp. 401–5.

5 This seems to have been in the mind of the Genoa impresario Giacomo Filippo Granara when he offered an *opera seria* company for a season at the Teatro Valle, Rome, in 1826. He talked exclusively about his costumes (and even offered fresh drapes for the boxes) without a word about singers or operas: 30 Nov. 1825 (intended for the Marchese Bartolomeo Capranica), BTBR Fondo Capranica, correspondence.

6 Gazzuoli to Lanari, 1 March 1838, BNF CV 365/16 (*Il Pirata* at La Pergola, Florence, CQ1838, in preference to *Norma*).

7 ATLaF Spettacoli b. 3; Pacini's letters to his wife, 1853, 1855, and his letterhead, 31 Dec. 1859 (no. 1087), Fondo Pacini, Biblioteca Comunale, Pescia.

8 Valle, *Cenni teorici-pratici*, pp. 14–15; Duke of Noja to Minister of the Interior, 3 Oct. 1821, 17 June 1822, Barbaja to Noja, 9 May 1822 ASN Min. Interno II inv. f. 4355.

9 Alberto Torri to M. Lopez, 13 Aug. 1853, ATRP carteggi 1853/2.

10 See Basso, ed., *Teatro Regio*, I, pp. 111–26; P. Cambiasi, *La Scala*, Milan, 1889; A. Paglicci-Brozzi, *Il R. Ducale Teatro di Milano nel secolo XVIII*, Milan, 1894; Mangini, *Teatri di Venezia*; C. Ricci, *I Teatri di Bologna*, Bologna, 1888; Gandini, *Modena*.

11 Basso, ed., *Teatro Regio*, II, pp. 178–204.

12 Lanari to Donizetti, 19 Aug. 1836, in *Studi Donizettiani*, III, 1978, p. 37.

13 Radiciotti, *Rossini*, I, p. 23.

14 Radiciotti, *Sinigaglia*, p. 48; A. Pellegrini, *Spettacoli lucchesi nei secoli XVII–XIX*, Lucca, 1914, p. 552. The dates of these episodes were 1762 and 1760.

15 BNF CV 365/35, 36, 51, 77; 410/120, 190; 411 s. v. Standish; Regli, *Dizionario biografico*; *Burke's Landed Gentry* s. v. Stephenson, Standish; F. Boase, *Modern English Biography*.

16 *Burke's Landed Gentry*; *Dictionary of National Biography* s. v. Harris, Augustus; family pedigree and tradition communicated by Capt. George Glossop, 1979; J. Booth, *The 'Old Vic' 1816–1916*, London, 1917, pp. 3–13; papers of Glossop *impresa*, ASN Teatri f. 98, and ASCM Sp. p. 56; G. Vaccaj, *Vita di Nicola Vaccaj*, Bologna, 1882, p. 86; AN AJ¹³ 228/1; B. Labat-Poussin, *Archives du Théâtre National de l'Opéra: Inventaire*, Paris, 1977, indexes s. v. Glossop, Bonneau de Méric. Glossop's two marriages (which according to family tradition were 'of a doubtful character') were to Elisabetta Ferron (Elizabeth Fearon) and to Joséphine Bonneau de Méric (known on the stage as de Méri, Demeri or Deméric).

17 Visconti correspondence, MTS CA 5640–9; Direttore generale della polizia, Milan, to Viceroy, 13 Jan. 1832, ASCM Sp. P. 56, police protocol, 13 Nov. 1835, ASCM Sp. P. 79/6.

18 A. Petracchi, *Sul reggimento de' pubblici teatri*, Milan, 1821; D. Isella, ed., *Le lettere di Carlo Porta e degli amici della Camerata*, Milan and Naples, 1967, p. 58 n.; Ebers, *King's Theatre*, pp. 150–1.

19 Marchese Domenico Andreotti to Lanari, 24 June 1836, BNF CV 343/28; G. Verdi, *I copialettere*, ed. G. Cesari and A. Luzio, Milan, 1913, pp. 10–12. Another Vincenzio Flauto, perhaps this one's father, printed the San Carlo libretti in 1785–6: ASN Casa Reale Antica f. 970.

20 Morini, *La Pergola*; Michael Kelly, *Reminiscences*, ed. R. Fiske, Oxford, 1975, pp. 46, 53. Kelly places Campigli's shop on the Ponte S. Trinita – an impossibility. He must have meant the next bridge, the Ponte Vecchio.

21 A. Manzi, 'I teatri di musica', in *Firenze d'oggi*, Florence, 1896, pp. 66–7. The Teatro Pagliano (1853) is now the Verdi.

22 A. Cametti, *Il Teatro di Tordinona poi di Apollo*, 2 vols., Tivoli, 1938, I, p. 229; ASR Camerale III Teatri b. 2137 nos. 24, 25.

23 Radiciotti, *Rossini*, I, p. 268 n.; Cartoni–Capranica correspondence, BTBR Fondo Capranica, and ASCR Archivio Capranica b. 459, R. De Felice, *Aspetti e momenti della vita economica di Roma e del Lazio nei secoli XVIII e XIX*, Rome, 1965, p. 270.

24 Correspondence with Capranica, BTBR Fondo Capranica.

25 Cametti, *Apollo*, I, pp. 246 *et seq.*

26 ASR Camerale III Teatri b. 2138 nos. 22–3, 30–1.

27 G. Cencetti to Pacini, 28 Aug. 1860 (copy), Fondo Pacini, Biblioteca Comunale, Pescia.

28 Abbiati, *Verdi*, II, p. 529; Verdi, *Copialettere*, pp. 570–1, 575–6. See also G. Janni, *Gioacchino Belli*, 2 vols., Milan, 1962, II, p. 634.

29 [B. Merelli], *Cenni biografici di Donizetti e Mayr raccolti dalle memorie di un vecchio ottuagenario dilettante di musica*, Bergamo, 1875, pp. 8–10.

30 Certificate signed Ragazzi, issued by the Imperiale Reale Tribunale Penale, Bergamo, 27 Sep. 1827, BTBR Fondo Capranica, correspondence. The certificate was issued at the request of the Marchese Capranica, who wanted information about Merelli as agent and used his own position as secretary to the Direzione Generale di Polizia, Rome, to secure it. This document settles the doubts raised by Walker, *Verdi*, pp. 39 *et seq.* The noblewoman from whom the attempted theft was said to have been made was Lodovica Cerri Farinelli.

31 Crivelli to Lanari, 1828–9, BNF CV 358/142 *et seq.*

32 Merelli to Lanari, 17 Dec. 1831, ibid. 396–8.

33 Merelli to Leon Herz, 1844, MTS CA 3747–9; Regli, *Dizionario biografico*.

34 O. Nicolai, *Tagebücher*, Leipzig, 1892, p. 109; F. Schlitzer, *Mondo teatrale dell'ottocento*, Naples, 1954, pp. 186–7; R. Mirate to G. B. Benelli, 1854, Piancastelli Autografi s. v. Benelli; L. Bretin to C. Balochino, 19 Nov. 1836, Wiener Stadtbibliothek, Balochino papers.

35 Abbiati, *Verdi*, I, pp. 539–46, 604–5, 673; Zavadini, *Donizetti*, pp. 696, 815.

36 Merelli to Lanari, 26 Aug. 1850, BNF CV 396/145 (in which he thanks Providence and the 'justice' of the Austrian government for his survival as impresario).

37 Regli, *Dizionario biografico*; [Merelli], *Cenni biografici*, pp. 8–10.

38 Janni, *Belli*, II, pp. 639–41; Gandini, *Modena*, II, pp. 367–9.

39 BNF CV 364/101, 108; 365/18; L. Trezzini, ed., *Due secoli di vita musicale: Storia del Teatro Comunale di Bologna*, 2 vols., Bologna, 1966, II, p. 25; *Teatro Arti e Letteratura*, Bologna, 1857–63, *passim*; Biblioteca dell'Archiginnasio, Bologna, Coll. Autografi XLI 11.101 *et seq.*

40 For a detailed account, and for other aspects of the Napoleonic gambling monopoly referred to in succeeding paragraphs, see J. Rosselli, 'Governi, appaltatori e giuochi d'azzardo nell'Italia napoleonica', *Rivista Storica Italiana*, XCIII, no. 2, 1981.

41 The sentence (which was to have been served off Tuscany) was commuted to imprisonment; Affligio was seen in 1781 cleaning out the baths at Bagni di San Giuliano near Pisa: Curiel, *Teatro San Pietro*, pp. 59–60; A. Zobi, *Storia civile di Toscana dal 1737 al 1848*, 2 vols., Florence, 1850–2, II, pp. 238–40; Kelly, *Reminiscences*, pp. 51–2.

42 Stendhal, *Rome, Naples et Florence*, ed. V. Del Litto, Lausanne, 1960, pp. 268–9.

43 Viceroy to Emperor, 4 Dec. 1822, ASCM Sp. P. 56; G. B. Villa to Lanari, BNF CV 415/163 *et seq.*

44 L. Mantovani, *Diario ecclesiastico-politico di Milano*, 1796–1824, Biblioteca Ambrosiana, Milan, Cod. H. 93–8, II, 12 Feb. 1803; Regli, *Dizionario biografico*; contracts, ASCM Sp. P. 60/5, 79/11; H. Berlioz, *Mémoires*, Paris, 1870, p. 351; Nicolai, *Briefe*, p. 297.

45 Balochino papers, Wiener Stadtbibliothek; Nicolai, *Briefe*, pp. 352–5; Berlioz, *Mémoires*, p. 351; R. Wallaschek, *Die Theater Wiens*, Vienna, 1909, section *Das K. K. Hofoperntheater*.

46 ASN Min. Interno II inv. f. 1773; *Storia di Napoli*, IX, p. 676. It is clear from the official papers that the story, often repeated, that Barbaja built the new San Carlo and San Francesco di Paola at his own expense is untrue. He was purely a building contractor. What he did over the San Carlo was to advance the cost of rebuilding; he was then compensated out of the proceeds of the gambling monopoly, to maximise which he was given a specially lax contract. The contract to build new government offices (where the present Naples city hall stands) was however taken away from Barbaja while construction was still going on: Barbaja to Luigi de' Medici, 18 Sep. 1822, Min. Interno II inv. f. 4355.

47 C. Angelini, A. Niccolini, and F. Rega, *Catalogo ragionato de' quadri del... Barbaja...*, Naples, 1819; 'Galleria Barbaja', *L'Omnibus*, Naples, VIII, no. 48, 1 April 1841.

48 C. Celano and G. B. Chiarini, *Notizie del bello, del curioso e dell'antico della città di Napoli*, Naples, 1856–60 edn., V, pp. 80–1.

49 Barbaja to Florimo ('Feloram'), no date but *c*. Sep. 1831, MTS Coll. Casati 1698. This autograph letter (of which translation can give only a pale idea) was prompted by allegations that Barbaja was not really interested in doing justice to a proposed new opera by Florimo's friend Bellini. See Bellini, *Epistolario*, pp. 282–6.

50 Barbaja to Medici, 18 Sep. 1822, ASN Min. Interno II inv. f. 4355.

51 Pacini, *Memorie artistiche*, p. 44.

52 A. Larussa, *Sulle cagioni del decadimento delli teatri in Napoli...*, Naples, 1850, p. 7; Radiciotti, *Rossini*, I, pp. 156–9.

53 Niccolini and Noja to Minister of the Interior, 29 Aug., 4 Dec. 1821, ASN Min. Interno II inv. f. 4355; G. Gioja to Count G. Melzi, 24 Apr. 1824, MTS CA 2303.

54 *L'Omnibus*, IX, nos. 25, 28, 1841.

55 P. Brunetti to Lanari, 1828, Gazzuoli–Lanari correspondence, 1837, *passim*, A. Basetti to Lanari, 14 Feb. 1837, BNF CV 350/94; 364; 365; 346/110.

56 *Inventario del R. Archivio di Stato in Lucca*, Lucca, 1872–80. II, p. 31, III, p. 410, IV, p. 380; ASL Direzione Scritture vol. 21, 1865, no. 2, 'Sul tabacco e la sua azienda in Lucca', Catasto Nuovo f. 57 no. 2. Bandini's banker partner was Giacomo Levi of Reggio Emilia.

57 To A. Perotti, 8 May 1838, in *Carteggi Verdiani*, ed. A. Luzio, Rome, 1935–47, IV, p. 148.

58 Lanari was not the ostensible impresario (because he had announced in 1849 his retirement from *impresa*) but all seasons at the Teatro Comunale, Bologna, from C1850 till his death in 1852 – including A1850 when Verdi prepared *Macbeth* and *Luisa Miller* – were run by him with Mauro Corticelli and Antonio Puglioli as his local representatives: ASB ASC Dep. Pub. Sp. tit. I rub. I, 1850–2.

59 G. Caroselli to Marchese Capranica, Ancona 5 June 1827, BTBR Fondo
    Capranica.
60 Verdi, *Copialettere*, pp. 444–9; *Studi Donizettiani*, III, p. 37.
61 Venier–Lanari correspondence, June 1841, BNV CV 415/110.
62 The operas were *I Capuleti e i Montecchi, Beatrice di Tenda, Attila, Macbeth*, and
    (besides *Lucia*) *Parisina, Rosmunda d'Inghilterra, Pia de' Tolomei*, and *Maria di
    Rudenz*. This account of Lanari's career is based on a large amount of
    correspondence in BNF CV and elsewhere. See also Regli, *Dizionario biografico*.
63 To R. and G. Morandi, 1819, Piancastelli 570. 1a; to G. Morandi, 1824, in
    G. Radiciotti, ed., *Lettere inedite di celebri musicisti...*, Milan, 1891.
64 G.-L. Duprez, *Souvenirs d'un Chanteur*, Paris, 1880, p. 79.
65 To Basetti, 14 Jan. 1837, to Bonini, March 1845, BNF CV 345/94, 348/141.
66 To F. Baldisseri, 1843, ibid. 344/63.
67 Duprez, *Souvenirs*, pp. 85–6.
68 Antonio Lanari to Pacini, 20 April 1862, Fondo Pacini, Biblioteca Comunale,
    Pescia.
69 Lanari's Paris agency was run in partnership with Lorini, an agent who
    specialised in American business: BNF CV 405/55.
70 Gazzuoli to N. Dottori, 31 July 1836, ibid. 364/91.
71 Alessandro Magotti, 1875, Biblioteca dell'Archiginnasio Coll. Autografi XLI
    11.102.

3 An industry in a hierarchical society

1 Cambiasi, *La Scala*, pp. xiii–xviii; prospectus of joint-stock *impresa*, 1780, ASB
   Assunteria di Camera, Diversorum, t. 128; Ferrari, *Spettacoli in Parma*, pp.
   89–90; Künigl to Nobile Associazione del Teatro alla Scala, 26 March 1788,
   ASCM Sp. P. 28; Petracchi, *Sul reggimento de'pubblici teatri*, pp. 17–21; E.
   Rosmini, *La Legislazione e la giurisprudenza dei teatri*, 2 vols., Milan, 1872, I,
   p. 171 n.; F. d'Arcais, 'L'Industria musicale', *Nuova Antologia*, 15 May 1879.
2 Berlioz, *Mémoires*, p. 378.
3 Radiciotti, *Rossini*, III, pp. 55–6; A. Asor Rosa, 'La Cultura', in *Storia d'Italia*,
   Einaudi, Turin, 1975, IV pt 2, pp. 964 *et seq.*
4 Government of Lombardy–Venetia to I. R. Chancellery, 20 March 1820,
   ASCM Sp. P. 60/3.
5 Valle, *Cenni teorici-pratici*, pp. 8–10.
6 Cambiasi, *La Scala*.
7 Deputazione dei Pubblici Spettacoli, Bologna, to Commissione Comunale, 12
   Jan. 1850, ASB ASC Dep. Pub. Sp. tit. I rub. I, 1850.
8 Lady Morgan, *Italy*, 2 vols., London, 1821, I, p. 102; Count Giuseppe
   Rangone to Count Francesco Rangone, Venice, 21, 24 Dec. 1835, Archiginnasio Carte Rangone B2827.
9 G. Crocioni, *I Teatri di Reggio nell'Emilia*, Reggio Emilia, 1907, pp. 66, 115,
   117.
10 Robinson, *Naples and Neapolitan Opera*, p. 9; Mme de Boigne, *Mémoires*, ed.
    J.-C. Berchet, Paris, 2 vols., 1971, I, pp. 291–2, quoted in Basso, ed., *Teatro
    Regio*, II, pp. 148–9.
11 Basso, ed., *Teatro Regio*, I, pp. 211–14; ASN Teatri f. 98, Barbaja to
    Soprintendente, 18 Nov. 1819, Min. Interno II inv. f. 4355, Barbaja petitions,
    1822–3.
12 Curiel, *Teatro San Pietro*, pp. 21–5, 142–3; C. Bottura, *Storia del Teatro
    Comunale di Trieste*, Trieste, 1885, pp. 107–8 n., 119, 293.

13 Contracts, 24 Dec. 1823, 31 Oct. 1829, Paterni–Capranica correspondence, ASCR Archivio Capranica b. 469; Notificazioni della Deputazione dei Pubblici Spettacoli, Teatri Valle e Metastasio, 16 March 1842, 4 Dec. 1846, Biblioteca dell'Istituto di Storia dell'Arte e Archeologia, Rome, Manifesti teatrali.

14 Tiby, *Teatro Carolino*, pp. 21–2; Mocenigo, *La Fenice*, pp.24–5; lists of box subscribers at the Teatro Apollo, Rome, C1848, Biblioteca dell' Istituto di Storia dell'Arte e Archeologia, Manifesti teatrali; and at the Teatro Valle, 1824, 1831–2, 1835, 1838, ASCR Archivio Capranica b. 469 (causa Paterni) and BTBR Fondo Capranica borderò, bilanci 8–12.

15 ASL Segreteria di Stato e di Gabinetto f. 87 no. 432, capitolato del Teatro Castglioncelli (early 19th century); G. Radiciotti, *Teatro, musica e musicisti in Recanati*, Recanati, 1904, pp. 12–21 (1823 plan for new theatre, by Monaldo Leopardi).

16 Cambiasi, *La Scala*; Tiby, *Teatro Carolino*, pp. 21–2; ASB ASC Dep. Pub. Sp. tit. 1 rub. 2, 1852; E. Papi, *Il Teatro Municipale di Piacenza*, no date but *c.* 1912.

17 La Scala stopped discriminating against 'foreigners' in 1797, Modena in 1820, Parma in 1830, Cesena in 1831: Cambiasi, *La Scala*; Gandini, *Modena*; Werklein to Sanvitale, 19 Dec. 1829, ATRP carteggi 1829; A. and L. Raggi, *Il Teatro Comunale di Cesena*, Cesena, 1906, pp. 26–7; Gazzuoli to Lanari, 1838–9, BNF CV 365/51, 58 (on the Teatro Alfieri, Florence).

18 Comando 3.a Divisione Militare to Deputazione, 24 Nov. 1852, ASB ASC Dep. Pub. Sp. tit. 1 rub. 1, 1852.

19 Anonymous pamphlet quoted in Cambiasi, *La Scala*, pp. 83–5.

20 BNF CV 344/41.

21 Pacini, *Memorie artistiche*, p. 20.

22 E. Santoro, *Il Teatro di Cremona*, 4 vols., Cremona, 1969–72, II, p. 114.

23 Lady Morgan, *Italy*, II, p. 411 (on the San Carlino).

24 I. R. Ufficiale Fiscale to Government of Lombardy–Venetia, 3 July 1820, ASCM Sp. P. 60/3.

25 Carlo Porta, 'Olter desgrazzi de Giovannin Bongee'.

26 Admission to the La Scala gallery in carnival seasons from 1823 to 31 varied from 0·65 francs to 0·87 francs; the daily wage of a builder's labourer in those years was 0·77 francs: Cambiasi, *La Scala*; A. De Maddalena, *Prezzi e mercedi a Milano dal 1701 al 1860*, Milan, 1974, p. 420.

27 Vaccaj, *Vita di Vaccaj*, p. 80.

28 A. Pellegrini, *Spettacoli lucchesi nei secoli XVII–XIX*, Lucca, 1914, pp. 514–15; Cambiasi, *La Scala*, pp. 63–4.

29 Ferrari, *Spettacoli in Parma*, p. 208; H. Taine, *Voyage en Italie*, 2 vols., Paris, 1884, I, p. 100.

30 Bonola to Lanari, 10 Oct. 1844, BNF CV 349/72.

31 Maldonati contract, 1789, ASCM Sp. P. 28; Ricci contract, 1811, and correspondence, 1814, ibid. 20.

32 Correspondence of Ricci and Lonati with Commissione Governativa, 1801, ibid. 29.

33 Promemoria serale, Teatro Comunale, Bologna, A1852, Conservatore Delegato to Deputazione, A1854, ASB ASC Dep. Pub. Sp. tit. 1 rub. 1, 1852, 1854.

34 Macchi and Maldonati progetti d'appalto, 1788, 1789, ASCM Sp. P. 28; Government of Lombardy–Venetia to Marchese Cagnola, 1 Feb. 1820, ibid. 60/3.

35 These were the contrasting arrangements in Venice at La Fenice (owned by the boxholders) at all times, and at the San Luca (owned by the Vendramin

family, with boxes owned by others) for an *opera seria* season in P1816: Museo Civico Correr, Venice, MSS PD buste C1419.

36 Valle, *Cenni teorici-pratici*, pp. 5–6, 189. Under a law of 1863 cash lotteries were allowed (subject to authorisation by the prefect) and prizes in kind forbidden; ASF Prefettura di Firenze, 1869, f. 164, 1870, f. 145.

37 Contracts for *impresa* of the Teatro del Cocomero, Florence, 1764–1806, ASCF f. 8374; Morini, *La Pergola*, pp. 29–31, 60–1, 103–6.

38 Radiciotti, *Sinigaglia*, pp. 21 *et seq.*; Gandini, *Modena*, I, pp. 82–3.

39 Hester Lynch Piozzi, formerly Thrale, *Observations and Reflections made in the course of a Journey to France, Italy, and Germany*, 2 vols., London, 1789, I, p. 89.

40 Valle, *Cenni teorici-pratici*, pp. iii–vi, 180–91.

41 C. Ivanovich, *Minerva al tavolino*, Venice, 1681, pp. 407–8; official statements of 1755, Rinaldi, *Argentina*, I, p. 91, and 1827, ASR Camerale III Teatri b. 2131, Teatro Capranica/24; Gazzuoli to Lanari, 23 Feb. 1837, BNF CV 364/118; Regli, *Dizionario biografico*, pp. xii–xiv; 'Il Liuto', 7 Nov. 1874, in Rinaldi, *Argentina*, II, p. 1069; D'Arcais, 'L'Industria musicale'.

42 Bandini to Sanvitale, 23 Sep. 1819, ATRP carteggi 1819.

43 W. J. Baumol and W. G. Bowen, *Performing Arts – The Economic Dilemma*, New York, 1966.

44 D'Arcais, 'L'Industria musicale', gave a model budget for a theatre such as the Regio, Turin, or the Carlo Felice, Genoa (both comparable to theatres in Table 1) which breaks down as follows:

Soloists	52
Music	8
Orchestra and chorus	20
Production	10
Other	10

45 Radiciotti, *Rossini*, I, p. 177; Berlioz, *Voyage musical en Allemagne et en Italie*, Paris, 1844, p. 164, and *Mémoires*, ch. 39; Verdi, *Copialettere*, pp. 681–2.

46 Basso, ed., *Teatro Regio*, II, pp. 674–7.

47 Robinson, *Naples and Neapolitan Opera*, pp. 63–4.

48 Rosmini, *Legislazione*, II, pp. 248 *et seq.*, 285 *et seq.* For Bellini's and Verdi's fees: Bellini, *Epistolario*, pp. 414–16, 488; Verdi, *Copialettere*, pp. 3, 5, 26–31, 35, 459–62.

49 ASCR Archivio Capranica b. 469, causa Paterni; BTBR Fondo Capranica, Capranica to Albertazzi, 29 Oct. 1832, to Barbaja, 22 Sep. 1835.

50 Lanari to E. Marzi, 15 April 1849, BNF CV 393/58; M. Barbieri Nini to Luigi Ronzi, 11 Jan. 1853, MTS Coll. Casati 45.

51 Correspondence of Capranica with A. Cuniberti and P. Cartoni, 1825–6, BTBR Fondo Capranica.

52 Basso, ed., *Teatro Regio*, I, p. 267 n.

53 At the Senigallia Fair – a season generally of twenty performances – the tenor Donzelli was paid 12,000 francs in 1835, nearly three times the highest fee recorded in the early 1820s (paid to the almost equally famous tenor Nicola Tacchinardi in 1823): Balducci to Lanari, 1835, BNF CV 346/14; Radiciotti, *Sinigaglia*.

54 To and from Alessandro Lanari, 1849, BNF CV 346/138, 393/55–60.

55 Verdi, *Copialettere*, p. 207.

56 Cametti, *Apollo*, I, pp. 255, 259.

57 Velluti, last of the great castrati, was paid 16,000 francs at La Fenice in

C1822, and then – without any intervening loss of reputation – 8,000 francs at the Grande, Trieste, in A1823: Bottura, *Comunale di Trieste*, p. 111.

58 Pasta received 1,000 francs per performance at La Fenice in CQ1833, as did Ronzi at the Valle, Rome, in P1836, and the tenor Mongini at La Scala in Q1860, while Malibran got about 1,080 francs a night at Senigallia in F1834: ATLaF Processi verbali convocazioni b. 5; BTBR Fondo Capranica (Ronzi); Mongini contract, ASCM Sp. P. 112/1; Radiciotti, *Sinigaglia*.

59 Merelli to Lanari, 17 Nov. 1828, BNF CV 395/178.

60 Based on L. Barilli to G. Morandi, 23 Dec. 1820, in Radiciotti, *Lettere inedite*, p. 44, and on actual takings (exclusive of subscriptions) of thirteen performances in July and twelve performances in December 1821: AN AJ^{13} 162, recettes journalières.

61 Takings for Jan. and April 1818, AN AJ^{13} 151; Quicherat, *Nourrit*, I, pp. 90, 101.

62 Figures for two performances of *Les Huguenots*, 1836, the first ten performances with Duprez of *Guillaume Tell*, 1837, and the first nineteen performances of Donizetti's *Dom Sébastien*, 1843: Quicherat, *Nourrit*, I, p. 262; H. Weinstock, *Rossini*, London, 1968, pp. 447–8, and *Donizetti*, London, 1963, pp. 195–6.

63 Prices in this and succeeding paragraphs are taken from the sources named in Table 6 and, for the Teatro Valle, from: ASR Camerale III Teatri b. 2138/2, 3, 16, 18; ASCR Archivio Capranica b. 513; Biblioteca dell'Istituto di Storia dell'Arte e Archeologia, Manifesti teatrali. Box prices used are for the best boxes in each tier.

64 Based on the price of boxes in the third tier, the only one for which the sources yield a near-complete series from 1802. Prices in other tiers, where they are available, seem to have moved at roughly the same rate.

65 Deputazione degli Spettacoli to Minister of the Interior, 23 Dec. 1823, ASN Min. Interno II inv. f. 4355. After 1823 there were variations in subscription prices, but strictly in proportion to changing numbers of performances. In the 1830s Barbaja was allowed to raise prices on special occasions up to twenty-four times a year.

66 President of the Società Proprietaria del Gran Teatro La Fenice, ATLaF Processi verbali convocazioni b. 3 (seduta 23 Apr. 1822).

67 Petracchi, *Sul reggimento de' pubblici teatri*, p. 173; Santley, *Student and Singer*, pp. 114–15.

68 ATLaF Processi verbali convocazioni b. 5, Spettacoli b. 3. Pasta did agree to give thirty-five instead of the stipulated forty performances, so saving the impresario 5,000 francs.

69 Cf. the Teatro Sociale, Voghera, a small-town theatre run on a shoestring by the boxholders, with increasing dependence on municipal subsidy but away from central government concerns: there the *ingresso* price went up more steadily, by 30% in 1848, 27% in 1862, 21% in 1873, and 25% in 1876: Maragliano, *Teatri di Voghera*.

70 Bottura, *Comunale di Trieste*, pp. 251, 254; Basso, ed., *Teatro Regio*, II, pp. 266–77.

71 Contract with Gaetano Maldonati, 31 July 1789, and preceding correspondence, ASCM Sp. P. 28.

72 Commissione Governativa per i Teatri, verbale seduta 20 Feb. 1821, ASCM Sp. P. 60.

73 The impresario of the Valle, Paterni enjoyed a kind of indirect subsidy, however: as impresario of the Apollo (C1831, C1834) he received a subsidy,

and his lease of the outdoor Anfiteatro Corea (used for bull-baiting, bareback riding, and fireworks) had been returned to him by the government on his surrendering the concession of weights and measures: ASR Camerale III Teatri b. 2137/25, 45.

74 BNF CV 393/117; S. Dalla Libera, 'Cronologia del Teatro La Fenice', p. 140, ATLaF.

75 Lanari to Merelli, 9 Jan. 1839, BNF CV 396/15.

76 Radiciotti, *Sinigaglia*, pp. 204–5.

77 Basso, ed., *Teatro Regio*, II, pp. 199–202, 266–77.

78 ATLaF Processi verbali convocazioni b. 3, 5, Sussidio comunale b. 1–3, Dalla Libera, 'Cronologia' and 'La Presidenza del Teatro La Fenice'.

79 Lanari to Donizetti, 19 Aug. 1836, *Studi Donizettiani*, III, 1978, p. 37.

80 C. de Boigne, *Petits mémoires de l'Opéra*, Paris, 1857, pp. 300–3; Quicherat, *Nourrit*, I, 179.

81 Poster dated 10 Apr. 1848, quoted in Rosmini, *Legislazione*, II, p. 38 n.

82 Count Künigl to Nobile Associazione del Teatro alla Scala, 26 March 1788, ASCM Sp. P. 28.

83 Rosmini, *Legislazione*, I, pp. 162–72.

84 G. Pannain in Comune di Napoli, *Il Teatro San Carlo*, Naples, 1951; Mocenigo, *La Fenice*; Morini, *La Pergola*. For general accounts see J. Budden, *The Operas of Verdi*, 3 vols., London, 1973–81, III, pp. 267–70, and M. Conati and G. Armani in S. Romagnoli and E. Garbero, eds., *Teatro a Reggio Emilia*, Florence, 1980, II.

85 H. Rosenthal, ed., *The Mapleson Memoirs*, London, 1966, pp. 172–3; MTS Canedi contracts, 1872–3, 1875, with A. Padovani and I. Giovannetti.

86 G. Depanis, *I Concerti popolari e il Teatro Regio di Torino*, 2 vols., Turin, 1914–15, II, pp. 40–1; MTS Coll. Casati 1082 (Stagno); A. Scalaberni to G. Marchetti, Nov. 1889, Piancastelli Autografi s.v. Marchetti; Santley, *Student and Singer*, pp. 89–90.

87 Cf. fees of little over 200 francs per performance for which the well-known prima donna Teresina Brambilla the younger was willing to sing at La Pergola in 1883: to Ponchielli, MTS CA 2536; and of 1,500 francs or 2,000 francs for a carnival season, paid to second-rank singers at (by then) second-rank theatres in Reggio Emilia and Bari: Candio and Rocchi contracts, Archiginnasio Coll. Autografi XLI 11.107.

88 To the Minister Guido Baccelli, 4 Feb. 1883, *Copialettere*, pp. 321–2.

4 The strong arm of authority

1 Contract with Gaetano Andreozzi, 11 March 1806, ASN Teatri f. 98.

2 Duke of Noja to Minister of the Interior, 30 April 1821, ASN Min. Interno II inv. f. 4355; Janni, *Belli*, II, p. 657; Cambiasi, *La Scala*, pp. 59–63; Maldonati petition, 22 Dec. 1789, ASCM Sp. P. 28.

3 Robinson, *Naples and Neapolitan Opera*, pp. 7–8.

4 Count Strassoldo, President of the Government of Lombardy–Venetia, to the Viceroy Archduke Rainer, 1 Aug. 1825, ASCM Sp. P. 56.

5 Deputazione degli Spettacoli to Pope Gregory XVI, 1834, quoted in Cametti, *Apollo*, I, pp. 244–5.

6 Vaccaj, *Vita di Vaccaj*, pp. 80–1.

7 G. Cassi, *Il Cardinale Consalvi ed i primi anni della restaurazione pontificia (1815–1819)*, Milan, 1931, p. 153.

8 Ferrari, *Spettacoli in Parma*, p. 175; ordnance of Gen. Menou, 8 Sep. 1808, Maire of Florence to Accademia degli Infuocati, 16 Sep. 1808, ASCF f. 8278 no. 84; Morini, *La Pergola*, pp. 110–11; E. Consalvi, *Memorie*, ed. M. Nasalli Rocca di Corneliano, Rome, 1950, pp. 149–51.

9 Cambiasi, *La Scala*, pp. 63–4.

10 ATLaF, Dalla Libera, 'La Presidenza del Teatro La Fenice', Processi verbali convocazioni b. 5, Sussidio comunale b. 1–3. (The composer was Coccia, proposed for C1832, the proposed Pasta season C1838; the mayor chiefly involved was Count Giacomo Correr).

11 Capranica to Pistoni, 19 Sep. 1826, other 1826 correspondence, BTBR Fondo Capranica.

12 ASB ASC Dep. Pub. Sp. tit. 1 rub. 1, 1850–4.

13 Gazzuoli to Lanari, 1835, BNF CV 364/86.

14 ASN Min. Interno II inv. f. 4355, *passim*.

15 ATRP carteggi 1819, 1829, *passim*.

16 Correspondence of Lanari, Count Amici-Pasquini, and Cardinal Albani, Feb. 1834, BNF CV 343/10.

17 Valle, *Cenni teorici-pratici*, pp. 11–24.

18 Eugenio Cavallini, maestro direttore, to Direzione, 9 April 1857, MTS CA 1063. (The impresari were Cattaneo and Pirola.)

19 Bandini, 'Progetto per l'appalto...osservazioni', 12 Oct. 1830, Count Stefano Sanvitale, 'Osservazioni...ai progetti...', 18 Oct. 1830, ATRP carteggi 1830.

20 Anon., 'Riflessioni intorno al quaderno de' patti compilato da S. E. il sig. Presidente delle Finanze', ibid.

21 Deputazione to Cesare Aria, maestro direttore of the Teatro Contavalli, 29 Dec. 1853, ASB ASC Dep. Pub. Sp. tit. 1 rub. 3, 1853.

22 Panzieri to Lanari, 23 June 1827, CV 400/46; Lanari to Donizetti, 23 June 1837, *Studi Donizettiani*, III, p. 52.

23 Rosmini, *Legislazione*, I, pp. 138–9, 140–2.

24 Luigi Alberti to Pacini, 8 Dec. 1855, Fondo Pacini no. 1139 (about *Margherita Pusterla*, San Carlo, Naples, C1856).

25 Rosmini, *Legislazione*, I, pp. 130–3 (case of Luigi Granci, 1842).

26 Baucardè and Crivelli to Deputazione, 3, 4 Dec. 1855, ASB ASC Dep. Pub. Sp. tit. 1 rub. 1, 1855.

27 Claudio Musi to Direttore, Parma, 17 Dec. 1844, ATRP carteggi 1844.

28 Vaccaj, *Vita di Vaccaj*, p. 112; BNF CV 343/139. For an early eighteenth-century view, see B. Marcello, *Il Teatro alla moda*, ed. A. D'Angeli, Milan, 1956, pp. 47–51. Much has been made in lives of Donizetti of the contralto Rosina Mazzarelli, whose part in *Pia de' Tolomei* had to be built up at the request of her 'protector' Giuseppe Berti, the La Fenice director in charge of productions. But Mazzarelli was a good singer and Lanari, then impresario, had her under four-year contract, so it may have suited him to use Berti's importunity as an excuse: Lanari–Donizetti correspondence, *Studi Donizettiani*, III, *passim*.

29 Gazzuoli to Lanari, 27 May 1837, BNF CV 364/143; to Pacini from Antonio Lanari, 28 March, from A. Ghina, 28 April 1857, Fondo Pacini nos. 968–9, 1000.

30 To Giorgio Frilli, 3 Jan. 1802, Accademia degli Infuocati, Copialettere, ASCF f. 8364.

31 Gazzuoli to Lanari, April 1837, BNF CV 364/129.

32 Lasina to Brenna, 6 Oct. 1851, and other correspondence. ATLaF Spettacoli b. 26; Lasina correspondence with V. Ortalli Laurent, President of Commissione Amministrativa, Parma, ATRP carteggi 1870.

33 ATLaF Processi verbali convocazioni b. 3 (1823).

34 To Donizetti, 25 Sep. 1837, *Studi Donizettiani*, III, p. 60.

35 ATLaF Processi verbali convocazioni b. 3, 5, Spettacoli b. 3. The former director was Count Tomà Mocenigo Soranzo, speaking in 1822.

36 Count Filippo Agucchi, head (conservatore delegato) of Deputazione, Bologna, to Senatore of Bologna, 23 March 1852, ASB, ASC Dep. Pub. Sp. tit. 1 rub. 1, 1852.

37 Merelli to Lanari, 15 Jan. 1839, BNF CV 396/87.

38 Gazzuoli to Lanari, 7 Nov.1837, ibid. 365/10.

39 Verdi to Tornielli, 12 May 1856, in D. Valeri *et al.*, *Verdi e la Fenice*, Venice, 1951, p. 53.

40 ASR, *Collezione di carte pubbliche, proclami, editti…[della] Repubblica Romana*, Rome, Year VII (1799), II, pp. 532–5.

41 Faenza free list and correspondence, Piancastelli 130.184, 200; 'Piano degli esenti…nel Pubblico Teatro Nuovo', 1763, contract with G. Mienci, 1769, ASB Assunteria di Camera, Diversorum, t. 128; Radiciotti, *Sinigaglia*, p. 192.

42 Maldonati contract, ASCM Sp. P. 28.

43 'Stato nominativo dei signori esenti…', ATRP carteggi 1829. See also Basso, ed., *Teatro Regio*, II, p. 660.

44 E.g. the impresari of the three main Florence theatres after an increase in the free list in 1806: ASF Segreteria di Stato 292 prot. 1 no. 2, 305 prot. 81 no. 4.

45 G. Cosentino, *Il Teatro Marsigli-Rossi*, Bologna, 1900, pp. 143–7; A. Comandini, *L'Italia nei 100 anni del secolo XIX giorno per giorno*, Milan, 1901–2, 29 Jan. 1806.

46 Correspondence of Presidenza of La Fenice and Prefect, 24 Sep., 22, 26 Dec. 1806, ASV Pref. dell'Adriatico b. 26; Presidenza to Direzione of Teatro Grande, Brescia, 1854, ATLaF Autografi diversi; Brunelli, *Teatri di Padova*, p. 379; Prefect of Arno to Minister of Police, 9 Jan. 1812, AN F⁷ 3655; Bulletin de police, Turin 7 nivose XIV (27 Dec. 1805), AN F⁷ 3817; Basso, ed., *Teatro Regio*, II, pp. 69 n., 112–13; Proclamation of Gen. Reille, Florence 6 April 1801, ASF Leggi e bandi.

47 Municipio di Napoli, *Concessione d'esercizio per le stagioni teatrali 1889–90 e 1890–91, Quaderno di oneri per la concessione del Teatro San Carlo* in the Biblioteca Lucchesi-Palli, Naples.

48 Ferrari, *Spettacoli in Parma*, p. 91.

49 Gazzuoli to Lanari, Feb. 1837, Jan. 1839, BNF CV 364/111, 365/63; V. Frajese, *Dal Costanzi all'Opera*, 4 vols., Rome,1977–8, I, p. 37.

50 Rosmini, *Legislazione*, I, ch. 5, II, p. 249.

51 M. Lavagetto, *Un Caso di censura: il 'Rigoletto'*, Milan, 1979.

52 Pacini, *Memorie artistiche*, p. 11; Presidenza of La Fenice to Verdi, 26 July 1843, Dalla Libera, 'Ernani–Cronologia', ATLaF. See also Radiciotti, *Rossini*, I, pp. 138, 269–70.

53 B. Brunelli, *I Teatri di Padova*, Padua, 1921, pp. 422–3; Ferrari, *Parma*, p. 116.

54 Gazzuoli to Lanari, Dec. 1836, BNF CV 364/104–7.

55 Dalla Libera, 'Ernani – Cronologia', ATLaF.

56 Angelo Tinti to Lanari, Bologna, 22 Nov. 1833, BNF CV 411/177.

57 C. Rossi-Gallieno, *Saggio di economia teatrale*, Milan, 1839, p. 30.
58 Many sets of regulations are printed in theatre histories, e.g. Ferrari, *Parma*, pp. 86, 94–5, 103; Cambiasi, *La Scala, passim*; Radiciotti, *Sinigaglia*, pp. 190–7. For the republican and Napoleonic period, see also ASCM Gride 6/123, MTS CA 244.
59 Pacini, *Memorie artistiche*, pp. 34–8 (*Alessandro nelle Indie*, San Carlo, Naples, 1824); Bellini, *Epistolario*, p. 79 (*Bianca e Fernando*, Carlo Felice, Genoa, 1828).
60 Brunelli, *Teatri di Padova*, pp. 327–8.
61 Pacini, *Memorie artistiche*, pp. 46–7; F. Melzi d'Eril to Marescalchi, 17 Dec. 1802, Melzi d'Eril, *Carteggi*, ed. C. Zaghi, 9 vols., Milan, 1958–66, III, p. 239.
62 A. Cametti, *Un Poeta melodrammatico romano (G. Ferretti)*, Milan, 1898, p. 212.
63 Ferrari, *Spettacoli in Parma*, pp. 174, 229; C. Masini to Deputazione, 30 Oct. 1853, Notificazione, 29 Sep. 1854, ASB ASC Dep. Pub. Sp. tit. I rub. 3, 1853, tit. II rub. 2, 1854.
64 Petitions of Maldonati, 22 Dec. 1789, ASCM Sp. P. 28; of Teatro Valle impresari, 1786, ASR Camerale III Teatri b. 2138 no. 12; of Barbaja, 17 Jan. 1822, ASN Min. Interno II inv. f. 4355.
65 Barbaja to Soprintendenza, 8, 12 April 1822, ASN Teatri f. 98 (arrest of minor singer for refusing to sing in the chorus); Deputazione to Minister, 10 June 1825, ASN Min. Interno II inv. f. 4356 (arrest of choreographer Henry and leading dancers Samengo and Brugnoli over failure to dance a *pas de deux* which had been announced); Gandini, *Modena*, I, p. 149; Crocioni, *Reggio nell' Emilia*, p. 71; Pasolini-Zanelli, *Faenza*, p. 67 (arrest of Giorgio Ronconi for giving an encore without permission); Brunelli, *Teatri di Padova*, pp. 432–3; Santley, *Student and Singer*, pp. 79–81; Ferrari, *Parma*, p. 102.
66 Promemoria serale per lo spettacolo autunnale 1852, Teatro Comunale, Bologna, ASB ASC Dep. Pub. Sp. tit. I rub. 1, 1853; Soprintendente to Minister, 14 Dec. 1817, ASN Min. Interno II inv. f. 4353; Vaccaj, *Vita di Vaccaj*, pp. 110–11.
67 A. Mackenzie-Grieve, *Clara Novello*, London, 1954, p. 119.
68 Gioanni Tacconi to Count Francesco Conti, 5 April 1788, Piancastelli 130.13.
69 L. Badolisani, *Per la signora Donna Luigia Boccabadati...*, Naples, 1832 in the Biblioteca della Società Napoletana di Storia Patria; ASN Giustizia, Decisioni civili f. 95, 27 March 1832.
70 Cambiasi, *La Scala*, p. 49; B. Gutierrez, *Il Teatro Carcano (1803–1914)*, Milan, 1914, pp. 41–3; Crocioni, *Reggio nell'Emilia*, pp. 51–4; ASCM Sp. P. 56 correspondence on arrest of Angelo Petracchi, 1819.
71 Noja to Minister, 30 April 1821, ASN Min. Interno II inv. f. 4355; Pacini, *Memorie artistiche*, pp. 58–9; Lanari to Presidenza of La Fenice, 16 Dec. 1831, ATLaF Spettacoli b. 3.
72 Balochino to Giorgio Ronconi, 18 Nov. 1839, Wiener Stadtbibliothek.
73 Barbaja to Panzieri, 12 July 1827, BNF CV 344/118; Radiciotti, *Sinigaglia*, pp. 92–3, 97; Rinaldi, *Argentina*, I, pp. 362–5.
74 Correspondence of 1826–7, BTBR Fondo Capranica; Basso, ed., *Teatro Regio*, II, p. 294; ATLaF Autografi diversi, s. v. Fanny Cerrito.
75 Rosmini, *Legislazione*, I, ch. 4, and pp. 2, 13–15, 336–7; correspondence of Prefect and Direzione of the Teatro Comunale, Parma, March 1870, ATRP carteggi 1870.
76 ASB ASC Dep. Pub. Sp. tit. I rub. 1, 3, 1860, *passim*.

77 Gandini, *Modena*, II; Raggi, *Cesena*, p. 132; Ferrari, *Parma*, pp. 246, 252, 257–8, 267, 271, 290, 295, 312.

5 The impresario as businessman

1 Verdi, *Copialettere*, p. 215 n. The impresario was Luigi Scalaberni.
2 Rosmini, *Legislazione*, I, pp. 196 *et seq.*
3 D'Arcais, 'L'Industria musicale', not very different from the satirical account of 159 years earlier in Marcello, *Teatro alla moda*, pp. 47–51.
4 Rossi-Gallieno, *Saggio di economia teatrale*, p. 22 n.
5 Papers of Faenza *impresa*, 1788, Piancastelli 130.1–14, 39–79, 119, 180, 184, 212; Rinaldi, *Argentina*, I, p. 346. Rinaldi refers to Caldesi as Calvesi; so does a Notificazione of 6 Dec. 1801 in the Biblioteca Casanatense, Rome, Editti. It is not clear whether he should be identified with the Vincenzo Calvesi who sang tenor parts in Vienna in 1785–6 and 1790–1 and created the part of Ferrando in *Così fan tutte*.
6 Cametti, *Apollo*, II, p. 396.
7 ASB ASC Dep. Pub. Sp. tit. 1 rub. 2, 1853. The lessee was Pasquale Brunetti, the nominee Antonio Magotti.
8 Examples of the first kind proposed to the baritone Giovanni Marchetti by the impresario F. Radicchi (for Chieti, P1886) and F. Moreno (for somewhere in Tuscany or Romagna, P1887), Piancastelli Autografi s.v. Marchetti; of the second kind, between the débutante soprano Zaira Tamburini and the (ultimately defaulting) impresario Salani, Teatro Contavalli, Bologna, P1860, ASB ASC Dep. Pub. Sp. tit. 1 rub. 3, 1860.
9 Somigli–Lanari correspondence, Dec. 1836, BNF CV 410/151.
10 To Lanari from Panzieri, June 1827, BNF CV 400/44, 47; from Tacchinardi, 9 April 1830, MTS Coll. Casati 1129.
11 Lanari to Merelli, 9 Jan. 1838, BNF CV 396/15.
12 Correspondence of Lanari with Crivelli, Merelli, and G. B. Villa, 1828–39, ibid. 358/142 *et seq.*, 396/7, 15, 32, 415/178, 180.
13 Correspondence of Lanari with F. Baldisseri, L. Campigli, and A. Gazzuoli, 1835–7, ibid. 345/161, 346/87, 351/162, 364/105–50.
14 See J. A. Davis, *Società e imprenditori nel Regno Borbonico 1815–1860*, Rome and Bari, 1979, pp. 148 *et seq.*
15 Foglio di associazione per un dramma serio in musica da rappresentarsi nel nuovo Pubblico Teatro la primavera dell'anno 1780 (printed prospectus), ASB Assunteria di Camera, Diversorum, t. 128. There seems to have been no 1780 season at the Comunale, Bologna: Trezzini, ed., *Due secoli di vita musicale*, II.
16 *Proposta di una società commerciale in anonimo per la intrapresa dei RR. Teatri*, and *Progetto di statuto della Compagnia d'Industria e Belle Arti*, both Naples, 1834, both in the British Library; Larussa, *Sulle cagioni del decadimento*, pp. 7–9; *Almanacco de' RR. Teatri...1834*; Zavadini, *Donizetti*, pp. 373–83; Lanari's correspondence with the Prince of Torella and with F. Capecelatro and Taglioni, BNF CV 352/175, 411/108.
17 Marchese Domenico Andreotti to Lanari, 28 Oct. 1837, BNF CV 343/35; [A. Starace], *Per alcuni socii nella impresa de' RR. Teatri contro il signor Domenico Barbaja socio impresario*, Naples, 1839, in the British Library.
18 A. Larussa, *Poche idee spontanee in rapporto alli teatri*, Naples, 1850; V. Torelli to Pacini, 2 Feb. 1858, Fondo Pacini no. 1080.
19 Andreotti to Lanari, Oct. 1837, Aug. 1838, BNF CV 343/35, 42.

20 Prospectus of Società Impresaria Romandiolo-Picena, ASB ASC Dep. Pub. Sp. tit. IV rub. 2, 1855; *Teatro Arti e Letteratura*, 1856, 1861.
21 Coccetti to Lanari, Lanari to Pecori, both 1849, BNF CV 353/169, 400/162.
22 Lanari to Torella and Capecelatro, April 1834, ibid. 352/175; Jacovacci to Pippo [Cencetti?], 1850, Piancastelli Autografi s. v. Jacovacci.
23 Correspondence of Lanari, Camuri, Ghelli, and A. Marchesi, BNF CV 365/120, 123–4, 132.
24 P. De'Capitani, minute on Government of Lombardy to I. R. Chancellery, 2 June 1828, ASCM Sp. P. 56.
25 Brunelli, *Teatri di Padova*, pp. 211–12, 271 *et seq.*
26 To Lanari from C. Brendoli, Leghorn, June 1841, from Gazzuoli, Bologna, Dec. 1836, BNF CV 350/43–4, 364/98, 100.
27 A. Vitti to Marchetti, Piancastelli Autografi s. v. Marchetti.
28 G. Cottrau, *Lettres d'un mélomane*, Naples, 1885, p. 24; A. Tassinari to Jacovacci, 6 June 1841, Piancastelli 690.69.
29 G. B. Cavalcaselle, *Tipi di scritture teatrali attraverso luoghi e tempi diversi*, Rome, 1919; Rosmini, *Legislazione*, I, p. 417.
30 Valle, *Cenni teorici-pratici*, pp. 24–34, 85–8, 91.
31 Barbaja maintained in 1837 that the writ of the Milan *camerino* still ran, but he had been out of north-central Italy for many years and was probably mistaken (or else was prevaricating): to Lanari, 6 Aug. 1837, BNF CV 344/167.
32 Draft contract, 1782, identical with actual contract of 1769 with G. Mienci, ASB Assunteria di Camera, Diversorum, t.128.
33 Cambiasi, *La Scala*, pp. 234–40; contracts for impresa of Cocomero, Florence, 1775–95, ASCF f. 8374; *Prospetti di appalto per lo R. Teatro S. Carlo*, in the Biblioteca Lucchesi-Palli, Naples; Consiglio comunale, Naples, deliberazione 20 May 1884, ASN Prefettura di Napoli f. 3487.
34 Depanis, *Concerti popolari*, I, pp. 171–2, II, pp. 66–7.
35 Balochino–Crivelli contract for La Scala and Cannobiana, 1820, ASCM Sp. P. 60/3; Guillaume contract for RR. Teatri, Naples, 1846, ASN Min. Interno II inv. f. 4359; De Nicola, *Diario napoletano*, 16, 28 Feb. 1816.
36 Valle, *Cenni teorici-pratici*, pp. 107 *et seq.*; Rinaldi, *Argentina*, I, pp. 474, 476; F. Montignani to Sanvitale, June–July 1819, ATRP carteggi 1819.
37 Gazzuoli to Lanari, 22 Feb. 1839, BNF CV 365/77.
38 Basso, ed., *Teatro Regio*, II, pp. 173–5; Rosmini, *Legislazione*, I, pp. 147–52, 265–71 (cases of 1858, 1864, 1865).
39 Rosmini, *Legislazione*, II, pp. 43–4, 364–5.
40 Cametti, *Apollo*, I, pp. 252–7; Antonio Lanari to Pacini, 20 April 1862, Fondo Pacini no. 1322. See also Notificazione by Reggente di Giustizia e Polizia di Roma e Giudice Privativo dei Teatri, 27 Feb. 1800, Biblioteca Casanatense, Rome, Editti; Gutierrez, *Teatro Carcano*, pp. 41–3.
41 G. Monaldi, *Impresari celebri del secolo XIX*, Rocca S. Casciano, 1918, p. 190; D'Arcais, 'L'Industria teatrale'.
42 Piozzi, *Observations and Reflections*, II, p. 139.
43 F. Bosdari, 'La Vita musicale a Bologna nel periodo napoleonico', *L'Archiginnasio*, Bologna, IX, 1914, pp. 16–17; ASB ASC Dep. Pub. Sp. tit. I rub. 7, 1850–60, *passim*.
44 Gaetano Bruni, impresario of Teatro Contavalli, Bologna, to Cesare Guermani, leader of the orchestra, 14 March 1850, ASB ASC Dep. Pub. Sp. tit. II rub. 7, 1850.

45 Ibid. rub. 1, 1854, rub. 7, 1855.
46 Lanari to P. Balducci, 17 May 1836, BNF CV 346/56.
47 Ibid. 42–56.
48 L. M. Viviani to Lanari, 23 Jan. 1836, ibid. 416/121.
49 H. Sachs, *Toscanini*, London, 1978, pp. 34, 46–7.
50 To Lanari from A. Bonini and from the Canovetti, 1833, 1841, 1845, BNF CV 348/137, 352/145–50.
51 ASB ASC Dep. Pub. Sp. tit. 1 rub. 2, 1852, 1853.
52 Contracts, 1764, 1770, 1775, ASCF f. 8374.
53 Contracts with Barbaja, 1822, 1824, with Guillaume, 1840, 1843, with Winter, 1848, with Prestreau, 1861, Commissione Amministrativa dei RR. Teatri di Napoli, 'Condizioni generali...alla concessione...', ASN Teatri f. 98, f. 105, Min. Interno II inv. f. 4359; *Quaderno di oneri per la concessione del Teatro San Carlo, 1889–91, Impresa Teatro San Carlo e masse orchestrali*, Naples, 1892, both in the Biblioteca Lucchesi-Palli.
54 Dr Paolo Cantoni, inspector of the Teatro del Corso, to Deputazione, 29 March 1855, ASB ASC Dep. Pub. Sp. tit. 1 rub. 2, 1855.
55 A. Carcano, 'Progetto d'ordinamento delle masse corali e d'orchestra del Teatro Comunale di Roma', 28 Nov. 1872, ASCR tit. xv. See also Lady Morgan, *Italy*, I, p. 269; *Mapleson Memoirs*, p. 262; Rossi-Gallieno, *Saggio di economia teatrale*, pp. 49–50; chorus regulations, Bologna 1852, Ravenna 1855, ASB ASC Dep. Pub. Sp. tit. 1 rub. 1, 1853 (Promemoria serale Autunno 1852), rub. 2, 1855; S. Dalla Libera, 'L'Archivio del Teatro La Fenice', *Ateneo Veneto*, 1 June 1968, p. 143.
56 C. Sardi, *Lucca e il suo Ducato*, Florence, 1912, p. 118; Papi, *Teatro Municipale di Piacenza*, p. 136; Proni, comandante dei Ducali Dragoni, to Sanvitale, 19 May 1829, ATRP carteggi 1829.
57 Gazzuoli to Lanari, 12, 31 Jan. 1839, BNF CV 365/64, 66 (Teatro Alfieri, Florence, C1839).
58 Correspondence of Gaetano Coccetti and Lanari, Jan. 1849, ibid. 353/173–4.
59 Correspondence of Tinti, Deputazione, and chorus, June–July 1860, ASB ASC Dep. Pub. Sp. tit. 1 rub. 1, 1860.
60 Monaldi, *Impresari celebri*, pp. 201–2. See A. Mazzucato to Giraldoni, 5 March 1867, MTS CA 2904 (chorus strike at La Scala).
61 Cencetti to Capranica, 1836, BTBR Fondo Capranica.
62 Gazzuoli to Lanari, 5 Jan. 1839, BNF CV 365/62. The Sartoria Lanari is documented chiefly in correspondence (1836–39) between Lanari and his assistants Antonio Gazzuoli and Francesco Baldisseri, and (in the 1820s) between him and his partner Lorenzo Panzieri: ibid. 343–4, 364–5, 400.
63 L. Dal Pane, *Industria e commercio nel Granducato di Toscana nell'età del Risorgimento*, 2 vols., Bologna, 1971–3, II, pp. 112–13.
64 Lanari to Taglioni, [1834], to Battistini, Nov. 1834, BNF CV 345/131, 411/108.
65 To Campigli, 25 Nov. 1834, to Baldisseri, 5 Dec. 1836, from Battistini, June 1848, ibid. 343/123, 346/117, 351/150.
66 To Lanari from Gazzuoli, 1 Aug., 4 Nov. 1837, from Romani, 1833, ibid. 364/156, 365/1, 405/151, 157.
67 Verdi to Tito Ricordi, 24 Oct. 1855, *Copialettere*, pp. 166–9.
68 Pacini to Jacovacci, 23 March 1861, Piancastelli Autografi s.v. Pacini.
69 Bellini, *Epistolario*, pp. 173–4, 379–80; *Studi Donizettiani*, III, p. 45.
70 Valle, *Cenni teorici-pratici*, pp. 35–45.

71 Goldoni, *La bella verità*, Bologna, 1762; B. Cavalieri, *L'Impresario d'opera*, Pisa, C1770 (music by Guglielmi), G. M. Diodati, *L'Impresario in angustie*, Reggio Calabria, C1789 (music by Cimarosa), both in the Biblioteca dell'Accademia di S. Cecilia, Rome; A. Sografi, *Le Convenienze teatrali*, Venice, 1794; and many others including G. Stephanie, *Der Schauspieldirektor*, Vienna, 1786 (music by Mozart).

72 G. Ricordi to Vaccaj, 9 Feb. 1825, 7 Feb. 1827, 17 Feb., 9 March 1845, Archivio Vaccaj, Biblioteca Comunale, Tolentino.

73 Pavesi to Count G. Melzi, 1, 4, 6 July 1830, MTS CA 4793–5 (the opera was *La Dama bianca d'Avenello*, Cannobiana A1830).

74 Gazzuoli to Lanari, 1836, 1837, BNF CV 364/99, 144. See Depanis, *Concerti popolari*, I, pp. 118–21.

75 Merelli to Lanari, 8 Dec. 1831, BNF CV 396/2.

76 *L'Impresario delle Smirne*, Act IV, scene 4.

77 Santley, *Student and Singer*, pp. 89–90.

78 Sanguineti to Lanari, 8 Jan. 1849, BNF CV 409/77.

79 Lanari to Luigi Pacini, 12 Oct. 1830, Archiginnasio Coll. Autografi LXXXVI; correspondence of Capranica and Giuseppina Ronzi, 1836, BTBR Fondo Capranica.

80 Tacchinardi to Lanari, 29 Jan. 1830, MTS Coll. Casati 1128.

81 Alessandro Magotti to Giordani, 1880, Archiginnasio Coll. Autografi XLI 11.119; Rosmini, *Legislazione*, II, pp. 86–9.

82 Balochino–Tacchinardi Persiani correspondence, 1837–45, Wiener Stadtbibliothek.

83 Rosmini, *Legislazione*, I, pp. 433–4, 436–44.

84 Merelli to Moriani, 30 Oct. 1847, MTS CA 3658; Quicherat, *Nourrit*, I, pp. 404, 433–4, 502.

85 P. Romani to Lanari, [early 1837], BNF CV 405/175.

86 Valle, *Cenni teorici-pratici*, pp. 58–63; Gandini, *Modena*, I, p. 288; contract with prima donna Maria Lafon, La Scala CQ1860 (exemption clause), ASCM Sp. P. 112/1.

87 Rosmini, *Legislazione*, I, pp. 500–1, 519–20. II, pp. 11–18.

88 Rinaldi, *Argentina*, I, p. 408.

89 Gazzuoli to Lanari, Feb. 1837 (Ducale, Parma, C1837, with Duprez), Oct. 1838 (Alfieri, Florence, A1838, with Strepponi), BNF CV 364/106, 111, 365/51–4; Santley, *Student and Singer*, p. 233.

90 Already noted in 1821 by Petracchi, *Sul reggimento de' pubblici teatri*, pp. 82–3.

91 To Lanari, 19 Sep. 1849, in Jarro (G. Piccini), *Memorie d'un impresario fiorentino*, Florence, 1892, p. 73.

92 E. Tadolini to A. Torri, 17 Feb. 1846, ATLaF Autografi diversi; Rigatti to Lanari, 10 Sep. 1851, BNF CV 405/55.

93 Valle, *Cenni teorici-pratici*, pp. 126–8; Rosmini, *Legislazione*, I, pp. 468–70, 509, II, p. 27; to Lanari from Merelli, 9 Oct. 1826, from P. Romani, [1836 to 1837], BNF CV 395/115, 405/171; Badolisani, *Per...Luigia Boccabadati ...*; ASN Giustizia, Decisioni civili f. 95, 27 March 1832; ASB ASC Dep. Pub. Sp. tit. 1 rub. 1, 1855, correspondence with Corticelli about 'indisposition' of Augusta Albertini Baucardè.

94 Contracts, MTS Coll. Casati 1427, 1448, Archiginnasio Coll. Autografi XLI 11.107.

95 Correspondence of Lanari with Barbaja, Merelli, G. B. Villa, 1836–7, BNF CV

344/128–32, 152, 415/180; Balochino to F. Taglioni, 23 Jan. 1836, Wiener Stadtbibliothek; Basso, ed., *Teatro Regio*, I, p. 231 (1778 attempt at Turin–Milan cartel).

96 Verdi to Giovanni Ricordi, 25 June 1850, ISVP 81/37. Cf. Radiciotti, *Rossini*, I, pp. 173, 271 n.

97 Verdi to Marie Escudier, 25 Aug. 1846, ISVP; *Copialettere*, pp. 125–8, 496–7.

98 Nicolai, *Briefe*, pp. 161, 169, 183–5, 232, 236–9.

99 Lanari to Dr E. Basevi, 1843, BNF CV 345/107. See Rosmini, *Legislazione*, II, pp. 346–9, 355–6.

100 Meyerbeer, *Briefwechsel und Tagebücher*, I, pp. 324–6, 387, 396, 399, 426–7, 466, 514.

101 Mayr to G. Morandi, 1808, in Radiciotti, *Lettere inedite*, p. 79 (about Ricordi piano score of *Adelasia*).

102 Lanari to G. and R. Morandi, 3 March 1820, Piancastelli 407.182; Lanari–Barbaja correspondence, 1836–8, BNF CV 344/132, 345/31, 37, 44; Gazzuoli to Lanari, 1837, BNF CV 364/120; Bellini, *Epistolario*, pp. 451–2; T. Ricordi to Verdi, 7 Nov. 1848, ISVP.

103 BNF CV 344/168, 345/19, 29, 31, 37, 44.

104 Ibid. 409/61–4.

105 Barbaja to Pacini, 19 June, 3 Aug. 1841, Fondo Pacini nos. 1148, 1151; Lanari to Donizetti, 30 June 1836, *Studi Donizettiani*, III, p. 33.

106 G. B. Lasina to G. Marchetti, 29 Nov. 1865, Piancastelli Autografi s.v. Marchetti. See also G. B. Bonola to Lanari, 1838, BNF CV 349/41 (referring to 'my dear Jacovacci', whom Bonola had yet to meet).

107 Correspondence of Lanari with Luigia Boccabadati, 1833, with Bonola, 1831, with Somigli, 1836, BNF CV 348/57–8, 165, 410/151; Jacovacci to N. Moriani, 1841, MTS CA 3828.

108 A. Batelli to Lanari, 1847, BNF CV 345/126–7; Trisolini to Marchetti, 1866, Piancastelli Autografi s. v. Marchetti.

109 Merelli to Lanari, 1837, BNF CV 396/33.

110 A. De Bassini to F. Lucca, 4 Jan. 1851, MTS Coll. Casati 319.

6 Agents and journalists

1 Radiciotti, *Sinigaglia*, p. 97; Basso, ed., *Teatro Regio*, II, p. 294.

2 Kelly, *Reminiscences*, p. 94. This Tamburini is not to be confused with the well-known baritone.

3 Papers of the Faenza *impresa*, 1788, Piancastelli 130.3–13, 39–79; G. Pasolini-Zanelli, *Il Teatro di Faenza dal 1788 al 1888*, Faenza, 1888, pp. 8–11, 16–27, 35–44.

4 Rinaldi, *Argentina*, I, p. 513; Radiciotti, *Rossini*, I, p. 31 n.; L. Pacini to G. C. Martorelli, 8 Dec. 1809, AN F^{1e} 139.

5 Circular of Società Commissionaria Teatrale sotto la ditta Rossi Maffei e Galeotti, BTBR Fondo Capranica, correspondence, 1 Dec. 1827.

6 For Ricordi's activities as agent: ibid. 1827–8, 1836, 1838; Zavadini, *Donizetti*, pp. 370–1.

7 Petracchi, *Sul reggimento de' pubblici teatri*, p. 20; *Teatro Arti e Letteratura*, Bologna, 19 March 1863.

8 C. Gatti, *Il Teatro alla Scala nella storia e nell'arte*, 2 vols., Milan, 1963, I, p. 47; E. Verzino, *Le Opere di Gaetano Donizetti: contributo alla loro storia*,

Bergamo, 1897, pp. 31–2; Santley, *Student and Singer*, p. 88; Cambiasi, *La Scala*, pp. xiii–xviii.

9 Crivelli to Lanari, 21 July 1829, BNF CV 358/147.

10 Basso, ed., *Teatro Regio*, II, p. 190.

11 Correspondence of Giovanni Marchetti, Piancastelli Autografi s.v. Marchetti.

12 Luigia Boccabadati to Lanari, 7 Sep. 1848, BNF CV 348/59.

13 Examples: ibid. 343/83–5 (Cesare Badiali, 1848); MTS CA 269, 273, 478 (Camilla Balsamini, 1809).

14 A clear example: Amato Ricci to Moriani, 21 July 1851, ibid. 3670.

15 Correspondence with Benelli, 1825, with Marchesi, 1828, with Galeotti, Gioanni Rossi, and the soprano Fischer, 1829, BTBR Fondo Capranica. See also A. Marchesi to Balochino, 17 June 1836, Balochino papers, Wiener Stadtbibliothek (according to which Merelli approached the soprano Fanny Tacchinardi Persiani through the Marchesi agency while also dealing with her direct).

16 G. B. Bonola to G. Brenna, 23 Sep. 1851, ATLaF Spettacoli b. 26; A. Torri to Dr Rossi, 29 Sep. 1852, Piancastelli 407.224.

17 Lanari to Marzi brothers, 18, 30 Sep. 1849, BNF CV 393/48, 72.

18 Ibid. 350/144–51, 395/124–74.

19 To Lanari from Merelli, 1828, from Burcardi, 1833, from Bonola, 1838, ibid. 349/35–6, 350/143, 395/138.

20 Burcardi to Zuccoli, 6 Jan. 1827, BTBR Fondo Capranica. The four were Burcardi, Gaetano Buttazzoni, Giulio Cesare Martorelli, and G. B. Bordese.

21 B. Bava to Lanari, 1850, BNF CV 346/120.

22 To Lanari from Burcardi, 24 Aug. 1833, from E. Marzi, 28 Sep. 1851, ibid. 350/141, 393/72; Galeotti to Presidenza of La Fenice, 16 Jan. 1831, ATLaF Spettacoli b. 3.

23 Correspondence of Pollione Ronzi, 1874, Archiginnasio Coll. Autografi LX 15940; of G. Lamperti, 1877, and M. Curiel, 1883 Piancastelli Autografi s. v. Marchetti; of C. D'Ormeville, 1885, MTS Coll. Casati 775.

24 Rosmini, *Legislazione*, II, ch. 10; Valle, *Cenni teorici-pratici*, pp. 140–52.

25 Ibid.; Piancastelli 407.157.

26 Bonola–Lanari correspondence, 1845, BNF CV 349/79; Bonola–Brenna correspondence, 1850–1, ATLaF Spettacoli b. 26.

27 Correspondence between Pollione Ronzi and Alessandro Magotti, 1877–8, Archiginnasio Coll. Autografi LX 15941–2.

28 Gazzuoli to Lanari, April 1838, BNF CV 365/35.

29 Petition of Evangelisti, ASB ASC Dep. Pub. Sp. tit. I rub. 1, 1853.

30 Valle, *Cenni teorici-pratici*, pp. 140–52; Contract with the baritone Senatore Sparapani, Teatro Dal Verme, Milan, P1876, MTS Coll. Casati 1436.

31 Printed contracts used by the agent G. B. Lampugnani, 1871, ibid. CA 5658.

32 Correspondence among Gioanni Rossi, Angelo Coen, and Giuditta Grisi, 1834–7, ibid. CA 3256–7, 3260, 3262; to Lanari from Benelli, 1849, from Cirelli, 1848, BNF CV 346/143–4, 419/76.

33 Piancastelli Autografi s. v. Jacovacci.

34 A. Ghislanzoni, *Storia di Milano dal 1836 al 1848*, published with *In chiave di baritono*, Milan, 1882, p. 135.

35 On Tenca: G. Lisio, 'Su l'epistolario di Casa Lucca', *Rendiconti del R. Istituto Lombardo di Scienze e Lettere*, XLI, 1908, p. 317; on Dolce: Prefect of Adriatico to Minister of the Interior, 28 July 1807, ASV Pref. dell'Adr. b. 94; A. Luzio,

'La Massoneria sotto il Regno Italico', *Archivio Storico Lombardo*, XLIV, 1917; R. J. Rath, *The Provisional Austrian Regime in Lombardy–Venetia, 1814–1815*, Austin, Texas and London, 1969, pp. 201, 225–6, 230, 240.

36 Lanari to Marchese G. Balbi, 30 Oct. 1849, BNF CV 343/92.
37 Fondo Pacini no. 1066.
38 Santley, *Student and Singer*, p. 122.
39 Dr Pietro Boniotti, editor of *Il Bazar*, Milan, to Lanari, 3 Aug. 1843, BNF CV 348/161.
40 Regli, *Dizionario biografico*, s. v. Prividali.
41 Santley, *Student and Singer*, pp. 232–3; correspondence of Marco Curiel, Piancastelli Autografi s. v. Marchetti; *Teatro Arti e Letteratura*, 26 June, 23 Oct., 27 Nov. 1862.
42 Bellini to Florimo, 11 Nov. 1834, Bellini, *Epistolario*, pp. 467–71.
43 D'Arcais, 'L'Industria musicale', pp. 141–2.
44 Zavadini, *Donizetti*, p. 493.
45 Cambiaggio to Felice Romani, 1843, MTS Coll. Casati 273; Merelli–Lanari correspondence, 1837, BNF CV 396/17, 22, 30; Donizetti to Pillet, 1844, Zavadini, *Donizetti*, pp. 742–3, 747–8.
46 Lanari to Barbaja, 1836, BNF CV 345/51.
47 Ibid. 411/108.
48 Antonio Lanari to Pacini, 15 April 1859, Fondo Pacini no. 1321.
49 Rosmini, *Legislazione*, II, pp. 151–4.
50 Correspondence between Lanari and Presidenza of La Fenice, ATLaF Processi verbali convocazioni b. 5; Rosmini, *Legislazione*, I, pp. 393–8.
51 Ibid. II, ch. 10.
52 G. Strepponi to Lanari, 23 June 1839, *Carteggi Verdiani*, IV, pp. 275–6; Moriani to Merelli, 9 Jan. 1838, MTS CA 3645; Duprez, *Souvenirs*, p. 84.
53 A. Boracchi to Lanari, Oct. 1838, BNF CV 405/108.
54 For Antonio Magotti: correspondence of Gazzuoli and Lanari, BNF CV 364–5 *passim*; *Teatro Arti e Letteratura*, 1857, 1861, 1863. For Alessandro Magotti: his papers and those of Pollione Ronzi, Archiginnasio Coll. Autografi XLI 11.101 *et seq.*, LX 15940 *et seq.*
55 Santley, *Student and Singer*, pp. 131–4; Bonola to Lanari, 1834, BNF CV 349/50; A. Catalani, *Lettere a Giuseppe Depanis*, ed. C. Gatti, Milan, 1946, p. 180.
56 Bonola to Brenna, 23 July 1851, ATLaF Spettacoli b. 26.
57 The volume of Merelli's correspondence can be deduced from the consecutive numbering of the letters in BNF CV 395–6. By 1837, when he was a good deal taken up with management rather than agency, he appears to have been down to about 5,000 letters a year.
58 BNF CV 395/185–9.
59 *Teatro Arti e Letteratura*, 15 July 1861.
60 Bellini, *Epistolario*, pp. 41, 84.
61 Santley, *Student and Singer*, pp. 131–4.
62 Adele Salvi Speck to Gaetano Giori, 23 Oct. 1857, MTS Coll. Casati 1071.

7   The impresario and the public

1 S. Arteaga, *Le Rivoluzioni del teatro musicale italiano*, Venice, 1785, II, pp. 321–2.

2 Berlioz, *Voyage musical*, pp. 218–20.

3 Verdi to Arrivabene, 5 Feb. 1876, *Copialettere*, pp. 687–9.

4 To Lanari from Cartoni and Camuri, 1841, BNF CV 352, 353/84; Stendhal, *Quelques promenades dans Rome*, Paris, 1829, entry for 16 June 1828.

5 A. Manzi, 'I Teatri di musica', in *Firenze d'oggi*, Florence, 1896, pp. 61–2.

6 To Pacini from Antonio Lanari, 27 April 1857, from L. Fioravanti, 24 April 1862, Fondo Pacini nos. 950, 1001.

7 Bellini, *Epistolario*, p. 172 n.; Bottura, *Comunale di Trieste*, p. 269 n.

8 Manzi, 'Teatri di musica', pp. 65–9.

9 Basetti to Lanari, 6 July 1833, BNF CV 345/97.

10 Examples: Alessandro Lanari at La Pergola, P1836, his son Antonio at the Argentina, Rome, P1844: *Studi Donizettiani*, III, p. 23; Rinaldi, *Argentina*, II, p. 779.

11 Jarro, *Memorie d'un impresario fiorentino*, pp. 8–11.

12 M. Novaro to Pacini, 22 Jan. 1862, Fondo Pacini no. 1026 (about Pacini's *Gianni di Nisida*, contracted for at the Carlo Felice).

13 'Avviso al rispettabile pubblico veneto di Clemente Riesch, impresario al Teatro San Luca nella primavera 1829', Museo Civico Correr, Venice, MS PD buste C.1419.

14 Radiciotti, *Rossini*, I, pp. 153–5.

15 Crocioni, *Reggio nell'Emilia*, pp. 51–4; Papi, *Municipale di Piacenza*, pp. 140–1; Gandini, *Modena*, II, pp. 279–83.

16 E.g. at *Marino Faliero*, Ducale, Parma P1838: Ferrari, *Spettacoli in Parma*, p. 193.

17 Weinstock, *Donizetti*, pp. 165–6.

18 Rinaldi, *Argentina*, I, pp. 58–9, 88–9, 200; Marcello, *Teatro alla moda*, pp. 64–5; Barbaja to Deputazione, 31 May 1822, ASN Teatri b. 98; Valle, *Cenni teorici-pratici*, pp. 171–4; Lalande, *Voyage en Italie*, V, p. 189.

19 Cambiasi, *La Scala*, p. 36; Edict of Direttore generale de'regio-ducali teatri, Piacenza, 1754, ASCM Gride 6/123; L. Bruni to Lanari, 1823, BNF CV 350/113.

20 Depanis, *Concerti popolari*, I, pp. 117–24; A. Cametti, *Un Poeta melodrammatico romano* (G. Ferretti), Milan, 1898, pp. 261–2.

21 Depanis, *Concerti popolari*, I, pp. 82–3, 98–101.

22 Verdi, *Copialettere*, p. 541; Quicherat, *Nourrit*, III, pp. 203–4.

23 Gandini, *Modena*, I, p. 181.

24 Basso, ed., *Teatro Regio*, II, pp. 292–3, 304; Maragliano, *Teatri di Voghera*, pp. 169–71; G. Forzano, *Come li ho conosciuti*, Turin, 1957, p. 11.

25 L. Dall'Olio to Pacini, 15 Dec. 1847, Fondo Pacini no. 1245. Cf. Pacini, *Memorie artistiche*, pp. 82, 87.

26 Ferrari, *Spettacoli in Parma*, pp. 279, 285, 312.

27 Rosmini, *Legislazione*, I, p. 328.

28 Prividali to Berti, 9 Feb. 1831, ATLaF Spettacoli b. 3.

29 Rinaldi, *Argentina*, I, p. 503; Bellini, *Epistolario*, pp. 343, 345–6.

30 Gen. Menou to Minister of the Interior, 1 complémentaire XII (18 Sep. 1804), AN F^{1e} 79; correspondence between Nardon and Minister, June–July 1807, AN F^{1e} 88.

31 Walker, *The Man Verdi*, pp. 14–20, 117–18, 127–8, 153–5.

32 C. Sardi, *Lucca e il suo ducato*, Florence, 1912, pp. 146–9 (*Lucrezia Borgia*, Teatro del Giglio; *Eleonora di Toledo*, Teatro Pantera).

33 Crocioni, *Reggio nell'Emilia*, pp. 69–70.
34 Raggi, *Teatro Comunale di Cesena*, p. 121 n.
35 Tiby, *Teatro Carolino*, pp. 182–92.
36 Gandini, *Modena*, II, pp. 116 *et seq.*, 301, 336–9; Bonola to Lanari, Nov. 1844, BNF CV 349/74.
37 Abbiati, *Verdi*, I, p. 782.
38 E. Surian, 'Lo Stato attuale degli studi verdiani', *Rivista italiana di musicologia*, XII, 1977, No. 2, p. 307; U. Volli in *La Repubblica*, Rome and Milan, 12 July 1980.
39 Mackenzie-Grieve, *Clara Novello*, p. 109.
40 E. Ciollaro to Pacini, 21 March 1846, Fondo Pacini no. 921.
41 Rossi-Gallieno, *Saggio di economia teatrale*, p. 56; Cametti, *Apollo*, I, pp. 297–8.
42 Depanis, *Concerti popolari*, II, p. 238.

8   The end of the impresari

1 Santoro, *Teatro di Cremona*, II, pp. 231–2, 262.
2 Abbiati, *Verdi*, I, pp. 414, 431.
3 'Sant' Ambrogio', 1846, in G. Giusti, *Opere*, ed. N. Sabbatucci, Turin, 1976, pp. 429–33.
4 Ghislanzoni, *Storia di Milano*, pp. 159–60.
5 P. Ginsborg, *Daniele Manin and the Venetian Revolution of 1848–49*, Cambridge, 1979, pp. 72, 76, 78–9, 81.
6 Martelli (direttore generale dell'ordine pubblico, Venice) to Presidenza of La Fenice, 9 Jan. 1852, ATLaF Autografi diversi.
7 C. Gagliani to A. Marchesi, Faenza 11 Jan. 1849, B. Winter to Lanari, Naples 25 Sep. 1849, BNF CV 364/36, 416/179; G. Ricordi to R. Morandi, 14 June 1848, Radiciotti, *Lettere inedite*, p. 105; Ricordi to Verdi, 21 Feb. 1849, ISVP (quoting Sanguineti, impresario of the Teatro Carlo Felice, Genoa).
8 G. Rovani, *Cento anni*, Milan, 1863, book XII, ch. 8.
9 Cambiaggio to Lanari, Aug. 1848, BNF CV 351/125.
10 Benelli to Lanari, 6 April 1849, ibid. 346/142.
11 Morini, *La Pergola*, pp. 208, 211.
12 Ferrari, *Spettacoli in Parma*, p. 265.
13 Morini, *La Pergola*, p. 118.
14 Lessona, *Volere è potere*, p. 298.
15 Meyerbeer, *Briefwechsel*, I, pp. 525, 529 (about *Il Crociato in Egitto*, 1824).
16 Balochino to F. Tacchinardi Persiani, 12 Feb. 1845, Wiener Stadtbibliothek; Basso, ed., *Teatro Regio*, II, pp. 263–5; *Prospetti d'appalto del Teatro San Carlo*.
17 Gatti, *La Scala*, II; *Prospetti d'appalto del Teatro San Carlo*.
18 Santley, *Student and Singer*, p. 234; Rosmini, *Legislazione*, I, p. 527; Parmeggiani to Marchetti, 1866, Piancastelli Autografi s. v. Marchetti.
19 Budden, *Operas of Verdi*, II, ch. 1.
20 M. Conati, 'La musica a Reggio nel secondo ottocento', in Romagnoli and Garbero, *Teatro a Reggio Emilia*, II, pp. 127–8.
21 *Storia di Napoli*, Naples, 1967–74, VIII, p. 773; Deputazione degli Spettacoli to Minister of the Interior, 29 July 1823, ASN Min. Interno II inv. f. 4355; Larussa, *Sulle cagioni del decadimento*, pp. 22–6.
22 ASR Camerale III Teatri b. 2137, nos. 6, 7, 19.
23 Rossini to P. Cartoni, 26 Oct. 1817, Piancastelli 405.39; *Cronache del giorno*,

1839 (broadsheet put out by Deputazione degli Spettacoli, Naples, in the possession of Architetto Franco Mancini).

24 B. Croce, *I Teatri di Napoli*, 1st edn., Naples, 1891, appendix x; ASN Min. Interno II inv. f. 706 (evidence of theatre building at Taranto and Lecce and in some small towns, 1830–50); Rosmini, *Legislazione*, II, pp. 581–97 (showing that of the 940 Italian theatres officially classified in 1871, only 170 were in the former Kingdom of the Two Sicilies, and many of these were small).

25 Varesi to Brenna, 28 Oct. 1852, ISVP.

26 Manzi, 'I Teatri di musica', pp. 66–8.

27 Cambiaggio to G. Lucca, 5 Jan. 1859, MTS Coll. Casati 279; Abbiati, *Verdi*, II, pp. 415–16, 444.

28 Arnold Bennett, *Florentine Journal...1910*, London, 1967, pp. 25–7.

29 ASF Prefettura di Firenze, 1868, f. 164 no. 11802; manifesto of Politeama Principe di Napoli, Lecce, E1885, Piancastelli Autografi s. v. Marchetti.

30 Pacini, *Memorie artistiche*, p. 20 (on opening night of the Argentina, Rome, C1821).

31 V. Frajese, *Dal Costanzi all'Opera*, Rome, 1977–8, I, pp. 25, 45–6.

32 Gatti, *La Scala*, I, pp. 49–52, 141–2, 154–5, 164–5; *Dizionario biografico degli italiani*, s. v. Artaria; Rosmini, *Legislazione*, II, pp. 228–81.

33 G. Viceconta to Marchese Bartolomeo Capranica, 18 Feb. 1836, BTBR Fondo Capranica.

34 Budden, *Operas of Verdi*, I, pp. 245, 364–5; Cametti, *G. Ferretti*, p. 245; Verdi, *Copialettere*, pp. 26–34; Mercadante to Lucca, 29 July 1853, MTS CA 3735. See also contract between the Marzi brothers on one side and Lucca and the composer Petrella on the other, for Petrella's *Il Duca di Scilla*, 30 March 1858, ASCM Sp. P. 112/1.

35 Verdi, *Copialettere*, pp. 37–40; Ricordi to Verdi, 27 May 1847, ISVP.

36 E.g. for *Simon Boccanegra* at Reggio Emilia, F1857: Ricordi to Verdi, 6 May 1857, ISVP.

37 Contract between Ricordi and Marzi brothers, Feb. 1858, ASCM Sp. P. 109.

38 A. Mazzucato to Giraldoni, 1865, MTS CA 2905; A. C. Gomes to Cattaneo, 2 July 1874, in Gomes, *Carteggi italiani*, ed. G. Nello Vetro, Milan, 1977, p. 101.

39 Depanis, *Concerti popolari*, I, pp. 187–8; Catalani, *Lettere*, pp. 83, 115.

40 Gatti, *La Scala*, I, pp. 164–7, 181–2.

41 Verdi to Boito, 18 Aug. 1889, *Carteggio Verdi–Boito*, ed. M. Medici, M. Conati, M. Casati, Parma, 1978, I, pp. 152, 184, 188.

42 Crivelli to Lanari, 7 Sep. 1829, BNF CV 358/151 (reporting the advice he had given the composer Persiani).

43 G. Coccetti to Lanari, 26 Jan. 1849, ibid. 353/173 (praising *Il Barbiere di Siviglia* in preference to Ricci's *Il Nuovo Figaro*, a rare disinterested comment).

44 P. Romani to Lanari, 14 May 1838, ibid. 365/39 (about Niccola Tilli, a lawyer and, until then, secretary to Bandini in the management of La Pergola).

Appendix

1 Rosmini, *Legislazione*, II, pp. 581 *et seq.*

2 At Bologna – important for our purposes – the standard length of the fashionable season (first spring, then autumn) was about twenty-four to

thirty performances, not unlike a short to middling carnival, whereas autumn and spring seasons elsewhere could go on for as long as three months and forty-eight or more performances: Trezzini, *Due secoli di vita musicale*, II.

3 First recorded performance at Naples, 1794, with music by Luigi Mosca: [C. Sartori], *Primo tentativo di catalogo unico dei libretti italiani a stampa fino all'anno 1800*, Milan, 1973–81. Libretto in the Biblioteca dell'Accademia di S. Cecilia, Rome.

4 Rinaldi, *Argentina*, II, p. 694; BTBR Fondo Capranica, borderò, bilanci.

5 Wallaschek, *K. K. Hofoperntheater*, pp. 105–6.

6 Marzi–Lanari correspondence, 1849, BNF CV 393/56, 65.

7 I have unfortunately not been able to consult the accounts and miscellaneous papers of Alessandro Lanari, of which M. De Angelis has lately published an inventory under the title *Le Cifre del melodramma* (Florence, 1982). The Lanari correspondence of 15,000 or so items in BNF CV has however been accessible.

8 There are tables in several volumes of the *Archivio economico del Risorgimento italiano*: G. Parenti, 'Monete e cambi nel Granducato di Toscana dal 1825 al 1859', U. Tucci, 'Le Monete del Regno lombardo-veneto dal 1815 al 1866', both in vol. II; G. Felloni, 'Corso delle monete e dei cambi negli Stati sabaudi dal 1820 al 1860', in vols. III–IV. Also in Felloni, *Il Mercato monetario in Piemonte nel secolo XVIII*, Milan, 1968; De Maddalena, *Prezzi e mercedi a Milano*; D. Demarco, *Storia del Banco di Napoli*, Naples, 1958; E. Martinori, *La Moneta*, Rome, 1915.

Note on further reading

This book is the first to attempt to deal systematically with Italian opera as a business, and with impresari and agents as a group. It follows that readers cannot be sent on to other works of a like kind. There is, however, a good deal to be picked up incidentally in works addressed to other aspects of opera.

Even the names of impresari, with few exceptions, were quickly forgotten. The most reliable published directory – even that mentions only the best known – appeared early in the period of decline: F. Regli, *Dizionario biografico dei più illustri poeti e artisti melodrammatici...in Italia dal 1800 al 1860* (Turin, 1860). I have myself compiled a directory or *Elenco degli impresari e agenti teatrali italiani*, listing some 400-odd names, with dates of seasons run and any available biographical information. This, in provisional computer print-out form, may be consulted in the following libraries: Music Library, Senate House Library, London; American Institute for Verdi Studies, New York University; Museo Teatrale alla Scala, Milan; Istituto di Studi Verdiani, Parma; Società Italiana di Musicologia, Bologna; Istituto di Bibliografia Musicale, Rome. I hope that it may attract additions and corrections and perhaps appear in print when these have been incorporated.

For the reader who wishes to understand the world of Italian opera in the nineteenth century, the best introduction – penetrating though necessarily brief – is the general background chapter in each of the three volumes of Julian Budden, *The Operas of Verdi* (London, 1973–81). Budden goes over some of the same ground in his contribution to W. Weaver and M. Chusid, eds., *The Verdi Companion* (London, 1980), where the chapter by Bruno Cagli is also useful. For the eighteenth century M. F. Robinson, *Naples and Neapolitan Opera* (Oxford, 1972) may be consulted; for the late nineteenth, G. Depanis, *I Concerti popolari e il Teatro Regio di Torino* (Turin, 1914–15), and F. d'Arcais, 'L'Industria Musicale', *Nuova Antologia*, 15 May 1879. The best contemporary guides are two manuals by and for practitioners: G. Valle, *Cenni teorici-pratici sulle aziende teatrali* (Milan, 1823), and E. Rosmini, *La Legislazione e la giurisprudenza dei teatri* (Milan, 1872).

In a class of his own is that opera lover Stendhal, whose writings offer a startling mixture of inside knowledge and wild misstatement, particularly his *Life of Rossini* (ed. and trans. R. N. Coe, London, 1956), *Rome, Naples et Florence* (1826 version; various modern editions) and his *Correspondance* (ed. H. Martineau and V. Del Litto, Paris, 1962).

If impresari have been ignored composers have had much notice, though even Rossini still awaits a satisfactory edition of his correspondence; meanwhile the life by G. Radiciotti (Tivoli, 3 vols., 1927–9) remains the most informative. The correspondence of Bellini (*Epistolario*, ed. L. Cambi, Milan, 1943) is a rich source, as is that of Donizetti (ed. G. Zavadini, Bergamo, 1948). Verdi's published letter-books or *Copialettere* (ed. G. Cesari and A. Luzio, Milan, 1913) are the most useful of several collections; all of them will ultimately be superseded by the edition of Verdi's complete correspondence now being prepared by the Istituto di Studi Verdiani at Parma.

The careers of once well-known but now forgotten composers can be revealing: witness the *Vita di Nicola Vaccaj* by his son (Bologna, 1882) and the lively though inaccurate *Le mie memorie artistiche* by Giovanni Pacini (Florence, 1875). So too can the correspondence of foreign composers trying their hand in Italy: see vol. I of G. Meyerbeer, *Briefwechsel und Tagebücher* (ed. H. & G. Becker, Berlin, 3 vols., 1960–75), and O. Nicolai's *Tagebücher* (Leipzig, 1892) and his *Briefe an seinen Vater* (ed. W. Altmann, Regensburg, 1924). Berlioz's *Mémoires* (Paris, 1870; English translation by D. Cairns, London, 1969) has some characteristically high-coloured descriptions of Italian theatre manners.

Biographies and autobiographies of singers are generally an unpromising genre, but four stand out from the rest: the autobiographies of Michael Kelly, the Irish tenor who sang in the original production of *Le Nozze di Figaro* (*Reminiscences*, ed. R. Fiske, Oxford, 1975), the English baritone Charles Santley (*Student and Singer*, London, 1892), and the great French tenor G.-L. Duprez (*Souvenirs d'un chanteur*, Paris, 1880); and L. Quicherat, *Adolphe Nourrit* (Paris, 3 vols., 1867), which has a good deal about that unfortunate singer's final Neapolitan period.

Histories of individual theatres are a genre much cultivated in Italy, where they feed on local patriotism. They are highly uneven in quality; we still lack satisfactory histories of the three most important opera houses (La Scala, Milan; La Fenice,

Venice; the San Carlo, Naples). Some of the most useful date from the late nineteenth and early twentieth centuries, inspired as they were by a positivistic belief in the value of accurate facts: P. E. Ferrari, *Spettacoli drammatico-musicali e coreografici in Parma* (Parma, 1884), A. Gandini, *Cronistoria dei teatri di Modena dal 1539 al 1871* (Modena, 1873), G. Radiciotti, *Teatro, musica e musicisti in Sinigaglia* (Milan, 1893), A. Cametti, *Il Teatro di Tordinona poi di Apollo* (Tivoli, 2 vols., 1938), C. L. Curiel, *Il Teatro San Pietro di Trieste* (Milan, 1937). Modern histories are seldom as satisfactory; welcome exceptions are A. Basso (ed.), *Storia del Teatro Regio di Torino* (Turin, 1976), N. Mangini, *I Teatri di Venezia* (Milan, 1974), and some of the articles on individual towns and theatres in the *Enciclopedia dello Spettacolo* (Rome, 1954–62).

The politics of opera is a subject that has begun to grow away from old clichés about opera as a carrier of Risorgimento nationalism, so far thanks mainly to a few musicologists and literary critics: M. Lavagetto, *Un Caso di censura: il 'Rigoletto'* (Milan, 1979), L. Baldacci, *Libretti d'opera* (Florence, 1974) (whose interpretation of *La Sonnambula* as a conservative document is controverted by F. Degrada, *Il Palazzo incantato*, Fiesole, 1979).

The student who wishes to work on manuscript sources will have a great deal to choose from among the following categories:

1. Papers of impresari: these are rare, apart from the papers of Alessandro Lanari in the Biblioteca Nazionale, Florence (two collections, one of them catalogued in the Carteggi Vari series, another, so far inaccessible, a catalogue of which has just appeared in M. De Angelis, *Le Cifre del melodramma* (Florence, 1982)) and those of Carlo Balochino in the Wiener Stadtbibliothek. But scattered papers may be found in

2. Miscellaneous collections of manuscripts, in particular those of the Museo Teatrale alla Scala, Milan, the Biblioteca Teatrale del Burcardo, Rome, the Collezione Piancastelli in the Biblioteca Comunale, Forlì.

3. Archives of individual theatres. Many theatres have none, among them some of the best known, but there are remarkable, largely unexploited archives at La Fenice, Venice, and the Teatro Regio, Parma.

4. Papers of composers. Those of Verdi at Sant'Agata near Parma are undoubtedly rich, but only very limited access has so far been granted. Photocopies of many of his letters (not including the Sant'Agata material) are in the Istituto di Studi Verdiani. Vaccaj's papers in the Biblioteca Comunale, Tolentino, are also of somewhat uncertain access. On the other hand the Fondo Pacini in the Biblioteca Comunale, Pescia, is both valuable and easily used. The papers of the conductor Angelo Mariani (two collections, in the Biblioteca Classense, Ravenna, and the Biblioteca Beriana, Genoa) may be of interest.

5. Manuscript chronologies and other papers relating to opera, compiled by local amateurs. These can be astonishingly detailed, like the Curti and Fantuzzi collections in the Biblioteca Comunale, Reggio Emilia.

6. Official papers, generally held in the State Archives in the relevant town, but sometimes in the municipal archives (or, for the Napoleonic period, in those series in the Archives Nationales, Paris, relating to Italian departments). Because the old Italian governments sought to control almost every aspect of opera production and performance, these papers are generally abundant, though particular series or years may be missing. Post-unification papers are sometimes thinner. The archives named in the list of abbreviations (p. viii) by no means exhaust those likely to contain relevant material.

Index

Individual operas and plays are indexed under the name of the composer or playwright. Cities of Spain, of Greece, and of the Americas are indexed under those headings. The words 'impresario' and 'opera' are not indexed; readers should consult particular topics.

Index

Index

Index

Index